BEING AND SOME PHILOSOPHERS

Nihil Obstat
          TERENCE P. McLAUGHLIN C.S.B.

Imp rimatur
          ✠ JAMES CARDINAL McGUIGAN
                  Archiep. Torontinus

March 4, 1949.

Being

and

Some Philosophers

ETIENNE GILSON

SECOND EDITION
CORRECTED AND ENLARGED

PONTIFICAL INSTITUTE OF MEDIAEVAL STUDIES

Toronto, Canada

1952

Second printing 1961

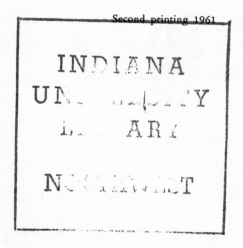
EUROPE PRINTING, THE HAGUE, HOLLAND

565, Meppelweg

CONTENTS

PREFACE

THE work of William James has largely been a defense of that type of philosophy which now goes by the name of "pragmatism." It is of the essence of pragmatism not to waste any time in defining abstract philosophical notions and, least of all, the notion of philosophy in general. Yet, in his well-known essay on *Philosophy and Its Critics*, James has felt it necessary at least once "to tarry a moment over the matter of definition." To this happy scruple we are indebted for a highly suggestive page, which I beg to reproduce in full, because its deepest significance lies perhaps less in what he says than in his peculiar way of saying it:

Limited by the omission of the special sciences, the name of Philosophy has come more and more to denote ideas of universal scope exclusively. The principles of explanation that underlie all things without exception, the elements common to gods and men and animals and stones, the first *whence* and the last *whither* of the whole cosmic procession, the conditions of all knowing, and the most general rules of human action—these furnish the problems commonly deemed philosophic *par excellence*, and the philosopher is a man who finds the most to say about them. Philosophy is defined in the usual Scholastic textbooks as 'the knowledge of things in general by their ultimate causes, so far as natural reason can attain to such knowledge.' This means that explanation of the universe at large, not description of its details, is what philosophy must aim at; and so it happens that a view of anything is termed philosophic just in proportion as it is broad and connected with other views, and as it uses principles not proximate, or intermediate, but ultimate and all-embracing, to justify itself. Any very sweeping view of the world is a philosophy in this sense, even though it may be a vague one. It is a *Weltanschauung* and intellectualized attitude towards life. Professor Dewey well describes the constitution of all the philosophies that actually exist, when he says that philosophy expresses a certain attitude, purpose, and temper of conjoined intellect and will, rather than a discipline whose boundaries can be really marked off.[1]

These remarkable lines are more than a mere statement of James' own views concerning the definition of philosophy in general. They actually re-enact the whole history of that definition from the time of the Greeks up to our own day. At the very beginning, James still seems to maintain the classical notion of metaphysics conceived as a wisdom, that is, as a knowledge of things in general by their ultimate causes. But it immediately appears that the causes he has in mind are neither things nor beings. As James conceives them, such causes are more or less ultimate according as they are more or less "general," so that philosophy becomes to him what has been termed by another philosopher as "the specialty of generalities." Thus transformed from the science of what is first in things into the science of what is most universal in thought, metaphysics presently undergoes a second metamorphosis, in that the intrinsic generality of its principles becomes itself broadness in scope. Now broadness is not quite the same as generality. The principles may be equally general without being equally valid, but if "a view of anything is termed philosophic just in proportion as it is broad," any broad view of things is as philosophic as any other equally broad one. In other words, generality was still related to things, whereas broadness is an attribute of the mind. But we must finally resort to it, be it only to account for the well-known fact that views of reality can be, though equally "sweeping," yet mutually conflicting ones. The generality of cognitions ultimately hangs on the aptness of a particular knowledge to be generalized, but the broadness in outlook is a mere attitude of the knowing subject towards reality. It is a matter of both intellect and will. In short, *quot capita, tot sensus:* there are as many philosophies as there are philosophers.

This situation has already prevailed for so long a time that it now appears as a perfectly normal and satisfactory one. There are countries where no professor of any science could hold his job for a month if he started teaching that he does not know what is true about the very science he is supposed to teach, but where a man finds it hard to be appointed as a professor of philosophy if he professes to believe in the truth of the philosophy he teaches. The only dogmatic tenet still held as valid in such philosophical circles is that, if a philosopher feels reasonably sure of being

[1] William James, *Some Problems of Philosophy* (New York, 1911), pp. 4-6.

right, then it is a sure thing that he is wrong, because it is of the very essence of philosophical knowledge merely to express "a certain attitude, purpose and temper of conjoined intellect and will." The man whose will uses every effort to let his own intellect see things just as they are, is then bound to appear as a self-satisfied fellow, a living insult to those who don't happen to see reality as he does. He is a man to steer clear of; in short, he is a fanatic.

It is, alas, only too true that dogmatic philosophers are liable to become fanatics, but they have at least an excuse, which is that they do believe in the truth of what they teach. Yet their excuse also accuses them. Precisely because they *believe* in philosophical truth, they don't *know* it. Hence their sometimes blind opposition to what they hold to be false, as if fundamental philosophical oppositions necessarily happened between truth and error, instead of being between partial truths and the whole truth. One can disagree with both Spinoza and Hegel, but understanding is a prerequisite to more than verbal disagreeing, and, once they are understood, they stand in no need of being refuted. For indeed it is one and the same thing to understand them in their fullness and to know them in their intrinsic limitations. The only will that should be found at the origin of philosophy should be the will to know, and this is why nothing is more important for a philosopher than the choice he makes of his own philosophical principles. The principle of principles is that a philosopher should always put first in his mind what is actually first in reality. What is first in reality need not be what is the most easily accessible to human understanding; it is that whose presence or absence entails the presence or absence of all the rest in reality.

The present book is not an attempt to show what comes first in reality, for all philosophers know it inasmuch as they are, not philosophers, but men. Our only problem will be to know how it is that what men so infallibly know *qua* men, they so often overlook *qua* philosophers. In order to solve such a problem, a good deal of historical material shall have to be taken into account. Yet this is not a book in the history of philosophy; it is a philosophical book, and a dogmatically philosophical one at that. The thesis it maintains is both so impersonal and so unpopular that its author cannot be suspected of fighting a personal battle. He simply wishes to state the truth which he himselfs feels duty bound to accept. Yet, he wishes at least to state it, and to state it as true.

This is why, as a history, this book would be entirely wrong. The choice of the philosophers singled out for special consideration, the selection of the theses to be discussed within their own particular philosophies, the intentional disregarding of all unnecessary display of historical erudition, everything in it is bound to appear as historical arbitrariness; and this is just what it is, since each and every line of this book is philosophic, if not in its form, at least in its purpose. Its author may well have committed historical mistakes; he has not committed the deadly one of mistaking philosophy for history. For the only task of history is to understand and to make understood, whereas philosophy must choose; and applying to history for reasons to make a choice is no longer history, it is philosophy. Exactly, it is that kind of philosophy which consists neither in thinking about thought nor in directly knowing reality, but in knowing the relation of thought to reality. It asks history what that relation has been in order to ascertain what it should be. Wholly free with respect to time, it is no more interested in the past as such than it is in the future. Unless such a philosophy be greatly mistaken, which is by no means impossible, its object has neither past nor future, for it *is*, that is, it is *being*, and the truth about it cannot be proved, it can only be seen—or overlooked. Such a dogmatism is singularly devoid of all metaphysical fanaticism either in fact or in intention only. It is and it can be nothing else than an invitation to look and see. And I frankly confess that it is an awkward and clumsy one, full of twists and turns, with nothing of that triumphant easiness which should characterize a direct statement of truth. Supposing it does it at all, this book can achieve its end only in a roundabout way, and here at least its author fully agrees with both William James and John Dewey—not indeed that there is such a thing as a personal truth, but that any approach to truth is bound to be a personal one. A dogmatic book may also be something of a personal confession, and this book is one. Bearing in mind possible brethren in metaphysical misery, it is the public confession of what has actually been a wandering quest of truth.

The matter of the present book has been taught during several years, under different titles, in Paris, at the Collège de France. Circumstances alone are responsible for the fact that it has found its final form in a series of lectures given in 1946 at the Pontifical Institute of Mediaeval Studies (Toronto). Its composition has mainly been a work of ascetic elimination. All that was, because merely historical, irrelevant or unnecessary to the philosophical purpose of the book, has been completely eliminated. I have often had to state what have been the ultimate intentions of some philosophers rather than their very words, and I know that such

undertaking is always fraught with considerable risk. It was my
good fortune to find in the Rev. Gerald B. Phelan, then President
of the Institute, a friend always ready to discuss and to clarify
the ultimate implications of Thomas Aquinas' metaphysics of
being. If that part of the work is not better than it is, the fault
is mine, not his. Furthermore, there are many other things which
I would have said in this book were it not for the fact that the
President of the Pontifical Institute, Professor Anton C. Pegis,
had said them himself quite adequately, and especially in his
essay, *The Dilemma of Being and Unity*.[2] I also feel indebted
to him for many an enlightening conversation. No more than
Father Phelan should Professor Pegis be held responsible for my
own metaphysical ventures, but I am afraid he could not well
decline all responsibility for their publication. He has kindly
assumed the thankless task of removing from my manuscript
blemishes which, perhaps excusable in a teacher who does not
use his own mother tongue, cannot be tolerated in print. Here
again, if this remains a book written in English by a Frenchman,
the fault is mine, not his; but good will is my excuse, and I hope
it will be kindly received by my English-speaking friends.

ETIENNE GILSON

Toronto,
December 15, 1948.

[2] A. C. Pegis, "The Dilemma of Being and Unity. A Platonic Incident in
Christian Thought," in *Essays in Thomism* (New York, Sheed & Ward, 1942),
pp. 151-183, especially pp. 179-183.

Chapter 1

On Being and the One

AFTER defining metaphysics as "a science which investigates being as being and the attributes which belong to this in virtue of its own nature," Aristotle had been careful to add, in order to preclude all possible confusion between metaphysics and the other branches of human learning: "Now this is not the same as any of the so-called special sciences; for none of these others deals generally with being as being. They cut off a part of being and investigate the attributes of this part."[1] Thus, for instance, the mathematical sciences deal with quantity, the physical sciences with motion, and the biological sciences with life, that is to say, with certain definite ways of being, none of which is being as being, but only being as life, as motion, or as quantity.

By making these very simple remarks, Aristotle was doing nothing less than granting metaphysics its charter as a distinct science specified by a distinct object. And his determination of it was so perfect that it contained, together with the definition of what metaphysics had to do in order to live, a clear intimation of what it should not do if it did not want to die. To cut off a part of being and to investigate the attributes of this part is a perfectly legitimate undertaking. In fact, it is to cultivate one of the so-called positive sciences. But to invest any conceivable part of being with the attributes of being itself, and to investigate the attributes of the whole from the point of view of any one of its parts, is to undertake a task whose very notion involves a contradiction. Anybody who attempts it is bound ultimately to fail. When he fails, he himself or his successors will probably blame his failure on metaphysics itself; and they then will conclude that metaphysics is a pseudo-science, which busies itself with problems impervious to the light of human reason. For this well-known form of metaphysical despair, skepticism is but another name. Skepticism is a philosophical disease which either moralism

---

[1] Aristotle, *Metaphysics*, Γ, 1, 1003 a 21-25 in *Aristotle Selections*, ed. by W. D. Ross (New York, Scribner, 1927), p. 53.

or pseudo-mysticism can ease, but for which there is no other cure than to come back to the science of being as being, namely, metaphysics.

If this be true, it should not be wrong to sum up the nature and unity of philosophical experience in the two following propositions: first, that since *being* is the first principle of human knowledge, it is *a fortiori* the first principle of metaphysics; next, that all the past failures of metaphysics should be blamed, not on metaphysics itself, but rather on repeated mistakes made by metaphysicians concerning the first principle of human knowledge, which is *being*.[2] If I now beg leave to use these conclusions as a starting point for a new journey to the land of metaphysics, the reason is not that I no longer hold them to be true; it rather is that I have always considered them as being, although true, yet almost fantastically paradoxical. For indeed, if *being* is the first principle of human knowledge, it must be the very first object to be grasped by the human mind; now, if it is, how are we to account for the fact that so many philosophers have been unable to grasp it? Nor is this all. That which comes first in the order of knowledge must of necessity accompany all our representations; now, if it does, how can *being* both be constantly present to the most common mind, yet prove so elusive that so many very great philosophers have failed to see it? If the ultimate lesson of philosophical experience is that the human mind is blind to the very light in which it is supposed to see both itself and all the rest, what it teaches us is worse than a paradox, it is an absurdity.

The only way for us to avoid this depressing conclusion is to suppose that the fault does not necessarily lie with the nature of the human mind, and that *being* itself might be partly responsible for the difficulty. There may well be something in its very nature which invites philosophers to behave as though the fear of *being* were the beginning of wisdom. What else could account for the curious eagerness of metaphysicians to ascribe the primacy and the universality of being to practically any one of its parts, rather than to accept *being* as the first principle of their philosophy?

As soon as we ask ourselves this question, the fundamental ambiguity of the notion of *being* begins to appear. In a first acceptation, the word being is a noun. As such, it signifies either *a being* (that is, the substance, nature, and essence of anything existent), or being itself, a property common to all that which can rightly be said to be. In a second acceptation, the same word is the

[2] E. Gilson, *The Unity of Philosophical Experience* (New York, Scribner, 1937), pp. 313, 316.

2

present participle of the verb *"to be."* As a verb, it no longer signifies something that is, nor even existence in general, but rather the very act whereby any given reality actually is, or exists. Let us call this act a *"to be,"* in contradistinction to what is commonly called *"a being."* It appears at once that, at least to the mind, the relation of *"to be"* to *"being"* is not a reciprocal one. *"Being"* is conceivable, *"to be"* is not. We cannot possibly conceive an *"is"* except as belonging to some thing that is, or exists. But the reverse is not true. Being is quite conceivable apart from actual existence; so much so that the very first and the most universal of all the distinctions in the realm of being is that which divides it into two classes, that of the real and that of the possible. Now what is it to conceive a being as merely possible, if not to conceive it apart from actual existence? A "possible" is a being which has not yet received, or which has already lost, its own to be. Since being is thinkable apart from actual existence, whereas actual existence is not thinkable apart from being, philosophers will simply yield to one of the fundamental facilities of the human mind by positing *being* minus actual existence as the first principle of metaphysics.

Let us go farther still. It is not enough to say that *being* is conceivable apart from existence; in a certain sense it must be said that *being* is always *conceived* by us apart from existence, for the very simple reason that existence itself cannot possibly be *conceived*. The nature of this paradoxical fact has been admirably described by Kant in the famous passage of his *Critique of Pure Reason* which deals with the so-called ontological proof of the existence of God: "Being," Kant says, "is evidently not a real predicate, or a concept of something that can be added to the concept of a thing."[3] In this text, in which being obviously means to be, Kant wants us to understand that there is no difference whatsoever between the conceptual content of our notion of a thing conceived as existing and the conceptual content of our notion of identically the same thing, not conceived as existing. Now, if the "to be" of a thing could be conceived apart from that which exists, it should be represented in our mind by some note distinct from the concept of the thing itself. Added to our concept of any one thing, such a note would make it represent that thing plus existence, whereas, subtracted from it, this note would make our concept represent the same thing, minus exist-

---

[3] Immanuel Kant, *Critique of Pure Reason*, Transcendental Dialectic, Bk. II, Ch. 3, sect. 4, in *Kant's Selections*, ed. by Theodore Meyer Greene (New York, Scribner 1929), p. 268.

ence. In point of fact, it is not so. There is nothing we can add to a concept in order to make it represent its object as existing; what happens if we add anything to it is that it represents something else. Such is the meaning of Kant's assertion, that the concept of the real does not contain more than the concept of the possible. If we mentally add a cent to the concept of a hundred dollars, we will turn it into the concept of another sum of money, namely, a hundred dollars and one cent; on the contrary, let us analyze the concept of a hundred possible dollars and a hundred real dollars: they are identically the same, namely, the concept of a hundred dollars. In Kant's own words: "By whatever and by however many predicates I may think a thing (even in completely determining it) nothing is really added to it, if I add that the thing exists."[4] In short, actual existence cannot be represented by, nor in, a concept.

Let us call this remarkable character of conceptual knowledge "existential neutrality." The fact that our concepts are existentially neutral has exercised a deep and continuous influence on the development of the history of philosophy, and the very commonness of the example used by Kant can help us in understanding why. Speculatively speaking, my concept of a hundred real dollars does not contain one cent more than my concept of a hundred possible dollars, but existentially speaking, there are a lot of cents in a hundred real dollars, whereas to own a million possible dollars is still to be a penniless man. It did not take a great philosopher to realize this, as Kant himself has been kind enough to grant: "In my financial position, no doubt there exists more by one hundred dollars than by their concept only,"[5] but this absolutely primitive fact is pregnant with an infinity of consequences which even Kant's genius has not been able to embrace in their totality. From the fact that existence is not includable in our concepts, it immediately follows that, to the full extent to which it is made up of concepts, philosophical speculation itself is existentially neutral. It will therefore remain identically the same whether its objects actually exist or not. The relation of a thus understood philosophy to reality will be practically the same as that of the mental multiplication by ten of our bank account to the amount of cash which we can actually draw from the bank. In short, a thus understood philosophy may perhaps be able to tell us everything about that which reality is, but nothing at all concerning this not unimportant detail: the actual existence, or non-existence, of what we call reality.

[4] *Ibid.*, p. 269.　　　　　[5] *Ibid.*

Let us now imagine some philosopher, quite willing to posit being as the first principle of his own doctrine, but still hesitating as to the exact meaning of this notion. Unless he has lost common sense, our man will be keenly aware of the fundamental importance of existence as such. If he himself did not exist, he would not be there to ask questions about the nature of reality, and if there were no actually existing things, he would have nothing to ask questions about. On the other hand, this fundamental fact, which we call existence, soon proves a rather barren topic for philosophical speculation. It belongs in the class of those "it-goes-without-saying" statements which, precisely because they are ultimate in their own order, have to be made once but do not need to be repeated, because they are not susceptible of any further elucidation. Such being the case, what is our philosopher going to do? His natural inclination will probably be to discount existence from his own notion of being. Leaving aside the actual to be of that which is, he will focus his attention on the nature of existence in general as well as on the attributes of all that which enjoys the remarkable privilege of being. If he does so, it will remain true to say that metaphysics is the science of being as being, but of being as a noun, not as a verb. Now, to leave a certain fact out because it cannot be represented by a concept is certainly not an *a priori* absurdity. It certainly looks like a waste of time to speculate about an object which is clearly recognized as inconceivable. Again, there is at least a chance that what is mentally inconceivable may be, at the same time, ontologically sterile. Now if "to be" means nothing more than "to be there," philosophers are wholly justified in taking existence for granted at the very beginning of their inquiries, and in never mentioning it again in the course of their investigations. Yet, this is taking a chance, for, after all, being itself might happen not to be existentially neutral. In other words, it is quite possible that actual existence may be an active force and an efficient cause of observable effects in those things of which we say that they are. If such were the case, all philosophies based upon an existenceless notion of being would be courting disaster, and eventually meet it. It would not take more than two or three disastrous experiments of that kind to convince philosophers that it does not pay to posit being as the first principle of metaphysical knowledge. Hence their repeated attempts to replace it by any one of its many possible surrogates, at the risk of multiplying philosophical failures, so to speak, *ad infinitum*.

We have now, I think, succeeded in identifying the new task which lies ahead of us. It will be to experiment on the following theme: what happens to the notion of being when actual existence is removed from its comprehension? I say to "experiment," because, widely accepted as it is, the conviction that sensible phenomena alone are resistant enough to be experimented upon is nonetheless an illusion. Abstract ideas have a resistance and, so to speak, a solidity of their own. The slightest alteration in their comprehension never fails to bring about a corresponding alteration in the whole series of their consequences. Now, in virtue of its very nature, the notion of being is one of those fundamental data which philosophers have envisaged from all conceivable points of view and scrutinized from all possible angles. Here, as everywhere else, the Greeks have come first, and one of the very first things they have done has precisely been to carry up to its absolutely ultimate consequences an existentially neutral conception of being.

When the early Greek thinkers initiated philosophical speculation, the very first question they asked themselves was: What stuff is reality made of? Taken in itself, this question was strikingly indicative of the most fundamental need of the human mind. To understand something is for us to conceive it as identical in nature with something else that we already know. To know the nature of reality at large is therefore for us to understand that each and every one of the innumerable things which make up the universe is, at bottom, identical in nature with each and every other thing. Prompted by this unshakable conviction, unshakable because rooted in the very essence of human understanding, the early Greek thinkers successively attempted to reduce nature in general to water, then to air, then to fire, until one of them at last hit upon the right answer to the question, by saying that the primary stuff which reality is made of is being.

The answer was obviously correct, for it is not at once evident that, in the last analysis, air and fire are nothing else than water, or that, conversely, water itself is nothing else than either air or fire; but it cannot be doubted that, whatever else they may be, water, air and fire have in common at least this property, that they are. Each of them is a being, and, since the same can be said of everything else, we cannot avoid the conclusion that being is the only property certainly shared in common by all that which is. Being, then, is the fundamental and ultimate element of reality.]

When he made this discovery, Parmenides of Elea at once carried metaphysical speculation to what was always to remain one of its ultimate limits; but, at the same time, he entangled himself in what still is for us one of the worst metaphysical difficulties. It had been possible for Parmenides' predecessors to identify nature with water, fire or air, without going to the trouble of defining the meaning of those terms. If I say that everything is water, everybody will understand what I mean, but if I say that everything is being, I can safely expect to be asked: what is being? For indeed we all know many beings, but what being itself is, or what it is to be, is an extremely obscure and intricate question. Parmenides could hardly avoid telling us what sort of reality being itself is. In point of fact, he was bold enough to raise the problem and clear-sighted enough to give it an answer which still deserves to hold our attention.

Such as we find it described in the first part of Parmenides' philosophical poem, being appears as endowed with all the attributes akin to the notion of identity. First of all, it is of the very essence of being that all that which shares in it is, whereas that which does not share in it, is not. Now if all that which is, is being, being is both unique and universal. For the same reason, a cause of its existence is inconceivable. In order to cause it, its cause would have first to be, which means that, since being is the only conceivable cause of being, it has no cause. Consequently, being has no beginning. Moreover, since any conceivable cause of its destruction would also have to be before destroying it, being can have no end. In other words, it is eternal. One cannot say of it that it once was, or that it will later be, but only that it is. Thus established in a perpetual present, being has no history because it is essentially foreign to change. Any modification in its structure would imply that something which was not is becoming, or beginning to be, which is an impossibility. Besides, being has no structure. It is not subject to division, since there is no place, within being itself, where it could possibly not exist. Let us therefore conceive it as absolutely full, and, if we find it easier to imagine its nature, let us picture it to our fancy like "the mass of a rounded sphere, equally distant from the centre at every point," wherein being is everywhere contiguous to, and equal with, being, immovable, necessary, eternally lying in the same condition and abiding in the same place. Such is the true nature of that which is; for being alone is, and there is no other alternative, for any conceivable reality, than either to be that which being itself actually is, or else not to be at all.[6]

[6] For an English translation of Parmenides' philosophical poem, see Milton C. Nahm, *Selections from Early Greek Philosophy*, 2nd ed. (New York, Crofts, 1941), pp. 113-117.

7

Today it is hard for us to read this philosophical poem, written between 500 and 450 B.C., otherwise than as a curious specimen of mental archeology, and, in fact, this is exactly what its plastic imagery is. But let us go beyond the poetic fiction of this rounded sphere of being, "perfected on every side," and "in the hold of great chains, without beginning or end;" let us try to reach, beyond these images, the rational exigencies of which the poet philosopher was trying to give us a concrete feeling, and old Parmenides will appear to us as he once appeared to Plato: "a man to be respected and at the same time feared."[7] There is in his thought something of the adamantine quality of his own notion of being. As early as the fifth century, B.C., Parmenides carried metaphysics, that is, our human science of the nature of being, up to one of its ultimate limits, and we will see that Plato himself has never been able to get out of this metaphysical dead end street. If we allow ourselves to be tricked into his own position on the problem of being, it is no longer Parmenides himself we are up against, but rather an unshakable law of the human mind.

What lies at the bottom of Parmenides' doctrine is this fundamental truth, that, however we look at reality, we fail to discover in it anything more important than its very existence. Hence his often-repeated statement that "being is," whereas "it is impossible that non-being be;" in other words, "either being exists or it does not exist," which means that, for reality, no intermediate condition is conceivable between existence and non-existence. In Parmenides' own words, "it is necessary that being either is absolutely or is not," and, since nobody would ever dream of maintaining that being is not, there is but one single path left open to philosophical speculation, "namely, that being is."[8]

So far, so good. The real difficulty begins when we try to interpret this very formula: being is. What makes Parmenides' position a permanently conclusive experiment in metaphysics is that it shows us what happens to reality when the proposition, *being is*, is held as a tautological one. For indeed it is evident that only that which is, is, or exists, but it is not at once evident that only that which answers Parmenides' description of being is, or exists. Because Parmenides has based his whole doctrine upon the evident assumption that being is, he still remains for us what he already was for Plato, a man to be respected; but because he has unreservedly equated existence with being, he still inspires us with as much fear as reverence. At first sight, it looks quite natural to

[7] Plato, *Theaetetus*, 183 E.
[8] Nahm, *Selections from Early Greek Philosophy*, pp. 115-116.

8

consider that to be a *being* is to exist and that, conversely, to exist is to be a being. Yet, if we grant Parmenides this seemingly necessary position, he will ruthlessly drag us through a series of such devastating consequences that very little will remain of what we usually call reality.

If to be a being and to exist are one and the same thing, it becomes imperative for us to exclude from actual existence whatever does not exhibit the genuine characters of being. Now being is one, but the world of sense we are living in appears to us as many. There is in it a variety of elements, each of which is identical with itself, but not identical with the others. Moreover, these elements are not only different; some of them are opposite: light and darkness, for instance; yet they seem to co-exist in the same world, so that, if we ascribe being to the world of sense, we shall have to say that being is neither one, nor homogeneous, nor simple, which we know to be impossible. Again, particular things are ceaselessly appearing and disappearing; we see them beginning to be, then progressively changing, decaying and coming to an end: plurality, diversity, mutability, caducity—so many characteristics that cannot be reconciled with our previous description of being. Now, if only that which deserves the title of being is, or exists, the world of sense as a whole must be said not to be. A strange yet unavoidable consequence with which, even today, each and every metaphysician still finds himself confronted. If reality is that which is, then there is nothing real but being only, and, since we have no experience of anything which we may consider as absolutely one, ingenerable and indestructible, wholly homogeneous, continuous and free from change, it follows of necessity that true reality is a pure object of the mind. Actual reality thus becomes the exclusive privilege of that object of thought to which alone our understanding can ascribe the attributes of being. All the rest, namely, this infinitely varied world of change, including ourselves who are living in it, cannot be said to be: it is but an appearance, a mere illusion.

Thus, as early as the fifth century before Christ, and without being in the least conscious of it, Parmenides was not only creating the science of being as being, but reaching at once one of those few philosophical positions that can rightly be called *pure*, in that they mark the absolute limits which, along certain lines of thought, are accessible to the human mind. If we call *existence* the definite mode of being which belongs to the world of change such as it is given in sensible experience—and it should not be forgotten that we have no experience of any other type of reality—it then becomes

obvious that there is a considerable difference between to be and
to exist. That which exists is not, just as that which is does
not exist. From the very beginning of the history of Western
thought, it thus appears that, if being truly is, nothing should
exist. In other words, there is nothing in being as such to account
for the fact of existence. If there is such a thing as existence,
either it has to be kept side by side with being, as something
wholly unrelated to it—which is what Parmenides seems to have
done—or else it will have already to pass for what modern existentialism says that it is: a "disease" of being.

Plato remains, on this point, the heir and continuator of
Parmenides, or, rather, of what had been his fundamental intuition.
Assuredly, nothing could be more different from the materialism
of Parmenides than Plato's idealism; but, since all that can be
said concerning being as being remains identically the same
whether being be conceived as material or not, the fact that
Parmenides' being was material whereas Plato's being was to be
immaterial, could not prevent it from obeying the same metaphysical necessities and, so to speak, from yielding to the same
law. In point of fact, *qua* beings, they are bound to be the same
being.

What Plato is seeking when dealing with this problem, is
what he himself has repeatedly called the *"ὄντως ὄν."* This expression is usually rendered in English by "really real," which is
undoubtedly correct; and yet, when it is thus translated, the Greek
loses a good deal of its original energy. For, indeed, the "real"
is less being itself than the thing (*res*) which a certain being is, but,
since we cannot say the "beingly being," we must accept "reality"
as a practical equivalent for "being." However we may choose
to translate it, the immediate meaning of Plato's formula is clear.
His intention obviously is to point out, amongst the many objects
of knowledge that are candidates for the title of being, the only
ones which truly deserve it. What makes it hard for us not to
betray Plato's genuine intention is that he himself, though
supremely apt at definition, seems more or less at a loss when
it comes to defining the nature of the "really real," that is, of
true being. As he never tires of repeating, really to be is to be
"its own self according to itself: *αὐτὸ καθ᾽ αὐτό."* The ultimate
mark of true being lies therefore in "selfhood." Now to say this
is merely to restate that relation, mysterious yet necessary, which
Parmenides had already discovered between identity and reality.
Such a relation is one of equality. To be, for any given thing, is
first of all to be that which it is. Abstract as it may seem, such a

formula assumes a concrete meaning as soon as we ask ourselves what it would mean, for any one of us, to "become another one." Strictly speaking, the question does not make sense. *I* cannot *become another*, for the very simple reason that, so long as I can say *I*, I am not yet another, whereas, as soon as the other is there, there appears on the scene a second *I* which is wholly unrelated to me. From my own *ego* to another one, no transition of any sort can possibly be conceived. When, in the *Golden Ass* of Apuleius, the hero of the novel tells us how, once a man, he later became a donkey, then a man again, it is well understood that, from the beginning of that entertaining tale up to its end, the very same being never ceases to exist, now under the shape of a man, now under that of a donkey. Were it otherwise, the tale could not even be told. All metamorphoses are conceivable, but only as superficial alterations of something which remains identically the same throughout the whole series of the transformations it undergoes. It is therefore one and the same thing, for all that which is, to be, and to be that which it is: the abolition of its self-identity amounts to its pure and simple annihilation.

In such a doctrine, in which self-identity is the condition and mark of reality, being necessarily appears as one, homogeneous, simple, and immune to change. These characteristics are much less attributes of being than various expressions of its essential self-identity. That which is, is bound to be one, because it is contradictory to conceive as belonging to a certain being something *other than* that being. Here is a lump of gold with a streak of silver in it; its being may be that of a jewel, it cannot be that of gold. If I want to name the beings which enter its composition, I must name at least two, and say: this is gold and this is silver. For indeed, gold *is* only inasmuch as it is *gold*. As Leibniz was fond of saying, it is one and the same to be *a* thing and to be a *thing*. In other words, the "really real" is free from otherness, because what we could ascribe to it as other than what it is would actually be "another being." For the same reason, being as such is free from change. In a doctrine where *to be* is *to be the same*, otherness is the very negation of being. Thus, in virtue of its self-identity, which forbids it to change unless indeed it ceased to be, true being is immutable in its own right.

This permanency in self-identity is the chief mark of the "really real," that is, of being. At the very beginning of our inquiry, we agreed with Kant that existence is not an attribute, but it now seems to appear that, according to Plato, being is one, and nothing shows better how wholly indifferent to actual exist-

11

ence his philosophy is. Reality is the very character which belongs to all that is a true being. Rather, it is what makes it to be a true being. In Plato's philosophy, as far as I can see, being in itself is not, but things that are real are so because they have it. There are beings about each of which it is true to say that either it is, or it is not, but there is no such thing as a self-subsisting being *qua* being.

This common property of all that truly is constitutes what Plato himself calls *οὐσία*, a word which can be correctly rendered by *essentia*, or *essence*, but which points out, beyond what we usually call the essence of the thing, the very reality of that which truly is. In other words, the *οὐσία* points to the property which belongs to the really real as such and makes it to be a being. Now, we know the metaphysical cause of that property: it lies in that very self-identity which, according to Plato, both constitutes being and justifies its attribution. In short, there is no difference whatsoever between being and self-identity. Let us recall the well-known passage of the *Phaedo* in which Plato himself, grappling with the difficulties of his own terminology, seems to be groping through words for a satisfactory formula of this fundamental equation: "But now let us return to those things we have been dealing with in the previous discussion. The very essence of being (*οὐσία αὐτὴ τοῦ εἶναι*) which we have accounted for by means of questions and answers, is it always in the same manner and in the same way, or is it now this way now that way? Equality itself, beauty itself, each and every itself (*αὐτὸ ἕκαστον*), which being is, are they liable at times to some degree of change? Or does each one of these things, whose form is single, remain always itself in itself, being changeless in every way and in every respect? They must remain always the same, Socrates, replied Cebes."[9] This text alone would suffice to justify R. Demos' statement: "Selfhood, self-identity, self-similarity, purity and rest are the fundamental requisites of being such as Plato himself understood it."[10]

In Plato's own writings, the thus-conceived "really real" is susceptible of several different names: Ideas, for instance, or Forms. However he may choose to call it, the really real is always for him, in virtue of its very reality, the supremely intelligible.

---

[9] Plato, *Phaedo*, 78 d, in *Plato Selections*, ed. by R. Demos (New York, Scribner, 1927), p. 178.

[10] R. Demos, *The Philosophy of Plato* (New York, Scribner, 1939), p. 160. We are leaving out of this list the note of "intelligibility," which Dr. Demos rightly includes, and which we will presently take into consideration.

As it will be seen later, there may be, in his doctrine, something that still remains to be found above both reality and intelligibility, but one thing at least is clear, and it is that, to him, the more a thing can be said to be, the more it can be said to be knowable. How could we possibly forget to recall, at the very moment we are reaching what still today remains one of the most solemn moments in the history of Western thought, the mysterious oracle already issued by old Parmenides: "To know, and that which is known, are one and the same thing"? If there be such things as pure metaphysical positions, here is one, for even as late as the nineteenth century, Hegel himself will have to posit it as the very basis of his own philosophical Encyclopaedia; but Plato can help us in understanding the limits as well as the nature of its necessity. If being and intelligibility can be strictly equated, the reason for it is precisely that being has first been equated with self-identity. Now, self- identity is the proper object of conceptual knowledge. To know that there is gold in a certain place is to know that what is to be found there is gold. If what is there is not gold, then there *is* no gold in that place. Now, beyond this unity of the particular thing, there is that of its species. And how can I obtain the species, if not through reducing the apparent diversity of individuals to the sameness and unity of their common Idea? Last, but not least, I need to unify in order to establish intelligible relations even between different things, a result which can be achieved only through linking them together by a continuous chain of identities: "I believe indeed, Sir, [Leibniz says] that the principle of principles is, so to speak, to make a correct use of ideas and of experiments; yet, if one looks deeper into one's principle, one will find that, in so far as ideas are concerned, it is nothing else than to link together definitions by means of axioms that are identical."[11] And why is it so? It is so every time and everywhere being happens to be defined by its self-identity. Now, thus to define being is one of the permanent temptations of the human mind. To equate reality and identity is merely to make reality be what it ought to be in order to be exhaustively intelligible to human understanding. In this sense and to this extent it is strictly true to say that being and thought are one, since

---

[11] Leibniz, in *Opera philosophia*, ed. by B. Erdmann, p. 311. The generality of this thesis has been remarkably established by E. Meyerson in practically each and every chapter of his works. Let it suffice to recall here the title of the best known among them: *Identity and Reality*. If E. Meyerson has always refused to draw from this fact any of its metaphysical implications, he must at least be thanked for having conclusively proved it.

being here finds itself reduced to a mere objectivation of what is for conceptual thought a fundamental necessity, namely, the principle of identity. Thought here does nothing more than to gratify itself by mirroring its very essence in an object made to order to suit its own needs.

Having accepted this Parmenidean standard of reality, Plato had necessarily to face its Parmenidean consequences, the first and most important of which naturally was: if to be is to be the same, what are we to do with otherness, that is to say, with the concrete world of change and of becoming? To this question, the obvious answer was that, if sameness alone is, otherness is not. As he himself once asked in a striking sentence of his *Timaeus*: "Which is the being that is eternal and is never born, and which is the being that is always being born, but never *is*?"[12] No hesitation is here possible. On the one hand, the genus of that whose form is always self-identical, ingenerable and indestructible: It is the world of what Plato has a hundred times described as divine, immortal, intelligible, made up of forms that are indestructible because they are simple and "enjoying always in the same way their self-identity;"[13] on the other hand, the genus of sensible things, which are ceaselessly being born and ceaselessly passing away, "always in motion, becoming in place and again vanishing out of place, which are apprehended by opinion and sense."[14] Clearly enough, if the first one of these two worlds is, the second one is not.

It would be rather foolish of us here to argue, against Plato, that the things whose reality he thus denies are indeed for us the very type of actual reality. This, Plato would say, is precisely the fundamental illusion one has to get rid of if one wants to become a philosopher. On the contrary, we are fully justified in asking him what he means by saying that an Idea *is*. It is especially legitimate to ask him the question in his own words, such at least as we read them in Jowett's daring, almost reckless, translation: "Is there any self-existent fire? and do all those things which we call 'self-existent' exist?"[15] Without taking unfair advantage of a translation, one cannot help wondering at the possible meaning of such propositions as: "Fire itself in itself" *is*, "Beauty *is*," "Equality *is*, or exists." To say that such realities

---

[12] Plato, *Timaeus*, 87 d.
[13] Plato, *Phaedo*, 80 b. Each one of these forms is endowed with a perfect internal homogeneity (μονοειδὲς), and, consequently, with an essential purity (καθαρὸν). It is one essence, and only one.
[14] Plato, *Timaeus*, 52, in Demos' edition, p. 614.
[15] Plato, *Timaeus*, 51, *loc. cit.*, p. 613.

14

exist is most confusing, because the only existence we can imagine is that of sensible things. Now, if Ideas *are*, in what sense can they be said *to be*? To write equality with a capital "E" does not help much in solving the problem. A plastic-minded reader of Plato may well imagine "justice itself in itself" in the guise of some white-clad, immovable and impassive figure, eternally holding a pair of scales wherein nothing is ever being weighed; but everybody knows that this is exactly what Plato wanted us not to do. If we are rightly to understand justice in itself, the very first condition to be fulfilled is *not* to imagine it. Then, once more, what do we mean by saying that justice *is*?

If we are here vainly looking to Plato for an answer, the reason probably is that we are asking him the wrong question. He has just told us what it is for him to be, and we keep on asking him what it is to exist. Having told us that to be is "to be the same," he has defined for us what was to him the very core of οὐσία, and to ask furthermore if, according to him, the "really real" really is, would only prove that we have not yet properly understood his answer. A concrete example will perhaps help in realizing the true nature of this metaphysical situation. In his remarkable book, *The Nature of Existence*, McTaggart has raised this highly interesting difficulty: "Is Mrs. Gamp real or not?"[16] If we could ask Dickens himself to give us his opinion, he would no doubt feel puzzled. To him, both Mrs. Gamp and her dram of whiskey probably were, as indeed they are to all his readers, incomparably more "real" than hundreds of people whose actual existence we hold as absolutely certain simply because we happen to meet them on the street. We feel quite sure that these people exist; yet, of how many among them could we reasonably suppose that they enjoy the wonderful self-identity and the perfect internal homogeneity by which Mrs. Gamp can be truly said to be? Not unlike a Platonic Idea, Mrs. Gamp is, but she does not exist, wheras most of us, who do actually exist, are not. Most men, as we say in our bad moods, and always excluding ourselves, are nonentities. The fundamental ambiguity of the word *"being"* is here so apparent that it can no longer be overlooked. It may mean either *that* which is, or the fact that it *is*. Of these two meanings, Plato resolutely ignores the second one. To the question: in what sense can it be said that a Platonic Idea is, there is but one answer: it *is* in the sense that it is wholly and exclusively that which it is. Plato gives us no other answer because he asks himself no other question.

[16] G. McTaggart Ellis McTaggart, *The Nature of Existence* (Cambridge University Press, 1921), Vol. I, p. 6.

Right or wrong, it looks at first sight as though such a radical decision were bound at least to simplify the task of the metaphysician. Yet, on closer inspection, this happy result does not materialize and the wonderful simplicity of Plato's notion of being soon appears full of many and unexpected complications.

The first recognizable characteristic of Plato's being is that it will always appear, throughout its various historical modifications, as a variable quantity. The position of Parmenides had been a very simple and an almost crude one: that which is, is, and that which is not, is not.[17] Not so with Plato, whose main speculative effort was addressed to the problem of accounting for the fact that certain things are, yet not quite, or, if we prefer to say it the other way around, that they not quite are not. Instead of juxtaposing being and non-being, that is, reality and appearance, Plato attempted to show that, even in appearance, there was a measure of reality. A both perfectly honest and exceedingly risky undertaking indeed, since from that very moment the problem would no longer be to distinguish between that which is and that which is not, but between that which is "really real" and that which, though real, is not really so.

The very formula of this new problem is enough to show us how indifferent to the order of actual existence Platonism is. In doctrines in which "to be a being" means "actually to be," or exist, it is hardly possible to think of an intermediate position between being and non-being. As Hamlet says, "to be or not to be, that is the question." Even without making Hamlet responsible for metaphysical decisions foreign to his personal difficulties, we can use his formula to express the fact that, in the order of actual existence at least, a thing either is, or is not, and there is no half-way house between these two positions. But things go differently in the Platonic world of οὐσία, in which there are "degrees of being," or of reality, which are proportioned to the degrees of selfhood and to the purity of essence in different beings. This is why Plato can say of sensible things that they are, yet not quite, without entangling himself in any hopeless contradiction. Of course, there are huge difficulties, but one cannot say that the doctrine does not make sense, as would be the case if for him *to be* meant *to exist*. In the world of Plato, sensible things are by as much as they share in the essence of what is "really real," that is to say, of that which can truly be said to be; yet these same

[17] J. Burnet, *Early Greek Philosophy*, 4th ed. (London, A. and C. Black, 1930) 174; *L'Aurore de la philosophie grecque* (Paris, Payot, 1929), p. 201, text 8.

sensible things are not, by as much as they are lacking in selfhood. The presence of Platonism can be detected, throughout the whole story of Western thought, by means of these two signs: first, being and non-being are variable quantities, between which innumerable degrees of reality can be found; next, all relations of being to non-being can and must be transposed into relations of sameness and otherness. In short, there is no difference whatsoever between the problem "to be or not to be" and the problem *de eodem et diverso.*

Every student in philosophy is fully aware of the difficulties that beset the Platonic doctrine of participation. Plato himself knows them better than anybody else, and we find them all, clearly stated, in his own dialogue, the *Parmenides.* Yet, the real difficulty is not to understand how several individuals can share in the same Idea without wrecking its unity; it is rather to understand how that Idea, taken itself in itself, can enjoy the privilege of its self-identity. How can it be self-identical without being other, as self, than it is as identical? Let us state the same question in different terms. It is indeed a problem to know how it is possible, for a multiplicity of things, to share in the unity of their common Idea, but is it not just as difficult to understand how one and the same Idea can share in its own unity? For, indeed, if an Idea is self-identical, it is one. Total, internal sameness is nothing else than total unity. Hence it is one and the same thing to say that an Idea is self-identical, that it is, and that it is one. But how can it be one? Justice, for instance, is what it is to be just; equality is what it is to be equal; fire is what it is to be fire; each of these Ideas is just that which it is; but since, at the same time, each of them is one, each of them is similarly sharing in another Idea, which is unity itself in itself. If it is so, unity is, to each one of the various Ideas, in a relation similar to that which obtains between a given Idea and its many individuals. Let us now generalize the problem and, instead of Ideas, let us speak of their common character, which is to be really real or truly to be. If the Idea is because it is one, being is because it is one. In other words, each and every "really real" is a "being that is one" or a "one that is." Now, this "one that is" appears to us as a compound of both being and the one. It is not simple, but it is made up of two parts, each of which is itself bound to be made of two parts, since it is always true to say that a being is one and that, for it, to be one is to be. It thus appears that even that simplest of all Ideas not only is not one, but includes a virtually infinite multiplicity. Of course, there is a way out of this maze: it is to consider the one

17

itself in itself, no longer as being, but merely as one. Only, if we do so, it then becomes true to say that the one is other than being, consequently that the one is not and that there are no relations between the one and being.[18] In other words, if we look at unity for the root of being, the being of unity is no more conceivable than the unity of being.

From Plotinus, who was to discover in it the very basis he needed for his own metaphysics of the One, down to A. E. Taylor, who thinks that the dialogue "is very largely of the nature of a *jeu d'esprit*,"[19] the *Parmenides* has received innumerable interpretations. In so far as our own problem is concerned, however, the ultimate meaning of the dialogue is by no means obscure. On the one hand, it is strictly impossible to conceive being without ascribing to it some sort of unity: "If the One is not, nothing is;" on the other hand, the relation of being to the One is inconceivable: whether you say that the One is or that it is not, and again whether you say that being is one or that it is not one, you get entangled in equally inextricable dialectical impossibilities. The abiding truth which we can still learn from Plato's *Parmenides* is that to be is something else than to be one; but then, what is it?

Defeated on the field of unity, we still may try to succeed on the field of sameness. Why, after all, should we say that self-identity is unity? Yet, if we attempt to solve the same problem by resorting to sameness, many difficulties will occur. To say that being is identical with sameness amounts to saying that there is absolutely no difference between the respective meanings of those two terms.[20] Now, should we accept this, being could no longer be ascribed to any two *different* things. In other words, things would then have either not to be, or not to be different. And, if anyone replies that we are not here concerned with the relation of *beings* to sameness, but with that of each "really real" being to its own self-identity, another difficulty would arise, namely, that otherness is actually and necessarily, if not included with sameness, at least coupled with it. What is it indeed to be *the same as* itself, if it is not to be *other than* all the rest? Sameness then entails otherness, and, since sameness has been posited as identical with being, just as otherness is identical with non-being, it is one and the same thing to say that sameness entails otherness and to say that being entails non-being. Consequently, the question

---

[18] Plato, *Parmenides*, 143-144.
[19] A. E. Taylor, *The Parmenides of Plato*, translated into English with Introduction and Appendices (Oxford, Clarendon Press, 1934), p. 39.
[20] Plato, *Sophist*, 255 b-c.

no longer is, to be *or* not to be, but, rather, to be *and* not to be. Nothing can be that which it is, without, at the same time, not being that which it is not. Moreover, each being is the same as itself only, whereas, it is other than all the rest. It is therefore the same but once, whereas it is "other" as many times as there are other things. Now, since to be is to be the same, and since to be other is not to be, any given thing can be called a being but once, against the infinite number of times when it must be said not to be. In short, according to the number of other beings that there are, so many times is it true to say that a given being is not, although, in respect of its own selfhood, this one being alone is, while all the other ones are not.[21] No more than unity, sameness alone does not suffice to account for reality.

If Plato found it hard to account for the being of any "really real" object, he could not but find it still harder to account for the mutual relations of such objects. Now, there are such relations. Even our sensible world is not made up of disconnected things; if it is a "world," a *cosmos*, it must needs enjoy an order of its own, and, since sensible things are but images of Ideas, Ideas themselves are bound to make up another world, the intelligible world. All the relations that can be observed in this world of sense must necessarily obtain in that intelligible world. Now, it is a fact that each sensible thing is actually sharing in a multiplicity of Ideas, and that they sometimes share in Ideas that are not only different, but opposite. I, for instance, may be taller than one person, yet smaller than another. Consequently, I am sharing in both tallness and smallness; but I also am mind and body, learned and ignorant, just and unjust. There is then in each concrete being a mixture of Ideas, but is there not a mixture of Ideas among Ideas themselves? Is not law sharing in justice, justice in equality, equality in quantity? Now, if each Idea entails a multiplicity of relations, yet is "itself in itself," it becomes useless for us to look at it in itself for the cause of its relations. Where are we going to find such a cause?

The problem is the more difficult to solve, as the relations which obtain between Ideas are really included within their very essence. They are, so to speak, constitutive of their very being: justice truly is, if not equality itself, at least an equality. Hence two consequences: first, that no Idea can be said to be solely that which it is; next, that in order to account for the fact that Ideas are what they are, we must needs posit such a principle as will account for both their internal consistency and their mutual

[21] *Ibid.*, 256, 258, 259.

19

compatibility. In other words, even though Plato does not seem to worry about the fact that Ideas are, he cannot help but worry about the fact that each of them is that which it is. Here again, the only way out is for him to posit, beyond being, some supreme principle and cause of that which being actually is. He does so in the *Republic*, where, after describing the order of appearance, then the order of true reality, which is the same as that of intelligibility, he says that even this "really real" is not supreme. Above and beyond οὐσία there still remains an ἐπέκεινα τῆς οὐσίας, that is to say, a principle which lies beyond being. Such is the Good, of which Plato says that it passes being in power as well as in dignity.[22]

In the ancient schools of philosophy, τὸ Πλάτωνος ἀγαθόν —Plato's Good—was a formula proverbially used to signify something very obscure. It had to be: how could we say what the Good is, since, in virtue of its very supremacy, it is not? We should therefore let that pass. What we cannot let pass unnoticed is the fact that, in a doctrine in which it is supposed to be the same as self-identity, true being is unable to account for itself. The "really real" then hangs upon something that is not real; the perfectly knowable hangs upon something that is not knowable, and whichever name we may choose to call their ultimate principle, be it the One or the Good, the fact remains that being and intelligibility no longer reign supreme. After following them as far as it can, the human mind loses their tracks, and they seem indeed to lose themselves, in the darkness of some supreme non-being and of some supreme unintelligibility.

Neoplatonism did not follow from Platonism by some mode of logical deduction, nor did it follow immediately in time. Many centuries separate Plotinus from Plato, and the spiritual needs of these two philosophers appear to us as having been, though akin, yet different. As has just been seen, Plato is called upon to go beyond being in his quest for ultimate truth, but he very seldom does it and, at any rate, he never stays there for any length of time. One can hardly breathe in such a metaphysical stratosphere, where to fly above being is to fly above intelligibility. Plato opens a door to mysticism, but he himself does not enter it. Not so with Plotinus. Plato had been a philosopher with a deep religious feeling; Plotinus looks rather as a theologian with deep philosophical insight. If, as Plato sometimes said there was, there is such a principle that is superior to being, then, Plotinus thinks, we should by all means make it the starting point of all philosophical

[22] Plato, *Republic*, VI, 509 b.

inquiry. Whatever question we may ask, let us always look to that principle for an answer. Now, there is such a principle, and, though Plotinus likes to remind us that it is an unnamable one, he has given it two names, which are precisely those already used by Plato to point out, beyond that which is, the ultimate root of being. These names are the One and the Good; but, here again, the problem is to know what they mean.

The Good and the One are one and the same thing, with two reservations, however: first, they are not *things*, and what they designate is not *a thing*; next, they point to two aspects, complementary yet distinct, of what they designate, the supreme unknown which lies beyond all names. Like that of Plato, the doctrine of Plotinus is largely a reflection on the nature of being, and in both cases the notion of being reaches its ultimate depth at the very point where it becomes apparent that, taken in its very essence, being itself hangs upon some principle that lies above or beyond it, namely, the radical opposition to multiplicity which is co-essential to being. Now, if being is because it is one, the ultimate principle of being is bound to be the One. Let us give it that name, at any rate, in so far as it ultimately causes being through giving it unity. As Plotinus himself says: "The non-one is preserved by the One, and it is owing to the One that it is what it is; so long as a certain thing, which is made up of many parts, is not yet become one, we cannot yet say of it: *it is*. And, if we can say of each and every thing what it is, it is owing to its unity as well as to its identity."[23] Now, in each one of those composite things which owe to it both their unity and their being, this self-identity still remains a participated unity. The One itself is entirely different: it is not one of those unities which are more or less perfectly achieved by some process of unification, but the origin and cause of all participated unity and therefore of all being. The One, then, is an immensely powerful principle, which is able to beget everything, and which, in point of fact, does beget everything. Now, if we look at it from this second point of view, which is that of its powerfulness, the first principle can rightly be called the Good. Thus, the first principle is both the One and the Good, as being the cause of "that which comes after the One, namely, multiplicity."

What is particularly striking in Plotinus' own position is its systematic character. Plato had here and there hinted that, in order to understand the ultimate nature of being, we need to go beyond being. Then he had once said that what lies beyond being was the Good, just as he had often suggested that, if being is, then

[23] Plotinus, *Enn.*, V, 3, 15.

the One also must needs be. Now, as compared with what Plotinus says, Plato's formulas appear as merely casual remarks. First of all, the One of Plotinus is not a rational principle to which, as in Plato's *Sophistes*, we are lead by dialectical speculation; it is beyond reality, more real than reality itself, and one still hesitates to call it a god, because it actually is much more than a god. Whatever we may choose to call it, the One of Plotinus is the highest object of worship.

Let us hasten to add, however, that, strictly speaking, the One is no object, precisely because it lies beyond being. The transcendence of the One in respect of being here becomes perfectly clear. In other words, it becomes perfectly clear that being no longer is the first principle, either in metaphysics or in reality. To Plotinus, being is only the second principle, above which there is to be found a higher one, so perfect in itself that it is not. More than that, it is precisely because the first principle is not being that it can be the cause of being. Should the first principle be itself being, then being would be first: it could have no cause. Thus, in Plotinus' own words: "It is because nothing in it is, that everything comes from it; so much so that, in order that being be, the One itself is bound not to be being, but the father of being, and being is its first-born child."[24]

Why is it necessary to put the One above being? Plato had already said it, but Plotinus now makes it quite clear. Each particular being is but a particular unit, which shares in unity itself, yet is not it. If the One were but "a certain one, it would not be the One itself; for indeed the One itself comes before what is but a certain one."[25] And this is precisely the reason why there really is no name for the One, not even the One. Whichever name we may choose to give it, we are bound to speak of the One as of a certain *it*. Now, the One is neither an *it*, nor a *he*, because the One is not a thing, and, if there is no thing which the One be, then we can boldly say that the One is nothing. In short, the One is nothing, because it is much too good to be something.

What all this comes to is that the One is unthinkable. Of course, the One is unthinkable for us, who are manifold, but Plotinus wants us to realize something much more important, namely, that, taken itself in itself, the One cannot become an object of thought. The better to understand this, let us recall the first and most elementary condition that is required for the simplest act of knowing. Where there is knowledge, there must be both a knowing subject and a known thing. True enough, the knower and the

[24] *Ibid.*, V, 2, 1.　　　　[25] *Ibid.*, V, 3, 12.

ON BEING AND THE ONE

known may happen to be one and the same, as it happens in;those cases when a man says: "I know myself." Yet, even then, for one and the same thing to be both knowing and known means for it to be no longer one, but two. Now, how could the absolutely One possibly be two? "If there is a reality that is the simplest of all [Plotinus says], it will have no self-knowledge. Had it such knowledge, it would be a multiple being. Consequently, it does not think itself, nor does one think it."[26] Such then is the reason why, since knowledge and being are inseparable, the One is both unreal and unthinkable, which precisely enables it to be the cause of both thought and being.

In Plotinus' philosophy, the relation of the One to thought and to being is so important, that the meaning of the whole doctrine hinges on its interpretation. Plotinianism has been not seldom labeled as a "monism," or as a "pantheism."[27] In point of fact, such problems are wholly foreign to the Plotinianism of Plotinus himself. What we call the "pantheism" of Plotinus is an illusion of perspective due to the interplay of two inconsistent doctrines of being. Such an illusion arises, in the mind of his interpreters, at the very point at which, identifying the One and the Good of Plotinus with the Being of the Christian God, they turn the Plotinian emanation of the multiple from the One into a Christian emanation of beings from Being. This, I am afraid, is an enormous mistake, for indeed we have not here to compare a certain ontology with another ontology but, rather, a certain ontology with, so to speak, a "monology." Now, strictly speaking, such a comparison is impossible, because each one of these two points of view on reality entails exigencies of its own, which are incompatible with those entailed by the other one. In a metaphysics of being, such as a Christian metaphysics, for instance, each and every lower grade of reality owes its own being to the fact that the first principle itself *is*. In a metaphysics of the One, however, it is a general rule that the lower grades of reality are only because their first principle itself is not. In order to give something, a cause is bound to be above it, for if the superior already had that which it causes, it could not *cause* it, it would *be* it.[28] Now, if a monism is a doctrine in which being is everywhere

<hr/>

[26] *Ibid.*, V, 3, 13. Cf. V, 6, 4. Let us note, however, that the One is not "unconscious;" only its self-knowledge is other than, and superior to, thought (*Enn.*, V, 4, 2); once more, we cannot imagine it.

[27] M. de Wulf, *Histoire de la philosophie médiévale*, 6th ed. (1934), Vol. I, p. 109. Cf. H. von Arnim, *Die europäische Philosophie des Altertums*, in *Allgemeine Geschichte der Philosophie* (Leipzig, Teubner, 1913), p. 259.

[28] Plotinus, *Enn.*, VI, 7, 17.

23

one and the same, no philosophy is farther removed from monism than that of Plotinus. To be sure, it would be a monism if its first principle were being; but, since we know that its first principle is above being, there can be no sharing by the world in the being of a first principle which itself *is not*.

Such is the exact meaning of the formulas by which Plotinus defines the problem of the origin of the world: "How did the One bestow what itself had not?"[29] And we already know the answer: "It is because nothing is in the One that everything comes from it. Thus, in order that being be, it is necessary that the One itself be, not being, but that which begets being. Being, then, is as its first-born child."[30] Let us be careful to remember this last formula, whose later history is inseparable from that of mediaeval metaphysics. For the moment, what we have to realize is this all-important fact, that a radical devaluation of being is taking place under our very eyes. From now on, wherever true and genuine Platonism shall prevail, οὐσία will not come first, but only second, in the universal order. In other words, the great chain of being as a whole, hangs upon a cause which itself completely transcends it. "It is manifest," Plotinus says, "that the maker of both reality and substance is itself no reality, but is beyond both reality and substance."[31] This is the authentic doctrine of Plotinus, and it is the very reverse of a Christian metaphysics of being. *"Quid enim est, nisi quia tu es?"*[32] Augustine will ask God in his *Confessions*. Had he been addressing, not the Christian God of *Exodus*, but the One of Plato, Augustine would have given his question an entirely different wording; no longer: "What is, if not because Thou art?" but, rather, "what is, if not because Thou art not?"

Thus correctly to situate Plotinus' own metaphysical position is not merely to add one more fact to the list of other historical facts; it is to grasp in its purity the authentic spirit of a great philosophical tradition, as well as to reveal the intrinsic necessity of that pure philosophical position which the metaphysics of the One finally is. Still imperfect in the mind of Plato, whose dialectic seems to have groped for rather than found it, the One was already there, weighted with its own necessary implications; but now, with Plotinus, those implications finally come out, so to speak, in full daylight, and with such blinding evidence that most of his historians do not seem quite able to keep them in sight.

[29] *Ibid.*, V, 3, 15.
[30] *Ibid.*, V, 2, 1.
[31] *Ibid.*, V, 3, 17.
[32] St. Augustine, *Confessions*, XI, 5, 7.

When Plotinus says, for instance, that the One is everything and yet is no thing,[33] it is an almost overwhelming temptation to infer that, though it itself is no one thing, the One is the being of all things. In a sense, since it is their cause, the One really is the being of all things; yet their being cannot be its own being, because the One itself has no being at all. The very stuff things are made of is being, that is to say, an emanation from the One, which itself is not. The gap that separates the world of Plotinus from its principle lies there, and nowhere else, but it is an infinitely wide one. Other philosophies will tirelessly repeat that the noun *"ens"* is derived from the verb *esse*, just as *beings* must necessarily come from a *Being*, which *is*. Now, the derivation of *being* suggested by Plotinus is an altogether different one, but it is no less expressive of its own metaphysical outlook: "In numbers," Plotinus says, "the sharing in unity is what gives rise to quantity; here, the trace of the One gives rise to reality [οὐσία], and being is nothing more than that trace of the One. And were we to say that the word *einai* [to be] is derived from *en* [one], we would no doubt tell the truth."[34] Let us therefore carefully distinguish the various philosophical orders and refrain from qualifying one of them by terms borrowed from another one. In a doctrine in which *ens* comes from *esse*, any essential community between beings and their principle would necessarily entail monism, and, if their principle be God, pantheism. Now, leaving aside the subtle problem of knowing whether the Plotinian One is God, we can at least safely affirm that it is not being. Consequently, in a doctrine where *einai* (to be) is derived from *en* (one), there can be no monism, that is, there can be no community of being between beings and a first principle which itself has no being. Besides, Plotinus himself says so: "When it comes to the principle that is anterior to beings, namely, the One, this principle remains in itself."[35] How then could such a principle become mixed,. at any point, with what it begets? "The Principle is not the whole of beings, but all beings come from it; it is not all beings, rather it is no one of them, so that it may beget them all."[36]

That, in Plotinus' philosophy, being comes from the One is therefore pretty obvious; but it is not equally clear why, in this same doctrine, being and knowing are one. Yet, Plotinus himself has said so: "To be and to know are one and the same thing."[37] The easiest way to realize the meaning of this statement is prob-

[33] Plotinus, *Enn.*, V, 2, 1.   [34] *Ibid.*, V, 5, 5.   [35] *Ibid.*
[36] *Ibid.*, III, 8, 9. Cf. III, 9, 4 and VI, 8, 19.
[37] *Ibid.*, III, 8, 8.

ably to approach it under this slightly different form: to be and to be an object of thought are one and the same thing.

To the question: what is a being? several different answers are possible, but all of them are bound to have in common this character, that they constitute so many determinations, by thought, of that *x* which we call *being*. True to Plato's tradition, and beyond Plato to that of Parmenides, Plotinus sees being arise, at the very point at which, circumscribing by definition an intelligible area, thought begets some knowable object, for which it is one and the same thing to be knowable and to be an object. Where there is knowledge, there is being, and, where there is being, there is knowledge. In other words, to be is to be thinkable, that is to say, to be is to be possessed of those attributes which are necessarily required in a possible object of thought.

Such is the reason why the notions of being, of reality, and intelligible nature, can all be rendered by a single term: οὐσία. Now we render it by "essence," now by "being," and always rightly; for, indeed, the essence of a being is nothing else than the very being in its own intelligibility. Now, the intrinsic reason for its intelligibility is its very reality. Such is essence, οὐσία, the realness of being. Nothing is farther removed from subjective idealism than Plotinus' doctrine. He does not mean to say that things are to be counted as real in so far as they are known, and still less does he say that, for any given thing, to be is to be known. The true position of Plotinus is, on the contrary, that intelligible relations are the very stuff that beings are made of. This may seem surprising to us, because the only intelligible relations we know are the loose and multiple ones which ceaselessly succeed each other in our own minds. In us, intelligibility is fragmentary, as well as disconnected, and its parts hold together only more or less through the never-ending patchwork of human dialectic. Yet, from time to time, even we may happen to grasp a multiplicity of relations within the unity of a single intellectual intuition. In such cases, the more intelligibility grows into a unity, the more it begins truly to be. And why should we not conceive all intelligible relations, blended together as it were in the unity of some supreme Intelligence, in which they would all be present at the same time, or rather out of time, since all its distinct consequences are simultaneously given in the unity of their common principle? Such, precisely, is the νοῦς of Plotinus. It is not the One, which soars above both intelligence and knowledge, but it is what comes immediately after the One in the order of subsisting principles. As has just been said, the One is no thing, but all things are in consequence of the One. Now, taken in itself, the supreme Intelligence (νοῦς) is the total intelligibility of the One. I am not saying that it is equal to the One; on the contrary, the One transcends all conceivable intelligibility, for the simple reason that, as soon as the relation of knower to known appears, unity steps out of the picture to make room for duality. The supreme Intelligence is therefore inferior to the One, yet, as an Intelligence, it is perfect, because it is the maximum of unity that is consistent with intelligibility.

It should by now become increasingly clear why, in such a doctrine, beings are identical with their own intelligible essences. If you attempt an intelligible explanation of something that is one, as much at least as any sensible thing may be one, you have to use a multiplicity of terms and of relations, which, ultimately, will leave out the very unity of the thing. In a desperate attempt to regain it, you will no doubt add one more intelligible relation to the preceding ones, which will merely increase their number, and, the more carefully you complete your picture, the more you increase the number of the intelligible relations you will add to the first one. Here again, I think, Leibniz may help in understanding Plotinus. His celebrated monads are just the substantial units of a world conceived by a Plotinus who, some fourteen centuries earlier, would have discovered the infinitesimal calculus. In point of fact, Plotinus knew nothing about the infinitesimal calculus, and this is why his "beings" are more simple than the monads of Leibniz; but they nevertheless belong in the same metaphysical family. Each of them is one of the innumerable, fragmentary and intelligible expressions of the One: "And this is why [Plotinus says] these things are essences, for, indeed, each of them has a limit and, so to speak, a form: being cannot belong to what lacks limits; being must needs be fixed in determined limits and stay there; this stable condition, for intelligible essences, is their definition and their form, whence they likewise draw their reality."[18]

After this has been said, there still remains a last illusion to be dispelled. Such intelligibles, or beings, are not "known by" the supreme Intelligence; they are that Intelligence, unless we prefer to say that the supreme Intelligence *is* such knowledge. The Intelligence is its objects just as its objects are that Intelligence, and, since each one of its objects, as determined by its intelligible definition, is a being, it can be said of that Intelligence, whose unity contains all possible beings, that it is being itself. Thus, being begins only after the One, in and with the supreme

---

[18] *Ibid.*, V, 1, 7.

Intelligence, so much so that, in Plotinus' own words: "The Intelligence is identical with being."[39] In these words Plotinus is merely restating, or, rather, quoting once more the oracle once issued by old Parmenides: "To be and to know are one and the same thing."[40] True enough, Plotinus is here doing more than repeating Parmenides, but the Plotinian hardening of the formula merely sets in relief the intrinsic necessity which it entailed from its very origin. The doctrine of Plotinus clearly shows, to the point of making it almost tangible, that, where being is posited as existentially neutral, it cannot play the part of a first principle, Q.E.D.

Thus to turn Plato's dialectic into a cosmogony was to embark upon the road which, by way of philosophical myth, leads philosophy to religion. Never did Plato himself frankly enter upon it, nor did Plotinus himself follow it to its very end. Some historians maintain that, in Plato's doctrine, the Good is God, but, as they have no text whatsoever to support their interpretation, there is no reason why we should feel obliged to discuss it. As to Plotinus, the question cannot be avoided, but it is not easy to answer it. In some texts, which are few and far between, he speaks of the One as of the supreme God; [41] but these are exceptional expressions, and the truth of the case has been objectively summed up in these words by one of his best historians: in Plotinus, "The One is a God sometimes." [42] Which serves at least to show that, if the One is truly a God, the fact does not strike Plotinus as particularly important. On the contrary, what fully deserves the title of God in his doctrine is Intelligence, of which Plotinus does not speak only as of a being that is divine, but as of a God. Intelligence is God *par excellence* in the doctrine of Plotinus.

These hints were not lost on the greatest successor of Plotinus, Proclus. In the doctrine of Proclus, metaphysics takes a decisive turn, not only to theology, but to religion. This fact alone would account for the remarkable popularity which Proclus was to enjoy among the theologians of the late Middle Ages. "The One is God," Proclus says; to which he presently adds this remark: "And how could it be otherwise, since the Good and the One are one and the same thing, and since the Good and God are one and the same thing?"[43] Having thus equated God, the Good and the

---

[39] *Ibid.*, V, 4, 2.   [40] *Ibid.*, V, 1, 8 and V, 9, 5.

[41] *Ibid.*, I, 8, 2; III, 9, 9 (?); V, 5, 3; V, 5, 9. See R. Arnou, *Le Désir de Dieu dans la philosophie de Plotin* (Paris, Alcan, 1921), p. 128.

[42] R. Arnou, *op. cit.*, p. 125, n. 13.

[43] Proclus, *Institutio theologica*, art. 113.

28

One, Proclus does not doubt for a single moment that, not only Plotinus, but Plato himself had already done it. This, of course, was taking a big chance, and very few historians, if any, would attempt to reconstruct the whole of Platonism along such lines. But Proclus himself was no historian and, after all, he was perfectly justified in loading the texts of Plato with all the truth that is consistent with their very wording. This is what he did, and the result was remarkable in itself, even though, to a historian, it looks almost fantastic.

Everyone remembers how, in the *Timaeus*, Plato describes the making of the world by the Demiurge. From beginning to end, the *Timaeus* is a myth, that is, a fiction. Having to describe the structure of this world, Plato fancies that it will make much better reading if he supposes that the universe has been made by a God, and if he tells us how the God has made it. Naturally, the very first thing which this God does is to read the complete works of Plato, after which he proceeds to make the world exactly as, had he been a God, Plato himself would have made it. Now, "The *Timaeus* refers everything to the Demiurge, while the *Parmenides* refers everything to the One; there must then be between them the following relation: the Demiurge is to the content of the universe as the One is to all beings." In other words, the Demiurge is to the sensible world what the One is to the whole of reality. This implies that, whereas the world-maker of the *Timaeus* is no more than a certain God (τὶς θεὸς), the One is God, pure and simple (ἁπλῶς θεὸς). If the Demiurge is a God, it is because the One grants him the necessary power to make the world. The *Parmenides* and the *Timaeus* should then be interpreted as dealing with two aspects of the same problem, the origin of the intelligible world and the origin of the world of sense, and as giving it the same solution. As was already the case in Plotinus, the One first begets the supreme Intelligence, that is, the first being, above which there is nothing to be found but the One.[44] Thus, being does not come first, but only second, in the order of metaphysical principles. As Proclus says, being comes first among created things,[45] which means that its creator is not a being. From beginning to end, Greek Platonism has thus kept faith with its own principles, but there still remains for us to indicate that it

[44] Proclus, *In Parmenidem Platonis*, in *Opera*, ed. by V. Cousin (Paris, 1821), Vol. IV, pp. 34, 35-36; *Institutio theologica*, art. 114, in *Plotini Enneades* (Paris, Didot, 1836), p. cxxxvii, and art. 129, p. xcii.

[45] Proclus, *Institutio theologica*, art. 138, *ed. cit.*, p. xcv.

did not betray them even after entering the domain of Christian speculation.

The very fact that Neoplatonism established early contact with Christian thought was, philosophically speaking, a mere accident. As a philosophy, Platonism itself certainly still had a few problems to solve in the fourth century, A.D., but it was quite capable of handling them in its own way. Yet, when all is said, the fact remains that Plotinus, and, still more, Proclus, had taken a considerable chance in turning what was essentially a doctrine of being into a doctrine of God, that is, a philosophy into a theology. This should account, at least up to a point, for the fact that some Neoplatonists, when they became converts to Christianity, felt much less like exchanging a philosophy for a religion, than like exchanging a religion for another religion. Plotinus and Proclus had invited men to join the One through both bodily asceticism and spiritual contemplation; Christianity was inviting men to do exactly the same thing. The main question, then, was to know how such a result could best be achieved, through the dialectic of Plato or through the grace of God in Christ. This indeed was an all-important matter to decide, but the fact that a philosopher became a Christian did not necessarily mean that he changed his philosophy. At a time when there was still no such thing as a Christian philosophy, one could go on thinking as a Platonist while believing as a Christian.

Yet there were difficulties, especially concerning the nature of being. There is no treatise on being in the Bible, but everyone remembers the famous passage of *Exodus:* III, 14, in which, answering Moses, who had asked Him for His name, God said: "I am He Who Is;" and again: "Thus shalt thou say to the children of Israel: He Who Is hath sent me into you." Now, no Christian needs to draw from this statement any metaphysical conclusions, but, if he does, he can draw only one, namely, that God is Being. On the other hand, the Christian God is the supreme principle and cause of the universe. If the Christian God is first, and if He is Being, then Being is first, and no Christian philosophy can posit anything above Being. Let us put the same thing differently. There is, in the Neoplatonic *Liber de Causis*, a famous aphorism which has been quoted and commented upon by countless mediaeval thinkers: *"Prima rerum creatarum est esse."*[46] This is straight

---

[46] O. Bardenhewer, *Die pseudo-aristotelische Schrift über das reine Gute, bekannt unter dem Namen "Liber de Causis"* (Freiburg, 1882), p. 166. The same sentence can easily be found in any edition of the Commentary of St. Thomas Aquinas on the *Liber de Causis*, lect. IV: *"Prima rerum creatarum est esse et non est ante ipsum*

Neoplatonism: the first principle is the One, and being comes next as the first of its creatures. Now this is, though self-consistent, yet absolutely inconsistent with the mental universe of Christian thinkers, in which being cannot be the first of all creatures for the good reason that it has to be the Creator Himself, namely, God. Psychologically speaking, one can philosophize as a Neoplatonist and believe as a Christian; logically speaking, one cannot think, at one and the same time, as a Neoplatonist and as a Christian.

Yet some Christian thinkers have attempted to do it, while others have realized that the thing could not be done. What makes the greatness of St. Augustine in the history of Christian philosophy is that, deeply imbued with Neoplatonism as he was, he yet never made the mistake of devaluating being, not even in order to extol the One. There is a great deal of Neoplatonism in Augustine, but there is a point, and it is a decisive one, at which he parts company with Plotinus: there is nothing above God in the Christian world of Augustine, and, since God is being, there is nothing above being. True enough, the God of Augustine is also the One and the Good, but He *is*, not because He is both good and one; rather, He is both good and one because He is *He Who Is*. Let this be said for the sake of those who might wonder at the absence of St. Augustine from even so sketchy a history of Christian Neoplatonism as this one. The Bishop of Hippo simply does not fit into the picture, because he parted from Plotinus on this fundamental principle of the primacy of Being.

The faultless rectitude of Augustine's Christian feeling in these matters is the more remarkable as he had read Plotinus in the Latin translation of Marius Victorinus. Now we know from the *Confessions* that, after professing for many years the doctrine of the *Enneads*, Marius Victorinus had become a Christian—an event which did not pass unheeded and made an especially deep impression on the young Augustine himself. After his conversion, the new Christian wrote a few treatises on theological questions, among which one is of particular interest to the history of our problem. Written in a highly technical and extremely obscure Latin, the book of Marius Victorinus *On the Generation of the Divine Word* shows us what Augustine himself would have said if, having imbibed the philosophy of Plotinus as he did, he had gone on thinking as a Neoplatonist after becoming a Christian.

God Himself, Victorinus says, is above all that which is and all that which is not. In a way, God is, because He is eternal;

---

creatum aliud," *i.e.*, the first among created things is being and nothing else has been created before it.

yet, since God is above even being, it can also be said of Him that he is not. Thus, God is not, inasmuch as He is above being. If He is superior to being, He can produce it. The Christian God of Victorinus is therefore a non-being who gives birth to being. Of course, since God is the cause of being, it can be said, in a certain sense, that God truly is (*vere ὄν*), but this expression merely means that being is in God as an effect is in an eminent cause, which contains it through being superior to it.[47] Strictly speaking, then, God is a supreme non-being, cause of all being.

Now, we should not forget that the Victorinus we are dealing with has already become a Christian. He therefore believes in the dogma of the Trinity, and, when he says God, we must understand God the Father. This is precisely what will enable him to follow Plotinus a bit further with at least the illusion that he is still speaking as a Christian. In the doctrine of Plotinus, the One begets the supreme Intelligence who, being the sum total of all intelligibility, is at the same time the first and supreme being. All we shall now have to say is that God the Father begets, through an ineffable generation, both being (*existentia*) and Intelligence (*νοῦς*). In this first born of the Father, every Christian reader will at once recognize the Divine Word and, consequently, Christ. With due respect to the memory of a convert who was certainly doing his best, one must say that, theologically speaking, this was a pretty mess. If the three Persons of the divine Trinity are coessential, and Victorinus, writing against the Arian Candidus, expressly means to prove it, it is hard to conceive that one of them is, while the other is not. Yet, here is God the Father Who is not, whereas, the Word is, but only because, and in so far as, He is begotten by the Father. Unbegotten, the Word would be the Father; He would not be a being. As Victorinus himself says: "God is the whole pre-being (*totum πρόον*); as to Jesus, He is that whole being itself (*hoc totum ὄν*); but already enjoying existence, and life, and intelligence; in short, the universally and in every way perfect being (*universale omnimodis τέλεον ὄν*)."[48]

It would certainly be unfair to say that Victorinus is here speaking as a pure Plotinian. He is not, but the fact that he does not want to be one does not make things any easier for him. In point of fact, he is doing about as well as could be done without giving up the supremacy of the One over being. Plotinus was not

[47] Marius Victorinus, *Liber de generatione Verbi divini*, in Migne, *PL*, Vol. VIII, col. 1022, and XIII, col. 1027.

[48] *Ibid.*, II, in Migne, *PL*, Vol. VIII, col. 1021; on the four types of non-being, IV, col. 1021-1022.

a Christian; he therefore saw no difficulty in positing the supreme Intelligence and supreme being frankly below the One. As he is a Christian, and writing against an Arian, Victorinus is bound to maintain that, although begotten by the Father, the Word-Being is in no way inferior to Him. Hence his repeated efforts to make clear that, even though He Himself be not, the Father is not deprived of being; for, indeed, the Word, Who is being, is in the Father as in His cause. The Being (ὄν) who is in potency in the Father becomes, owing to this self-generation of God, being in act.[49] In this sense, God as begotten is in no way inferior to the begetting God; rather, God is cause of Himself (*sui ipsius est causa*); and it is through Himself that God is God.[50] All we can do here is to recommend Victorinus to the indulgence of modern theologians. But what is unusual in his own position clearly appears when he deals with the famous text of *Exodus:* III, 14, which we have quoted above. Such a text is, so to speak, the acid test which infallibly detects the true nature of being in any Christian philosophy. In this case, the problem can be defined as follows: If a Christian maintains, with Plotinus, that being is the first-born of a higher principle, who, according to him, will be *He Who Is?* All we now have to do is to let Victorinus speak for himself: "It is Jesus Christ. For, He Himself has said: *And should they ask thee, Who hath sent thee? tell them, Being* (ὁ ὤν). For, indeed, this sole being (*solum enim illud* ὄν), who always is (*semper* ὄν), is being (ὁ ὤν *est*)."[51] It is a bit hard to imagine Jesus Christ speaking to Moses in the Old Testament. This time we should recommend Victorinus to the indulgence of modern exegetes. But we ourselves should not lose sight of our own objective. The fact that Neoplatonism makes bad theology and worse exegesis is no philosophical argument against the Platonic notion of being. Yet, it goes a long way to prove something else, which is the only point I am now trying to make. If any being ever entailed the notion of existence, it is Yahweh, the God whose very name is, I AM; and here is a Christian theologian who, because he still conceives being after the manner of Plato, cannot even understand the very name of his God. A tangible proof indeed that the Platonic notion of being is not only foreign to existence, but inconsistent with it.

Marius Victorinus is a highly instructive case, but he is not the only one. The unknown author of the treatises which, written at

[49] *Ibid.*, XVI, col. 1029 B.
[50] *Ibid.*, XVI, col. 1028 C, and XVIII, col. 1030.
[51] *Ibid.*, XIV, col. 1028 B. Cf. XV, col. 1028 BC.

an unknown date, bear the name of Dionysius the Areopagite, hails from the same philosophical country. Whoever wrote them, he certainly was a Christian, yet he did not hesitate to posit the Good even above being, with the unavoidable consequence that, once more, the Christian God had to be conceived as the supreme non-being. True to the leading principle of Plotinus, Dionysius maintains that God must not be what He gives, in order precisely that He may give it: "If, as is indeed the case, the Good is above all being, then we are bound to say that what itself is without form gives form; that He who remains in Himself without essence is the acme of essence; that, being a lifeless reality, He is supreme life; that, being a reality without intelligence, He is supreme wisdom, and so on, since any form denied to the Good points out His informing power."[52] As a Christian, Dionysius knows that God has claimed for Himself the name of Being, but since, as a Platonist, he knows that God is even above being, all he can do is to see in this highest of all "divine names" the supreme denomination of God as known from His effects. God is not being qua God, but in so far as He is the author of being, which is the first of His creatures. In Dionysius' own words: "God Himself is not being, but He is the being of beings;"[53] which means: He is that because of which beings are. And what is it that accounts for the being of all beings? Once more, it is the Good. Let us now go back to the sixth book of Plato's Republic: "You must admit that knowable objects owe the Good not only their aptness to be known, but even their being and their reality (τὸ εἶναί τε καὶ τὴν οὐσίαν), although the Good is no reality (οὐκ οὐσίας ὄντος τοῦ ἀγαθοῦ), but far surpasses reality in both power and majesty."[54] Whoever he was, Dionysius was certainly thinking along the same lines. To this Christian, He Who Is is the cause of all beings, only because He Himself is not.

The paradoxical character of this interpretation was so apparent that comparatively few Christian thinkers ever accepted it. Yet some of them did, and always with the same results. In the ninth century, a disciple of Dionysius, John the Scot, gave a complete description of what was to him the universe of Christian thought, without for a single moment betraying the spirit of his master. His Division of Nature is a complete cosmogony, which itself is a sort of concrete dialectic whose particular moments are so many definite "natures." In other words, the world of John the Scot is a deduction from its first principle, and each term of

[52] Dionysius, De divinis nominibus, IV, 3.   [53] Ibid., V, 4.
[54] Plato, Republic, VI, 509 b.

this deduction constitutes a certain nature. As to Nature itself, it signifies all that about which something can be said because it is included in the general order of the universe. We do not need to suppose that every nature is "a being." At least, we don't know that yet, and maybe it is not true: "Nature [John says] is the general name of all that which is and of all that which is not."[55]

What are these natures? As we have just said, each nature is a particular moment of the universal dialectic which we call the universe. Among these moments, or terms, some can be grasped by intellectual knowledge. We can say what they are and, consequently, that they are. Hence they are beings. But there are other terms which, though we feel bound to posit them at the origin or during the course of our deduction, escape both understanding and definition. It is not only that *we* cannot define them; rather they themselves are of such nature that *they* cannot be defined. Some of them are above being, some others are below being; in any case, such natures are not. In short, if John the Scot has written a book on the *Division of Nature* rather than on the *Division of Reality*, the reason for it is that he needed a wider name than reality to include non-beings as well as beings.

The first principle is, of course, such a non-being. Himself a Christian, John identifies his first principle with the divinity, but, since its effects *are*, the divinity itself *is not*. As he himself says, using the language of Dionysius, "The being of all things is the divinity which is above being: *esse omnium est superesse divinitas*."[56] Now, we have said that beings come from what is above being by way of deduction, which, in a sense, is true; yet, it must not be forgotten that John himself calls it a division, which means that, as soon as you posit the first principle, the whole series of beings develops itself both before the eyes of the mind and in reality. In John's doctrine, the First is, before anything else, goodness, generosity. The world of beings makes up a dialectical system because it obeys intelligible laws; but it does not owe its origin to an analytical deduction from its principle, it rather flows from its goodness and fecundity.

Modern historians have accused John the Scot of monism and of pantheism. I am afraid that this is a mistake. We are perfectly free to disagree with him, but we should not ascribe to him a philosophical position which was never his. In point of fact, his

---

[55] J. Scotus Erigena, *De divisione naturae*, I, in Migne, *PL*, Vol. CXXII, col. 441 A.

[56] *Ibid.*, I, 3; col. 443 B.

own case exactly repeats that of Plotinus. The being of creatures cannot be, in any sense of the word, part and parcel of the being of God, for the simple reason that God Himself has no being. Between Him Who is not and things that are, there is an unbridgeable metaphysical gap. It is not even an ontological gap of the sort which, in other doctrines, separates the supreme Being from finite beings. God and creatures are here so wholly distinct that we cannot apply to God the name of being, either in a univocal, analogical or even equivocal way. The doctrine of the analogy of being would have very much disturbed John the Scot, as smacking of pantheism, and the doctrine of the univocity of being would have looked to him as being nothing else. What he himself wanted to do was, on the contrary, to raise God so much above beings that no confusion between them remained possible; and, of course, the easiest way to do it was to raise God even above being, which he did. "God," John says, "is not the genus of creatures, nor creatures a species of the genus God. And the same applies to the relation of the whole to its parts. God is not the whole of His creation, nor is His creation part of God; and, conversely, the creation is not the whole of God, nor is God a part of His creation."[57] Such statements are as explicit as they are clear. How is it, then, that so many historians have understood his doctrine as a pantheism? The reason for it is simple. As they themselves are not Platonists, they think of everything in terms of being. Now, *if* the first principle of John the Scot were Being, it would be both monistic and pantheistic to say, as he indeed often does, that God is the being of all things. But he says just the reverse. The repeated condemnations of his doctrine by the Church do not mean that John's philosophy was inconsistent as a philosophy; they mean precisely that, as a Christian philosophy, it was wrong. For, indeed, since He himself says so, the Christian God *is;* consequently, if a Christian philosopher maintains that God can be the being of creatures because He himself is not, that philosopher is wrong. Even before any Christian philosopher had understood in what sense it is true, the Christian Church had known, having read it in the Bible, that the first principle is the supreme act of existence. The only mistake of John the Scot was to imagine that the existentially neutral philosophy of Plato suited the supremely existing Christian God.

It could easily be shown how many similar difficulties John the Scot had to overcome in his undertaking. One of them at least should be mentioned because of its typical nature and its historical

[57] *Ibid.,* II, 1; col. 523.

importance. It is a well-known fact that practically every Christian philosophy makes room for the Platonic doctrine of Ideas; only, since the Christian God is being, Plato's Ideas must then become the divine Ideas. So much so that, rather than being in God, they are God. To quote but a few great names, St. Augustine, St. Anselm, St. Bonaventura and St. Thomas Aquinas all agree on this fundamental point.

It is most remarkable that, in spite of what seems to be an abstract necessity, at least some Christian philosophers ultimately denied it. John the Scot was one of them and, discounting some scanty indications left to him by Dionysius, the first one to do so. Not without some hesitations, however. If being coincides with intelligibility, the first intelligibles must also be the first beings; but the divine Ideas are the first intelligibles; hence they are the first beings. Now, it is sound Neoplatonism that if being is the first creature of God, the Ideas are creatures. On the other hand, since the Christian God is Being, He is His own Ideas, which means that the divine Ideas are God. This obviously leads us to assert two utterly irreconcilable positions, namely, that the Ideas are created, and that they are God. How could a Christian thinker maintain that there are creatures in God and that such creatures are God? Obviously, John the Scot is here torn between two conflicting, yet equally absolute abstract necessities, and we may well wonder how he ever succeeded in getting out of such a dilemma.

As a matter of fact, he never did. To this intricate problem, the answer of John the Scot is that the divine Ideas are creatures, and yet they are not creatures. They are not creatures because no true creature is eternal; now, there is no doubt that Ideas are eternal: the Ideas of God have always been and always will be with God. Yet, they are creatures in this sense at least that, in their quality of being, they are eternally being created by Him Who is above being, namely, God. In short, they are eternal but not co-eternal with God. Here again it would be much less instructive to criticize than it is to understand. What John the Scot is obviously trying to do is to identify the divine Ideas with God as much as his own philosophical principles allow him to do so. But they don't quite allow him to do it. In so far as they *are*, his divine Ideas have to be created, and, since the notion of a "co-eternal creature" is inconsistent, he has to fall back upon that of a merely eternal creature. Yet, when all is said, his divine Ideas remain creatures; how then can they still be divine? John can find no way out of his difficulty, because there is none; but, if he leaves us without an answer, he gives us something much more precious to keep, namely, the key which opens the interpretation of all similar doctrines during the whole Middle Ages: in any doctrine in which there is the slightest gap between the Christian God and the divine Ideas, the breadth of that gap is exactly in proportion to the ontological Platonism of the doctrine. Plato's being is too existentially neutral ever to coincide with *Him Who Is.*

It is hardly possible to conclude this part of our inquiry without at least mentioning another similar experiment, which took place around the beginning of the fourteenth century, at a time when the *Elementatio Theologica* of Proclus had just been translated into Latin and was beginning to be read. One never feels safe in talking about Meister Eckhart. He seldoms speaks twice in identically the same way, and the problem always is to know whether he is saying the same thing in a different way or if he is saying different things. Yet, his *Quaestiones Parisienses* are of such interest for our own problem that we cannot well afford to ignore them.

One cannot expect a fourteenth century theologian to repeat Plotinus or Proclus. Eckhart had read St. Thomas Aquinas carefully, and he knew his theology well. Yet, he was going his own way, which was, for a Christian, an unusual one. God, Eckhart says, does not know because He is, He rather is because He knows. His very act of intellection is the very root of His being.[58] Such a God closely resembles, if not the One of Plotinus, at least his supreme Intelligence. Being a theologian, Eckhart must find in Scripture a text to support his assertion, and quoting *Exodus* would be here entirely out of place. But why not quote the very first lines of the Gospel according to Saint John: "In the beginning was the Word"? For, Eckhart remarks: The Evangelist has not said: "In the beginning was Being, and God was Being," but only this: "In the beginning was the Word", or, as the Lord Himself says a little further, the Truth. Such is the name which God Himself has claimed for His own: "I am the Truth" [John XIV. 16]. Let us therefore posit intellection as the first of the divine perfections, and being after it.[59] After all, there is for us no other way to understand what Saint John goes on to say, *"All things were made by Him,* so that being belongs to them after they are made. Hence what the author of the *Liber de Causis* says: The first creature is being."[60]

[58] Eckhart, *Quaestiones et Sermo Parisienses*, ed. by B. Geyer (Bonn, P. Hanstein, 1931), p. 7.
[59] *Ibid.*, p. 9. [60] *Ibid.*, p. 7.

38

This should now begin to sound familiar to our ears, and we know more or less where we are. It does not come to us as a surprise to hear Eckhart saying: "To be does not belong to God, nor being, and He is something higher than being: *Deo non convenit esse, nec ens, sed est aliquid altius ente.*" And again, still more explicitly: "There is in God neither to be nor being; for, indeed, if a cause is truly a cause, nothing of the effect should be formally in its cause. Now, God is the cause of all being. Hence being cannot formally be in God. Of course, if it pleases you to give to 'intellection' the name of 'being' I have no objection. Even so, if there is in God something which you may call being, it belongs to Him through intellection."[61] In short, "Since being belongs to creatures, it cannot be in God, except as in its cause. Thus, in God, there is no being, but *puritas essendi*,"[62] a formula which obviously means, not the purity of being, but the purity *from* being.

It was somewhat paradoxical to define *Him Who Is* as a God in Whom no trace of being can be found. No wonder, then, that Eckhart got into trouble with ecclesiastical authorities. But what could he do? When, in order to placate his judges, he made up his mind to preach that God is, he singled out for the text of his sermon, not *Exodus:* III, 14, but *Deuteronomy:* VI, 4: "Listen, Israel, the Lord our God, the Lord is One." And here indeed he had something to say! This was a text on which Eckhart would never tire of preaching or of writing, but in his whole commentary on these words two lines seem to me more precious than all the rest: "*Deus est unus:* God is one; this is confirmed by the fact that Proclus, too, and the *Liber de Causis* frequently call God the One or Unity."[63]

What more could we hope for? Because existence as such seemed inconceivable, metaphysical reflection has spontaneously conceived being as "that which is," irrespective of the fact "that it is." Being then became selfhood, and, because selfhood could not be understood otherwise than as unity, the metaphysics of being gave birth to a metaphysics of the One. Thus, having reduced the whole of being to self-identity, metaphysics finally subjected being to a transcendent cause radically different from being; and, since what is above being is not intelligible, the will to achieve exhaustive intelligibility by eliminating existence drove metaphysics to subject to an unintelligible non-being the whole

[61] *Ibid.*, pp. 10, 11. [62] *Ibid.*, p. 10.
[63] Text in G. dello Volpe, *Il misticismo speculativo di Maestro Echkhart nei suoi rapporti storici* (Bologna, 1930), p. 147.

BEING AND SOME PHILOSOPHERS

order of intelligible reality. This is why all Platonisms sooner or later lead to mysticism, and sooner rather than later. Now, mysticism in itself is excellent, but not *in* philosophy, and especially not in a philosophy whose professed ambition is to achieve perfect intelligibility. It was not easy to guess what would happen to being if existence was left out of it. Plato cannot be blamed for having tried it, but history shows us to what consequences such an undertaking was bound to lead: once removed from being, existence can never be pushed back into it, and, once deprived of its existence, being is unable to give an intelligible account of itself.

But is it certain that what is lacking in Plato's being is existence? Being may be more complex than Plato's selfhood, without including existence. It might be, for instance, substance. Our problem cannot be solved correctly unless we first take the answer of Aristotle into consideration.

Chapter II

Being and Substance

AMONG all the objections directed by Plato himself against his own doctrine of being, there is an outstanding one, namely, that, if there are Ideas, we are no better off for knowing this, because we cannot know them and, anyhow, they have nothing to do with the world of sense in which we live. Slaves, Plato says, are not enslaved to mastership, but to concrete beings that are their masters. Likewise, masters do not have dominion over slaveness, but over their own slaves; thus, these real things around us can do nothing to those yonder realities, any more than those yonder realities can do anything to this world of ours. Whence it follows that, even if it were proven that there are Ideas, we could not possibly know them. Gods, perhaps, know them, but we don't, because we have not science in itself, which is the only possible knowledge of things in themselves. The world of Ideas remains unknowable to us, and, even though we did know it, such knowledge would not help us in understanding the world we live in, because it is different from and unrelated to it.[1]

If there were such a science as a phenomenology of metaphysics, Platonism would no doubt appear as the normal philosophy of mathematicians and of physico-mathematicians. Living as they do in a world of abstract, intelligible relations, they naturally consider number as an adequate expression of reality. In this sense, modern science is a continually self-revising version of the *Timaeus*, and this is why, when they philosophize, modern scientists usually fall into some sort of loose Platonism. Plato's world precisely is the very world they live in, at least *qua* scientists. Not so with biologists and physicians, and, if we want to clear up the difference, all we have to do is to quote two names: Leibniz, Locke. Physicians seldom are metaphysicians, and, when they are, their metaphysics is very careful not to allow its *meta* to lose sight of its *physics*. Such men usually follow what Locke himself once called "a plain historical," that is, descriptive, "method." Aristotle

---

[1] Plato, *Parmenides*, 133 d-134 c.

was such a man. When a French physician said, "There are no sicknesses, but there are men who are sick," he was not aware of summing up, in a terse sentence, the whole Aristotelian doctrine of being. Yet he did. The metaphysics of Aristotle is the normal philosophy of all those whose natural trend of mind or social vocation is to deal, in a concrete way, with concrete reality.

Like his master, Plato, Aristotle is interested in οὐσία: that which is. Only, when he speaks of it, what he has in mind is something quite different from a Platonic Idea. To him, reality is what he sees and what he can touch: this man, this tree, this piece of wood. Whatever other name it may bear, reality always is for him a particular and actually existing thing, that is, a distinct ontological unit which is able to subsist in itself and can be defined in itself: not man in himself, but this individual man whom I can call Peter or John. Our problem then is to find out what there is, in any concretely existing thing, which makes it to be an οὐσία, a reality.

There is a first class of characteristics which, although we find them present in any given thing, do not deserve the title of reality. It comprises whatever always belongs to something, without being itself some thing. Aristotle describes such characteristics as "always given in a subject," which means that they always "belong to" some real being, but never themselves become "a being." Such are, for instance, the sensible qualities. A color always belongs to a colored thing, whence there follows this important metaphysical consequence, that such characteristics have no being of their own. What they have of being is the being of the subject to which they belong; their being is its being or, in other words, the only way for them to be is "to belong" and, as Aristotle says, "to be in." This is why such characteristics are fittingly called "accidents," because they themselves are not beings, but merely happen "to be in" some real beings. Clearly enough, accidents are not the οὐσίαι we are looking for, since their definition does not fulfill the requirements of what truly *is*.

Let us now turn toward another aspect of reality. To say that a certain being is "white" means that the quality of whiteness is present in this particular being. On the contrary, if we say that a certain being is "a man," we do not mean to say that "manness" is something which, like whiteness, for instance, happens to belong to, or to be in, this particular being. The proof of it is that it is possible to be a man without being white, whereas, to be a man without being man is impossible. Manness then is not a property that belongs *in* certain subjects; rather, it is a characteristic which

42

can be ascribed to those subjects. "Man" is what can be "said of" any actually given man. Let us call "predicability" this particular property. As in the case of accidents, it appears that such characteristics have no actual reality of their own. "Manness" and "stoneness" do not exist in themselves; they only represent what I can truly ascribe to real "men" or to real "stones;" so much so that to turn them into real beings would be to repeat Plato's mistake. It would be to substitute Ideas for actual realities.

This twofold elimination ultimately leaves us confronted with those distinct ontological units we spoke of in the first place. In point of fact, all we know about them is that they are neither abstract notions, such as "man" or "stone," nor mere accidents, such as the color of a man or the size of a stone. Yet, this twofold negation can be turned into a twofold affirmation. If real being is not a mere abstract notion or, as we say, a concept, it follows that what truly is, is individual in its own right. Moreover, to say that actual being is to be found only *in* a subject implies that actual being is a subject. Now, what is it to be a subject? It is to be that in which and by which accidents are. In other words, οὐσία, reality, is that which, having in itself all that is required in a thing so that it may be, can moreover grant being to those added determinations which we call its accidents. As such, every actual subject receives the title of "substance" (*sub-stans*), because it can be figuratively fancied as "standing under" accidents, that is, as supporting them.

The indirect character of this determination of being is obvious in Aristotle's own formulas: "Being (οὐσία), in the true, primitive and strict meaning of this term, is that which neither is predicable of a subject, nor is present in a subject; it is, for instance, a particular horse or a particular man."[2] But this seems to be little more than a restatement of the problem, for, if it tells us that Plato was right in refusing actual being to sensible qualities, while he was wrong in ascribing it to abstract notions, it still does not explain what makes reality to be real. We now know where to look for it, but we still do not know what it is.

It looks, then, as though the problem has to be approached in a different way. The question is to know what there is, in an individual subject, that makes it to be a being. In our sensible experience, which is the only one we have, the most striking indication we have that a certain substance is there is the operations it carries and the changes which it causes. Everywhere there is action, there is an acting thing, so that we first detect substances

[2] Aristotle, *Categories*, I, 5, 2 a 11.

by what they do. Let us call "nature" any substance conceived as the intrinsic principle of its own operations. All true substances are natures: they move, they change, they act. And this leads us to a second characteristic of substances. In order thus to act, each of them must first of all be a subsisting energy, that is, an act. If we follow Aristotle thus far, we are entering with him a world entirely different from that of Plato: a concretely real and wholly dynamic world, in which being no longer is selfhood, but energy and efficacy. Hence the twofold meaning of the word "act," which the mediaeval disciples of Aristotle will be careful to distinguish: first, the act which is the thing itself or which the thing itself is (*actus primus*); secondly, any particular action exercised by that thing (*actus secundus*). Now, if you take together all the secondary acts which a given thing performs, you will find that they constitute the very reality of the thing. A thing is all that it does to itself as well as to others. In such a philosophy, "to be" becomes an active word, which, before anything else, signifies the exercising of an act, whether it be the very act of "being," or that of "being-white," or any other one of the same sort. We said that "whiteness" is not, and rightly, but "a white man" *is* white, so that, through him, whiteness also is, as sharing in his own being. It still remains to be seen whether Aristotle is here talking about existence, but he certainly is talking about existing things; and, because, such as he describes it, reality is an actually real nucleus of energy, its very core lies beyond the grasp of any concept. Nothing is more important to remember in Aristotle's philosophy of being, and yet nothing is more commonly overlooked: in their innermost reality, substances are unknown. All we know about them is that, since they act, they are, and they are acts.

Having reached this point, Aristotle had to stop, leaving his doctrine open to every possible interpretation and misinterpretation. He knew full well that to be is to be in act, that is to say, to be an act, but to say what an act is, was an altogether different proposition. The only thing he could do about it was to point to actuality as to something which we cannot fail to know, provided only we see it. Or else he would point out its contrary, that is, potentiality or possibility, but even this does not help much, since to understand act through potency is much more difficult than to understand potency through act. When worrying about the problem, Aristotle first reminds his reader that "we must not seek a definition of everything;" then he invites him to figure out for himself, by comparing a number of analogous cases, the meaning of those two terms: "As that which is building is to that which is capable of building, so is the waking to the sleeping, and that which is seeing to that which has its eyes shut but has sight, and that which is shaped out of the matter to the matter, and that which has been wrought to the unwrought." Assuredly, a bare inspection of these examples clearly shows what Aristotle had in mind when he said: "Actuality means the existence of the thing;"[3] they help us, so to speak, in locating actual reality: we now know where to look for it, and that is all.

It is typical of Aristotle's realism that, though fully aware of the bare and ultimate "givenness" of act as such, he never thought of setting it aside as irrelevant to reality. There is something which is not above being, as was the Good of Plato, but which is *in* being or, rather, which is the very reality of being, yet escapes definition. Real things are precisely of that sort, and philosophy should take them such as they are. If there remains something mysterious in the nature of actuality, it is at least a mystery of nature, not a mystery created out of nothing by the minds of metaphysicians.

We must now proceed in our inquiry and ask Aristotle one more question which, I am afraid, will prove a puzzling one. This very being which reality is inasmuch as it is act, what sort of being is it? In other words, what do we mean exactly by saying of a being in act, that it *is*? The first answer which occurs to the mind is that, in this case at least, to be means to exist, and this, probably, was what it meant to Aristotle himself when, in every-day life, he forgot to philosophize. Nothing is more widespread among men than the certitude of the all-importance of existence: as the saying goes, a living dog is better than a dead king. But we also know that, what they know as men, philosophers are liable to forget as philosophers, and our problem is here to know if, when Aristotle speaks of actual being, what he has in mind is existence or something else.

To this question, we are fortunate in having Aristotle's own answer, and nothing in it authorizes us to think that actual existence was included in what he called being. Of course, to him, as to us, real things were actually existing things. Aristotle has never stopped to consider existence in itself and then deliberately proceeded to exclude it from being. There is no text in which Aristotle says that actual being is not such in virtue of its own "to be," but we have plenty of texts in which he tells us that to be is

[3] Aristotle, *Metaphysics*, Θ, 6, 1048^a 38-1048^b 4, in *Aristotle Selections*, ed. by W. D. Ross (New York, Scribner, 1927), p. 82.

something else. In fact, everything goes as if, when he speaks of being, he never thought of existence. He does not reject it, he completely overlooks it. We should therefore look elsewhere for what he considers as actual reality.

"Among the many meanings of being," Aristotle says, "the first is the one where it means *that which is* and where it signifies the substance."⁴ In other words, the *is* of the thing is the *what* of the thing, not the fact that it exists, but that which the thing is and which makes it to be a substance. This by no means signifies that Aristotle is not interested in the existence or non-existence of what he is talking about. On the contrary, everybody knows that, in his philosophy, the first question to be asked about any possible subject of investigation is, does it exist? But the answer is a short and final one. Once evidenced by sense or concluded by rational argumentation, existence is tacitly dismissed. For, indeed, if the thing does not exist, there is nothing more to say; if, on the contrary, it exists, we should certainly say something about it, but solely about that which it is, not about its existence, which can now be taken for granted.

This is why existence, a mere prerequisite to being, plays no part in its structure. The true Aristotelian name for being is substance, which is itself identical with what a being is. We are not here reconstructing the doctrine of Aristotle nor deducing from his principles implications of which he was not aware. His own words are perfectly clear: "And indeed the question which was raised of old and is raised now and always, and is always the subject of doubt, namely, what being is, is just the question: what is substance? For it is this that some assert to be one, others more than one, and that some assert to be limited in number, others unlimited. And so we also must consider chiefly and primarily and almost exclusively what that is which is in this sense."⁵ All we have now to do is to equate these terms: what primarily *is*, the *substance* of that which is, *what* the thing is. In short, the "whatness" of a thing is its very being.

Such is the principle which accounts for the metaphysical structure of reality in the doctrine of Aristotle. Each actual being is, so to speak, made up of several metaphysical layers, all of which necessarily enter its constitution, but not on the same level nor with equal rights. On the strength of what has been said, it is clear that what is most real in substance is that whereby it is an act. Now, a corporeal substance is not what it is because

⁴ Aristotle, *Metaphysics*, Z, 1, 1028 a 13.
⁵ *Ibid.*, 1028b2-8, in *Selections*, ed. by Ross, n. 26, p. 64.

of its matter. To use a classical example, a statue is not what it is because it is made of wood, of stone or of bronze. On the contrary, the same statue can almost indifferently be made of any one of those matters, and we will say that it is the same statue, provided only its shape remains the same. This, of course, is but an image. Natural forms are less easily detected than artificially made ones, but the reason for it is that shapes are visible, whereas natural forms are the intelligible core of visible reality. Yet, there are such forms. Materially speaking, an animal is made up of inorganic matter, and nothing else. The chemical analysis of its tissues reveals nothing that could not as well enter the composition of entirely different beings. It is nevertheless an animal, and therefore a substance, because it has an inner principle which accounts for its organic character, all its accidents, and all the operations it performs. Such is the form. Obviously, if there is in a substance anything that is act, it is not the matter, it is the form. The form then is the very act whereby a substance is what it is, and, if a being is primarily or, as Aristotle himself says, almost exclusively *what* it is, each being is primarily and almost exclusively its form. This, which is true of the doctrine of Aristotle, will remain equally true of the doctrine of his disciples, otherwise they would not be his disciples. The distinctive character of a truly Aristotelian metaphysics of being—and one might feel tempted to call it its specific form—lies in the fact that it knows of no act superior to the form, not even existence. There is nothing above being; in being, there is nothing above the form, and this means that the form of a given being is an act of which there is no act. If anyone posits, above the form, an act of that act, he may well use the technical terminology of Aristotle, but on this point at least he is not an Aristotelian.

This fundamental fact entails many puzzling consequences, the first of which is that, when all is said, we are coming back to Plato. It has often been remarked, and rightly, that the forms of Aristotle are but the Ideas of Plato brought down from heaven to earth. We know a form through the being to which it gives rise, and we know that being through its definition. As knowable and known, the form is called "essence." Now, it is a fact that forms or essences remain identically the same in all these individuals that belong to a same species. If the main objection directed by Aristotle against Plato holds good, namely, that *man* in himself does not exist and that, if he exists, we are not interested in him, because what we need to know is not *man*, but men, the same reproach seems to apply to Aristotle. Like that of Plato, his own

47

doctrine has neither use nor room for individuals. The only difference is that Plato made open profession not to be interested in individuals, whereas Aristotle makes open profession to be interested in nothing else, and then goes on to prove that, since the form is the same throughout the whole species, the true being of the individual in no way differs from the true being of the species.

All this is very strange, yet it was unavoidable. On the one hand, Aristotle knows that *this* man alone, not *man*, is real; on the other hand, he decides that what is real in this man is *what* any man is; how could his *this* and his *what* ever be reconciled? True enough, Aristotle has an explanation for individuality. Individuals, he says, are such in virtue of their matter. Yes, but the matter of a being is not *what* that being is, it is what is lowest in it; so much so that, of itself, it has no being. However we look at it, there is something wrong in a doctrine in which the supremely real is such through that which exhibits an almost complete lack of reality. This is what is bound to happen to any realism which stops at the level of substance; not the individuals, but their species, then becomes the true being and the true reality.[6]

The radical ambiguity of the doctrine is best seen by its historical consequences. During the Middle Ages, thinkers and philosophical schools were divided between themselves on the famous problem of universals: how can the species be present in individuals, or how can the multiplicity of individuals share in the unity of the species? At first sight, this centuries-long controversy has the appearance of a purely dialectical game, but what really lies at the bottom of the whole business is the very notion of being. What *is?* Is it, as Ockham says, only individuals? Then the form of the species is absolutely nothing but the common name we give to individuals similar among themselves. This is nominalism. If, on the contrary, you say that the form of the species must needs be, since it is owing to it that individuals are, then you are a realist, in this sense, at least, that you ascribe to specific forms a reality of their own. But what kind of reality? Has the form a sort of self-subsisting reality? Then it is a Platonic Idea. Has it no other existence than that of a concept in our mind? Then in what sense can we still say that it is the very core of

---

[6] This is why so many disciples of Aristotle will stress the unity of the species. The famous Averroistic doctrine of the unity of the intellect for the whole human species has no other origin. The species alone is substance. At the very extremity of the development, and beyond Averroes, looms the metaphysics of *the substance:* Spinoza.

actual being? Now it is by no means unusual to see philosophers disagreeing among themselves; what is really puzzling here is that, should we believe them, they all agree with Aristotle. And I rather think they do. At any rate, I would not undertake to convince any one of them that he does not, because Aristotle himself had bungled the whole question.

The primary mistake of Aristotle, as well as of his followers, was to use the verb "to be" in a single meaning, whereas it actually has two. If it means that a thing is, then individuals alone are, and forms are not; if it means *what* a thing is, then forms alone are and individuals are not. The controversy on the being of universals has no other origin than the failure of Aristotle himself to make this fundamental distinction. In his philosophy, as much as in that of Plato, *what* is does not exist, and that which exists, is not.

Had Plato lived long enough to read, in the First Book of Aristotle's *Metaphysics*, the criticism of his own doctrine of ideas, he might have written one more dialogue, the *Aristoteles*, in which it would have been child's play for Socrates to get Aristotle entangled in hopeless difficulties:

"I should like to know, Aristotle, whether you really mean that there are certain forms of which individual beings partake, and from which they derive their names: that men, for instance, are men because they partake of the form and essence of man."

"Yes, Socrates, that is what I mean."

"Then each individual partakes of the whole of the essence or else of part of the essence. Can there be any other mode of participation?"

"There cannot be."

"Then do you think that the whole essence is one, and yet, being one, is in each one of the things?"

"Why not, Socrates?"

"Because, one and the same thing will then at one and the same time exist as a whole in many separate individuals, and will therefore be in a state of separation from itself!"

"Nay, Socrates, it is not so. Essences are not Ideas; they do not subsist in themselves but only in particular things, and this is why, although we conceive them as one, they can be predicated of many."

"I like your way, Aristotle, of locating *one* in many places at once; but did you not say that essence is that whereby individual beings are?"

"Yes, Socrates, I did."

"Then, my lad, I wish you could tell me how it may be that beings are through sharing in an essence, which itself is not!"

The history of the problem of universals has precisely been such a dialogue, and it could have no conclusion. If essences exist, they cannot be shared in without losing their unity and consequently their being. If individuals *are*, then each of them should be a distinct species and there could not be, as in point of fact there are, species that include in their unity a multiplicity of individuals. What is true is that essences are and that individuals exist, so that each essence exists in and through some individual, just as in and through its essence every individual truly is. But, to be in a position to say so, one must first have distinguished between individuation and individuality, that is, one must have realized that, no less necessarily and perhaps more deeply than essence, existence enters the structure of actual being.

Thus, the world of Aristotle is made up of existents without existence. They all exist, otherwise they would not be beings; but, since their actual existence has nothing to do with what they are, we can safely describe them as if they did not exist. Hence the twofold aspect of his own work. He himself is a *Janus Bifrons*. There is a first Aristotle, who wrote the *Historia Animalium*. He was a keen observer of actually existing beings, deeply concerned in observing the development of the chick in the egg, the mode of reproduction of sharks and rays, or the structure and the habits of bees. But there is a second Aristotle, much nearer to Plato than the first one, and what this second Aristotle says is: "The individuals comprised within a species, such as Socrates and Coriscos, are the real beings; but inasmuch as these individuals possess one common specific form, it will suffice to state the universal attributes of the species, that is, the attributes common to all its individuals, once for all"[7] This "once for all," is indeed dreadful. It is responsible for the immediate death of those positive sciences of observation which Aristotle himself had so happily fostered. For centuries and centuries men will know everything about water, because they will know its essence, that which water is; so also with fire, with air, with earth, with man. Why indeed should we look at things in order to know them? Within each species, they are all alike; if you know one of them, you know them all. What a poverty-stricken world such a world is! And how much deeper the words of the poet sound to our ears: "There are more things in heaven and earth, Horatio, than are

[7] Aristotle, *De partibus animalium*, A, 4, 644^a 23-27, in *Selections*, ed. by Ross, n. 54, pp. 173-174.

dreamed of in your philosophy." Yes, indeed, but this was the same poet who knew that what matters is "to be or not to be," and it should matter in philosophy if it does in reality.

For those who fancy that philosophy is bound to follow the march of time, and that what was held as true a hundred years ago can no longer be held to be such, it is an instructive experiment to glance at the commentaries of Averroes on Aristotle, especially in those passages in which he himself comments on the nature of being. What happened to Averroes was simply this: In the twelfth century after Christ, Averroes, himself an Arab established in Spain, happened to read the works of Aristotle, and he thought that, on the whole and almost in every detail, Aristotle was right. He then set about writing commentary after commentary in order to clear up the obscure text of Aristotle and thereby to show that what that text said was true. He could not well do the one without doing the other. To him, Aristotle was *the* Philosopher: to restate his doctrine and to state truth itself were one and the same thing.

What makes the case of Averroes an eminently instructive one, especially for the discussion of our own problem, is the new turn which, between the time of Aristotle and that of his commentator, religion had given to the problem of being. Inasmuch as it is an abstractly objective interpretation of reality, philosophy is not interested in actual existence; on the contrary, inasmuch as it is primarily concerned with human individuals and the concrete problems of their personal salvation, religion cannot afford to ignore existence. This is why, in Plato's philosophy, the gods are always there to account for existential events. Ideas alone cannot account for any existence, because they themselves are, but do not exist, whereas the gods, whatever they may be, do at least exist. In the *Timaeus*, not an Idea, but a god, makes the world, and, though Ideas account for the intelligibility of what the god makes, they themselves do not make it. It takes something that *is* to cause an existential happening.

In the twelfth century after Christ, two religions, both stemming from the Old Testament, agreed in teaching that there is a supreme God, Who truly is and Who is the Maker of the world. "To make" means here "to create." First, there was God, but there was no world. Next, there still was God, but there also was a world, because God had made it to be, and for God to make it to be is what we call creation. Now, if we believe that the world has been created, what is the very first thing that happened to it at the very time when it was created, if not *to be?* The sovereign importance of existence and its factual primacy cannot possibly be overlooked by men who believe that things have been created out of nothing. Existence, and existence alone, accounts for the fact that any given thing is not nothing. This is why, even before the time of Averroes, another Arabian philosopher, whose own position we shall later examine, had taught that, since to exist is something that happens to beings, existence itself is an "accident."

When he read this statement of Avicenna, Averroes felt not only surprised, but scornfully indignant. And no wonder. Having learned from Aristotle that being and substance are one,[8] he was bound to conceive substance as identical with its actual reality. Now, to say that something is actually real, and to say that it *is*, is to say one and the same thing. In Aristotle's own words: "A man, an existent man, and man, are just the same."[9] How indeed could it be otherwise in a philosophy in which the very being of a being is to be "that which it is?" Now, it is very remarkable that, when confronted with the doctrine of Avicenna, Averroes made no mistake about its origin. That was a religious origin, and Averroes immediately said so: "Avicenna is quite wrong in thinking that unity and being point to determinations superadded to the essence of a thing, and one may well wonder how such a man has made such a mistake; but he has listened to the theologians of our religion and mixed up their sayings with his own science of divinity,"[10] that is, with his own metaphysics. Now, this is precisely what Averroes himself has always refused to do. Religion has its own work, which is to educate people who are too dull to understand philosophy, or too untutored to be amenable to its teaching. This is why religion is necessary, for what it preaches is fundamentally the same as what philosophy teaches, and, unless common men believed what it preaches, they would behave like beasts. But theologians should preach, not teach, just as philosophers should teach, not preach. Theologians should not attempt to demonstrate, because they cannot do it, and philosophers must be careful not to get belief mixed up with what they prove, because then they can no longer prove anything. Now, to preach creation is just a handy way to make people feel that God is their Master, which is true even though, as is well known by those who truly philosophize, nothing of the sort ever happened. The fundamental mistake which accounts for the distinction be-

---

[8] Aristotle, *Metaphysics*, Z, 1, 1028b4.
[9] Aristotle, *Metaphysics*, Γ, 2, 1003b.
[10] Averroes, *In IV Metaph.*, c. 3, in *Aristotelis Stagiritae . . . opera omnia* (Venetiis, apud Juntas, 1552), Vol. IX, p. 43ᵛ.

tween being and its existence is Avicenna's illusion that a religious belief can assume a philosophical meaning.[11]

What makes the case of Averroes a highly instructive one is that, in so far as Averroes was Aristotle, Aristotle found himself inescapably confronted with the metaphysical problem of existence so that he could no longer ignore it. If there was room for existence in a world in which being is identical with "what it is," now was for the new Aristotle the time to tell us where it fits; if, on the contrary, existence was just a word which added nothing to what we already know about being, the new Aristotle was bound to tell us that it was so, and why. This last is exactly what Averroes has done, so that his metaphysics constitutes a crucial experiment, in so far at least as the relation of pure substantialism to existence is concerned.

Who, Averroes asks, says that real beings "exist?" In a way, everybody does, but how do they say it? Arguing from the root of the verb which means "to be" in Arabic, Averroes remarks that, in common language, when people want to say that a thing exists, they say that it is "to be found," just as, in order to convey that a certain thing does not exist, they say that it is "not to be found." We ourselves would now say that, to Averroes' compatriots, as to some German philosophers, *to be* is *to be there: sein* is *dasein*. This is nothing more than a crude and popular way of talking, but if any philosopher takes it seriously, he will have no other choice than to make existence an accidental determination of being. The thing must then be imagined as a reality, let us say an essence, which is in itself distinct from and prior to the bare fact that it happens to be or not to be there. Such is, according to Averroes, the mistake made by Avicenna when he said that existence is an accident that happens to the essence: *"Quod esse sit accidens eveniens quidditati."*

Several errors necessarily follow from this first one. If the very fact that a certain being *is*, is distinct from *what* that being is, each and every real being will have to be conceived as a compound of its essence and its existence. If we so conceive it, the essence will have to be further conceived, not as a being, but only as that which becomes a being when it happens to exist. Now, since essence no longer deserves the title of being, except in so far as it receives existence, or *esse*, the distinction of essence and existence becomes a distinction between two constituents of being, one of which is conditioned by and subjected to the other.

---

[11] Averroes, *Destructio destructionum*, disp. VIII, *ed. cit.*, Vol. IX, f. 43^v; and disp. I, f. 9^v.

In other words, essence then deserves the title of being only inasmuch as it has already received its existence. Consequently, apart from its existence, essence in itself is a bare possible, not a being, but a possible being. A world made up of such essences is a world in which no being contains in itself the reason for its existence, for its necessity, for its intrinsic intelligibility.

Such a world was exactly what Avicenna wanted, in order to placate theologians. When all is said, there is one necessary being, and only one. He is "the First," eternally subsisting in virtue of His own necessity and eternally drawing possibles from potency to act. Now, to actualize a possible is to give it actual existence, so that an existing being is a possible which happens to be actualized. It now is because, in the eternal flow of changing things, it was its turn to be. Let us now single out one of these existing beings and look at its structure. Out of itself, it was but a possible, but it now is in virtue of the power and fecundity of the First and, while it is, it cannot not be. It is therefore necessary, and it is so on two accounts: first, while it lasts, it cannot not be; next when actual existence happens to it, it cannot not happen to it, because every being is only in virtue of the necessity of the First. What flows from the First flows from Him according to His own internal intelligible law. Every existing being then exhibits two opposite faces, according as we look at it as it is in itself or as it is in its relation to the First. In itself, it is but possible; in its relation to the First, it is necessary As Avicenna himself says, it is a *possibile a se necessarium ex alio*, that is, as it were a single word, a "possible-by-itself-necessary-by-another." In short, this is among the sort of beings which can be produced by a first cause, since their own existence is entirely deprived of necessity. To say that existence is an accident which happens to essences is but a shorter way of saying the same thing.

Such a doctrine is perfectly consistent, yet Averroes rejects it as a whole because there is something wrong in its very principle, namely, its notion of existence. What is existence, Averroes asks, and how are we supposed to conceive it? Avicenna says that it is an accident, but we know how many kinds of accidents there are, we know which they are, and existence is not among them. Of the ten categories of Aristotle, the first is substance, while the nine following ones designate all possible accidents, such as quantity, quality, place, relation, and so on. We don't find existence there. Now, since it is supposed to happen to a substance, it cannot be substance, and since it is not one of the known accidents, it cannot be an accident; hence it is nothing, because all that is,

54

is either substance or accident. A very remarkable argument indeed, at least if we look at it in the proper way. To Averroes, as to Aristotle himself, the ten categories cover the whole domain of what can be known and said about things. If existence answers none of the only questions concerning reality which make sense, then existence does not make sense, it is unthinkable, it is nothing.

To this conclusion, the obvious objection is that Aristotle himself might well have overlooked a category. After all, nothing proves that his list was complete, and, were we to say that there are ten accidents instead of nine, there would be no harm in it. Perhaps, but let us try. Existence then is an accident, but, as soon as we look at it that way, our new accident exhibits most disturbing properties. At least its properties seem entirely different from those of any other accident. When I add quantity to a substance, I give it size, or bulk, whereby I alter its appearance; if I add quality to it, I make it look white or black, and I still alter its appearance, and so on with all the other accidents of place, relation and so on, each of which contributes a specific determination of the substance, in itself distinct from all the other types of determination. In other words, quantity gives to a substance what quality cannot give; quantity is not quality, but they are two irreducibly distinct categories of accident. Not so with existence. If to be were a category, it would indiscriminately apply to all the other categories, and to all of them in the same way. When I say that a certain substance has both quality and quantity, I do not mean that quantity is the same thing as quality, nor that both quantity and quality are the same thing as substance. Three distinct notions are here present to my mind, but, if I say that a substance is, that its quantity is, or that its quality is, what am I doing? The very accident which I am supposed to add to any one of those three terms blends itself, so to speak, with them and vanishes from sight as being identical with them. "This substance is black" is a meaningful proposition, because blackness is not the substance of which it is predicated. "This substance is," if it means anything, means that this is a substance, and to maintain the contrary would be to maintain that a real substance is distinct from its own being. The same reasoning likewise applies to all the nine accidents. If existence were an accident, then quantity, for instance, could not be, because, were it existence, it could no more be quantity than it can be quality, and so on with the rest. The proposition, "quantity is," either means that quantity is quantity or it means nothing. In short, one cannot consider as an accident that which can be said of any substance and of any accident without adding anything to its notion. The very idea of a category common to all the other categories is absurd. All that business, Averroes says, is censurable and wrong: *hoc totum est falsum et vituperabile.* There is no place, in metaphysics, for an existence conceived as distinct from that which is.

Mistakes, however, have to be overcome, and what precedes would leave us with a divided mind, unless we were to account for the very confusion which is responsible for so many misunderstandings. Such propositions as "x is" do indeed make sense, and what they say may be true or false as the case may be. But what do they mean? When a judgment is true, it is so because it says "that which is." Any true judgment then asserts the reality of something which is indeed a reality. To say that "a man is" merely means that "there is a man," and, if this proposition happens to be true, it is so because what is there is indeed a man. But let us generalize the proposition. When I say that "something is," whatever that may be, the proposition merely means that a certain being is there. What matters here is the intrinsic reality of the being at stake, and precisely the verb "is" expresses nothing else than that very reality. Avicenna wants us to imagine that "is" adds something to the notion of being. But this does not make sense, since, as a word, "being" signifies nothing else than "is." "Being" is the noun derived from the verb "is," so that its meaning can be nothing else than "that which is." We might as well maintain that "humanity," which is derived from "man," signifies something else than "what man is," or that "individuality," which is derived from "individual," signifies something more than "what an individual is." What has Avicenna done? He has simply imagined that the "is" of our judgments, which is the bare statement of the actual reality of a certain essence, signifies something which, when added to essences, turns them into so many realities, whereas, to say that a certain being is merely means that it is a being.[12]

The world of Averroes thus appears as made up of truly Aristotelian substances, each of which is naturally endowed with the unity and the being that belong to all beings. No distinction whatsoever should then be made between the substance, its unity and its being. In a fearfully concise statement, Averroes tells us: "The substance of any one being, by which it is one, is

---

[12] Averroes, *Epitome in librum Metaphysicae Aristotelis,* tract. I, *ed. cit.,* Vol. VIII, f. 1692; *Destructio destructionum,* disp. V; *ed. cit.,* Vol. IX, f. 34ᵛ. Cf. A. Forest, *La Structure métaphysique du concret selon saint Thomas d'Aquin* (Paris, J. Vrin, 1931), p. 143, n. 2.

its to be, whereby it is a being: *Substantia cujuslibet unius, per quam est unum, est suum esse, per quod est ens.*[12] The equation of *substance, one, to be* and *being* is here absolutely complete, and, since substance comes first, it is the whole of reality.

Thus far, Averroes seems quite successful in his effort to rid philosophy of existence, but it still remains for him to solve a problem, namely, the very one which Avicenna himself had tried to solve: the relation of possible beings to their actual existence. After all, there are such things as actualized possibilities, and their being cannot be the same, as actual, as it was as a mere possible. Under this definite form, at least, the problem of existence cannot be eliminated. Averroes is clearly conscious of it, but he thinks that, even then, it remains a pseudo-problem; so much so that a philosophy worthy of the name can and must establish its futility. In the mind of Avicenna, the whole difficulty is tied up with his notion of what he calls the "possible out of itself." Of course, if there are such beings which, out of themselves, are merely possible, the problem arises to know what must be added to them in order to give them actual reality. But is the pure possible of Avicenna an intelligible philosophical notion? We can understand what Avicenna means by the First, Who is the only necessary being, and Who subsists in virtue of His own necessity. We also can understand that all that which is, outside the First, is necessary in virtue of the necessity of the First. Had he said this, and nothing more, Avicenna would have said nothing but the truth and the whole truth; for, indeed, all that which is, is necessary either by itself or by its cause, and the proposition can be proven.

Let us consider the case of any one of those beings which Avicenna holds to be "necessary in virtue of another." Since it is, and since it is necessary that it be, in what sense can we still say that it remains "possible?" Avicenna's answer is that such a being remains possible in itself. But what is its "itself," apart from what it is? Avicenna says: it is its essence. Which is true. But, if we take a certain essence prior to its actualization, it is indeed a pure possible, precisely because it does not yet exist and has no necessity whatsoever; if, on the contrary, we take it as already actualized, it does then exist, but it has become necessary and there is no trace in it of any possibility. When it was possible, it was not, and, now that it is, it no longer is possible. To imagine it as being both at one and the same time, one has to suppose that it actually is, and that, while it is, it still remains in itself as if

[12] Averroes, *In IV Metaph.*, c. 3, *ed. cit.*, Vol. IX, f. 43ᵛ.

it were not. The unrealized possibility seems here to survive its actual realization and, so to speak, to receive from its very negation some sort of vague reality. But this is absurd. "If the thing is necessary, however it may have been posited, possibility is wholly absent from it. Nothing can be found in the world of such a nature that it be possible in a certain way, yet necessary in another way. For, it has already been shown that what is necessary is in no way possible, since possible and necessary contradict each other. Where there is possibility in a certain being, it is that such a being contains, over and above what is necessary from the point of view of its own nature, something that is merely possible from the point of view of another nature. Such is the case of the heavenly bodies, or of what there is above them (namely, the *primum mobile*) for, such things are necessary as regards their being, but they are possible with respect to their motion in space. What has led Avicenna to that distinction was his opinion that the heavenly bodies are necessary by another, and yet possible out of themselves."[14]

To complete his criticism, Averroes had only to identify the cause required by Avicenna in order to account for the existence of the "possible out of itself," with the cause of existence required by religions in order to account for the creation of the world. And he did it. "You must know" [Averroes says] "that the newness ascribed by religious law to this world is of the same nature as the newness of things as it is understood in this doctrine."[15] Let us pause a moment to pay homage to the remarkable philosophical insight of Avicenna's great adversary. What he clearly sees in the doctrine of his predecessor is a kind of philosophical substitute for the religious notion of creation. The God of Avicenna is a God Who *is*, so much so that, rather than say that His essence is identical with His existence, we had better say that He has no essence at all. Yet, Avicenna does not consider his God as having created the world by an act of will. As has been said, the world flows from God's intrinsic necessity, according to the laws of intelligible necessity. There is no true creation in Avicenna's doctrine, but to the keen eyes of Averroes there still is too much of it, or, at least, there still is something which looks too much like it. The world of Avicenna remains a world of happenings. Assuredly, they all are necessary happenings, but still they do happen. Possibles that were mere possibles become actual beings, then pass away and make room for the actualization of other

---

[14] Averroes, *Destructio destructionum*, disp. VIII, *ed. cit.*, Vol. IX, f. 43^v.
[15] *Ibid.*, disp. I, Vol. IX, f. 9^v.

possibles. There remains in such a philosophy at least some faint trace of what any true philosophy of the concept hates above everything else, novelty.

A universe in which nothing new ever happens—such is the universe of Averroes himself. To the question: "How do you account for the fact that motions begin and then come to an end?" his answer is that motions may seen to begin and to end, but that motion itself never has either beginning or end. It cannot either begin or end, because to move essentially entails both a before and an after, so that, wherever you look for motion there always is a "before" whence it comes, as surely as there is an "after" whither it goes. The modern principle of the conservation of energy in the world would have been welcomed by Averroes. All the motions of the heavenly bodies and all the motions which are caused by them on earth, that is to say, all the motions there are, constitute for him a single motion, indefinitely perpetuated, whose sum total remains indefinitely the same: "And this is why, when theologians have asked philosophers if the movements anterior to the present ones have ceased, the philosophers have answered that those movements have not ceased, because, as philosophers see it, just as those movements have had no beginning, so they have no end."[16] And let us not forget that what is true of motion holds good for any event in general. All that happens is a motion of some sort, so that all that is, is always there, identically the same, in spite of its apparent mutability.

One could hardly wish for a world better made to suit the taste of abstract conceptual thinking. Existence is no more to be feared here than it will be in the philosophy of Spinoza. No provision is made for it in this eternally self-identical world, not even the smallest corner where that unpredictable element may threaten to play the most harmless of its tricks. Perfectly proof against newness, it remains eternally such as it is. Since generations and corruptions are but particular kinds of motion, individual beings can come and go without disturbing the peace of the world. Some beings, such as the heavenly bodies and the pure intelligences which move them, are naturally eternal and incorruptible; taken all together, they make up the divine world, which is free from change in its own right. As to the other beings, which, like ourselves, are born, and whose life is so short, it is true to say that they themselves are subject to change, but they do not count, for their only function is to ensure the perpetuity of their own species, which itself always is owing to them and never changes. Individuals

[16] *Ibid.*

pass away, the species never pass away. They do not pass away because, just as a motion never ends except in giving rise to another motion, so that motion is always there, so also "man" never ends, owing to the perpetual substitution of those who are born for those who die. The world has always been just what it is; humanity has always been just what it is; human knowledge has always been just what it is, for the totality of intelligible forms is being permanently radiated and, so to speak, broadcast by the subsisting Intelligence Who thinks for us and in us from above, the intellectual differences between human souls having no other cause than the individual abilities of their respective bodies to catch the divine message, that is, to receive those intelligible forms. Intellectual intelligibility, then, may happen to be received by one man better than by another, in which case we say that he is more intelligent, or even that he has genius, but, when a philosopher dies, philosophy itself remains. It may now exist in the West, now in the East, but philosophy always remains because there always are philosophers, and, if true philosophy seems at times to perish, it is but an illusion. Total knowledge is always present in the Intelligence which is the unique intellect of the human species, and, though you can't take it with you when you die, because you have no individual intellect to take it in, nothing of it is lost. True enough, the divine message may be blurred for a while, but not forever. Once caught by Aristotle in Greece, it is now being heard by Averroes in Spain, and we need not fear that it will ever be completely lost. In short, individual men are mortal, and wholly so, but all the true, all the good and all the beautiful of which they partake for a little while is immortal in its own right. If the future of such things is what makes men uneasy when they die, they can die in peace, for truth, goodness and beauty always come to them from above and they abide there. They are eternally safe and bright in that Intelligence which perpetually enlightens mankind; they are still more so in each one of the higher intelligences, and they are eminently so in the first and supreme Thought, Who eternally thinks Himself in the solitude of His own perfection and is the Supreme Being because He is the Supreme Intelligibility. All that is here, is eternally there, and it is there much more really than it is here. In spite of all appearances, the world of being is one solid block of intelligible necessity. Such is the ultimate reason why being always is and cannot be conceived apart from its being. A perfect instance, indeed, of a mental universe in which, for any conceivable being, to be and to be that which it is are one and the same thing.

Obviously, nothing could be more unpalatable than such a doctrine to theologians of any persuasion. That Averroes himself had his troubles with Moslem divines not only is a fact, but should cause us no surprise. Later on, Spinoza, whose doctrine largely is a revised version of Averroism rewritten in the language of Descartes, will also have his trouble with the Synagogue, and for the same fundamental reason: in any religious world there is novelty, because there is existence. But, if there is a religious world in which newness reigns supreme, it is the Christian world, in which at least two extraordinary things once happened—its creation by God and its re-creation through the Incarnation of the Divine Word. One of the most paradoxical episodes in the history of Western thought has been the rise, in the thirteenth century, of a philosophical school whose members imagined that they could think as Averroists while believing as Christians. If there is a crucial experiment on the compossibility of existence with being in a metaphysics in which being is identified with substance, here is one, and there is good reason to hope that its study will throw some light on the true nature of their relation.

One of the most famous Averroists of the thirteenth century, Siger of Brabant is exactly the man we need to help us with our problem. Not only was he a Christian—and I personally do not know of any reason to doubt the perfect sincerity of his faith— but he also was, around 1270, a Master of Arts in the University of Paris. A Master of Arts was then a professor in charge of teaching philosophy to students who, for the most part, were later to study theology. As such, the Parisian Master of Arts had nothing to do with theology itself; his only business was to introduce his students to the philosophy of Aristotle, from his logic to his metaphysics, ethics and politics. On the other hand, it must be borne in mind that 1270 is a rather late date in the history of mediaeval philosophy. When Siger of Brabant had to deal with any philosophical problem, he could not avoid taking into account what some of his predecessors had already said on the question. The Commentaries of Averroes were at his disposal and, to him, what they said was the adequate expression of Aristotle's own thought, which itself was one with philosophical truth. But he had read many other philosophers, such as Avicenna among the Arabs, Albertus Magnus and Thomas Aquinas among the Christians.

This, I think, should account for the remarkable decision made by Siger of Brabant when, having to raise questions about Book IV of Aristotle's *Metaphysics*, he found himself confronted with

61

the definition of this supreme science: a science whose object is being *qua* being. The problem was not for him to find something to say about it; in fact, he had only too much to choose from, but he made an unusual choice. The very first question asked by Siger on this occasion was: "Whether, in created things, being (*ens*) or to be (*esse*) belongs to the essence of creatures, or is something added to their essence."[17] Obviously, we are now reaching a time when the problem of the distinction of essence and existence has already been openly raised and widely discussed. For Siger to have asked it in the very first place, the question must have already become, if not, as it now is, a perennial question, at least a question of the day. Between Siger and his own favorite master, Averroes, there stands Thomas Aquinas. For him, that is the trouble, but for us, that is what makes his case extremely interesting. If, as he naturally will do, Siger wants to identify essence and existence, it won't be enough for him to play Averroes against Avicenna, whom Averroes had both known and already refuted; he will have to play Averroes against Thomas Aquinas, whom Averroes could not refute, because he could not foresee his coming.

The whole discussion of the problem is somewhat obscured by a certain ambiguity, for which Siger himself is not responsible, because its source lies in the very position of the question. Averroes was right at least in this, that the origin of the notion of existence, as distinct from the notion of essence, is religious and tied up with the notion of creation. No one can read the Old Testament and try to formulate what it teaches about the origin of the world, without reaching the conclusion that, if there has been a creation, then the world is something that both is new and exists. As compared with its eternal idea in God, existence happens to it as a novelty.

When Christian theologians want to express this relation of the created world to its Creator, they all say that creatures do not exist out of themselves, but owe their existence to God. This is a point on which they all agree, and, although their agreement is here unavoidable, it has been, for many of them as well as for more than one of their historians, the source of a dangerous confusion.

The only way to express such a relation is to say that, since creatures do not exist by themselves, they receive their existence

---

[17] M. Grabmann, *Neuaufgefundene "Quaestionen" Sigers von Brabant zu den Werken des Aristoteles* (Clm. 9559), in *Miscellanea Francesco Ehrle*, (Roma, Bibiotheca Apostolica Vaticana, 1926), Vol. I, pp. 103-147. The above-quoted text is to be found on p. 133

from God. Their own being is not something that belongs to them *per se;* it is given to them from above, and, precisely because their being is a received being, they are distinct from the only *per se* Being there is, namely, God, their Creator. It can therefore be said that in all Christian theologies no creature *is* in its own right. Now, if creatures do not owe their own existence to themselves, there must needs be in each of them some sort of composition of what they are with the very fact that they are. In short, the distinction between creatures and their Creator entails, in creatures themselves, a distinction between their existence and the essence of their being.

If this were true, all theologians and philosophers of the Middle Ages should have taught the distinction of essence and existence, for, indeed, all of them have realized the distinction there is between the self-existent Being, Who is God, and the being of His creatures, who have it only because they receive it. But it is not so. The problem of the distinction of essence and existence is an altogether different problem. It is a purely philosophical problem, which consists in determining whether or not, within a created being, after it has been created and during the very time when it is, there is any reason to ascribe to it a distinct act in virtue of which it *is*. Now, if all theologians agree on the fact that creatures owe their being to God, it is not true to say that they all agree on the second point. They do not; far from it. Many mediaeval theologians, to whom the distinction of essence and existence has been wrongly ascribed, have in fact never thought of it. What is true is that, if a mediaeval theologian professes, as a philosopher, the distinction of essence and existence, he will find in it, as a theologian, the sufficient and ultimate reason we have for distinguishing the self-existent Being of God from the received being of creatures. But those who hold different metaphysics of being will find at their disposal many other ways of distinguishing God from His creatures, which proves at least this, that, when a theologian teaches the distinction of essence and existence, it is not because Christian theology necessarily requires it, but because he thinks that, as a philosophical doctrine, it is true. The very fact that great Christian theologies, such as those of Duns Scotus and of Suarez, manage perfectly well without this distinction, is a sufficient proof that it is not a dictate of revelation, but a purely rational view of the nature of being.

Siger of Brabant was too near the very origin of the doctrine not to fall victim to this confusion. Observing that, in those doctrines in which essence is distinct from existence, theologians

63

resort to it in order to justify the distinction of beings from the Supreme Being, he jumped to the conclusion that this very use they made of their thesis was, in their eyes, both its origin and its justification. This mistake is apparent in the initial remark of Siger's own answer to the question: "There are several different opinions on this point. Some say that a thing *is* in virtue of a disposition added to its essence, so that, according to them, "thing" and "being" have not the same meaning. Thus, "to be" is something added to the essence. This is the opinion of Albert in his Commentary. His reason is that of the *Liber de Causis*, namely, that things have their being from their first principle."[18] Now, whether or not Albertus Magnus has taught the distinction of essence and existence in creatures, I am not prepared to say, but, if he did, it cannot have been for that reason. True enough, if a certain being is a creature, we can easily imagine that it *might* not exist, as indeed would be the case if God had not created it. Consequently, practically all theologians admit that there is, between any given creature and its being, what they call a distinction of reason. The actual thing *is*, but, after all, it does not contain in itself the sufficient reason for its own existence, so that we can abstractedly conceive it as a non-existing thing. Such a statement does not necessarily imply that the thing in question is itself composed of its own essence and of its own existence; it merely expresses the relation of effect to cause which obtains between any creature and its Creator. And this indeed is what the *Liber de Causis* means when it says that the first principle is, to all things, their own being.

The same mistake occurs under another form towards the end of his question, when Siger of Brabant remarks: "Every thing that subsists by itself, below the First, is composite This last reason has been the main one for Brother Thomas."[19] No, it has not. After admitting that nothing below God is simple, and that created things include both essence and existence, Brother Thomas has naturally concluded that the first and fundamental lack of simplicity in things was due to their composition of essence and existence, but he did not need such a composition in order to account for their lack of simplicity. Even without resorting to the composition of matter and form which some theologians, like Augustine and Bonaventura, for instance, admitted in all created beings, Brother Thomas could have resorted to the distinction of act and potency, which occurs in all creatures, but not

[18] Siger of Brabant, *op. cit.*, p. 135.
[19] *Ibid.*, p. 137.

in the cause of their being, the Pure Act Whom we call God. And this is what Siger himself very clearly shows by proving that, without resorting to the distinction of essence and existence, it still remains possible to account for the lack of simplicity in creatures, as opposed to the perfect simplicity of God. If this be true, as I think it is, the fact that, below the First Cause, everything is composite cannot have been for Brother Thomas the main reason for positing the distinction of essence and existence in created things.

But how does Siger himself account for the difference in simplicity which there must needs be between God and His creatures? True to the spirit which prevails in the metaphysics of both Averroes and Aristotle, he does not feel impressed by the fact that created beings *might* not be. Let us rather say that, to him, this is far from being a fact. If they were not necessary, be it only through their cause, they would not be at all. What makes them different from the first principle cannot lie in the very fact that they are, but in their peculiar way of being, that is, in *what* they are. Because He is Pure Act, the First is one and simple. On the contrary, below Him, all the rest is mere participation in the pure actuality of the First. Now, a participation always is a certain degree of participation. Some created beings even participate more or less in the actuality of their cause, and this is why they have different essences, according as they approach more or less the simplicity of the First. Just as numbers differ from one another in species because of their various relations to unity, which is the principle of number, so beings differ from one another in essence because of their various relations to the pure act of being. Now, what a certain creature lacks in act is exactly measured by its potency. There is then a lack of simplicity in all creatures, because what makes them to be creatures is the amount of potency which specifies the essence of their own act. But we do not even need to assert this in order to avoid the difficulty. Let us take a creature that is not made up of form and matter, that is, a purely spiritual substance. Like the First, it is bound to be a self-subsisting act of thought, yet it still will lack the simplicity of the First. For, indeed, the First is a self-thinking thought; He does not need to receive from any source His own intelligibility, whereas, below the First, all knowing substances know their objects only through intelligible species. *"Omne aliud a Primo intelligit per speciem quae est aliud ab ipso:* Every being other than the First knows through some species that is something else than that very

65

being."[20] In other words, the Aristotelian notion of substance is so foreign to existence that existence plays no part in this description of created being.

The whole argumentation of Siger obviously entails that the actuality of substance as such be the whole of the actuality of being as such. In such a world, to be is to be substance, that is, either a pure form, if the substance at stake be an incorporeal one, or a substantial unit of form and matter, if the substance at stake be a corporeal one. In both cases, substances *are* in virtue of their form, which is act by definition, and, since there is nothing above act, the whole reality of any given being is completely accounted for by the actuality of its very form.

We are now in a position to see what must have been, from the point of view of Siger of Brabant, the main mistake made by both Brother Albert and Brother Thomas. Albert was right in saying that, God alone excepted, each and every creature is *per aliud* in the order of efficient causality; but this does not prevent each created thing from being a being *per se*. For, if it is at all, then it is a substance, and every substance is as such both *a se*, *ex se* and even *per se*, since it is by itself, out of itself and through itself that it is the very being it is. To which Albert will no doubt rejoin that, anyhow, it is not the cause of its own being. Of course it isn't! Unless it were created, it would not be at all, but, now that it has been created, it is a *per se* because it is a substance. When the old English poet exclaims: "O London, thou art of townes a *per se!*"[21] he does not mean to say that London is without having been made, but, rather, that London is such a city as stands alone among all the others and, for this reason, eminently *is*. London eminently is for being the very city it is. In other words, a created thing is *per aliud* in the order of efficient causality, yet it is *per se* in the order of formal causality, which, in the realm of substance, reigns supreme. Albert has therefore intermingled the two orders of the efficient cause and of the formal cause; hence his curious illusion that an existing thing still needs existence in order to exist. A perfectly valid argument indeed for anyone who, taking existence for granted, cannot see in what sense an actually given substance may still need to have it.

But, if the case of Master Albert is bad, that of Brother Thomas is worse. For, instead of merely saying that substances owe their being to something else, he has attempted to find, in substances

[20] *Ibid.*, p. 138.
[21] Ascribed to William Dunbar. *The Poems of William Dunbar*, edited by W. Mackay Mackenzie (Edinburgh, Porpoise Press, 1932), poem no. 88, l. l, p. 177. Cf. Appendix C. pp. 240-241.

66

themselves, some definite room for the very existence they are supposed to receive. And he cannot do it because the thing simply cannot be done. Thomas does not want existence to be substance itself, because he wants it to be the existence *of* the substance, that is, the very principle which, present *in* the substance, makes it to be. As if anything were still wanting in that which is, in order to make it to be! On the other hand, Thomas fully realizes that Avicenna was wrong in making existence an accident. As an accident, existence would fit nowhere in philosophy; which means that it has to be something else. But, if it is neither a substance nor an accident, *what* is it?

No more pertinent question could be asked by a philosopher to whom to be is necessarily to be a *what*. And the reason for Siger's attitude is clear: where there is no "whatness," there is no conceptual intelligibility. If we cannot say "what" the thing at stake is, then no thing is really at stake, and we are merely talking about nothing. Plato may have been mistaken in putting the One and the Good above being, but he had been right in saying that, if reality is only "what" it is, there must be some higher principle above even reality. Here, on the contrary, the very notion of a "higher-than-whatness" principle completely vanishes, because the summit of reality is itself, though an act, yet a what. The Aristotelian God is a being of which we can say what He is, namely, the pure act of an eternally self-thinking Thought. There is no trace of any invitation to rise above substance in such a metaphysics, no inducement therefore to wonder if, after all, whatness is truly the whole of reality. Of course, Siger *might* have asked himself the question, but our whole point is precisely to show that, however deep and keen a mind he has, no philosopher can see what lies beyond his own position of the question.

This is precisely what is happening to Siger, and not to understand what one is talking about is such an advantage in any kind of discussion that one is bound to score along the whole line. For, what he does is to ask Brother Thomas: *"What* is existence?" and, of course, Brother Thomas cannot answer. Unfortunately, unable as he was to say what existence is, he had at least tried to point it out, that is, to call our attention to it, so that we might at least realize *that* it is. In order to do so, he could not help using words, each of which means something whose "whatness," if so desired, we could define. While so doing, Brother Thomas obviously gives the impression of trying to define existence, although as a matter of fact, he is merely pointing to it. For an onlooker who sees it as a would-be definition, each and every such attempt can result only in failure. With diabolical cleverness Siger has singled out, among the innumerable formulas of Thomas Aquinas, the one which, were it a definition, would certainly be the worst of his failures. Quoting verbatim, Siger says that, according to Brother Thomas: "To be (*esse*) is something superadded to the essence of the thing, that does not belong to the essence of the thing, yet which is not an accident, but is something superadded as if it were, so to speak, constituted by the essence, or out of the principles of the essence."[22] As regards obscurity, this is a masterpiece. Everything in it is wrong, and it is so according to Thomas Aquinas himself: To be is not something (*aliquid*), because it is not a thing (*quid*); moreover, it is not even true to say that *esse* does not belong to the essence (*non pertinens ad essentiam rei*), because, though it be not the essence, it certainly is *its* to be; last, but not least, if it does not belong to the essence, how can it, at the same time, arise from its constitutive principles? Are we to suppose that existence originates in the constitutive principles of an essence which, apart from its existence, is not? With such an opportunity, Siger could not help but score. Let us admit, he says, that existence is constituted, or, rather, as it pleases Brother Thomas to say it, *quasi* constituted by the principles of reality. Now, what are those principles? There are but three: matter, form (whose union constitutes the substance), accident. If it be anything at all, existence has to be either matter, or form, or accident. Now, Thomas himself says, and rightly, that it is not an accident; on the other hand, he does not say that existerce is matter, because matter is potency, whereas, to be is an act; nor does he say that existence is form, because, if he said so, existence would not have to be added to essence: *qua* form, essence would exist in its own right. Siger's victory is here complete. To say, with Brother Thomas, that existence is superadded to form, to matter and to accident is nothing less, Siger scornfully remarks, than *ponere quartam naturam in entibus*, that is, to add a fourth one to the three known constituent principles of reality.

To us, this does not have the appearance of a high crime. If three principles are not enough, why not a fourth one? But the irony of Siger is quite excusable if we remember that he was a disciple of Aristotle through the commentator *par excellence*, Averroes. Now, here is a man, Brother Thomas, who calls Aristotle *Philosophus, the* Philosopher; who speaks Aristotle's own philosophical language: matter, form, essence, substance, accidents, and who nevertheless attempts to say something for which such

[22] Siger of Brabant, *op. cit.*, pp. 135-136.

a language has no words. Here again Siger of Brabant *might* have guessed that Thomas Aquinas' philosophy was *not*, after all, the philosophy of Aristotle, but all the appearances were against it, and it is no wonder that he mistook the new position of his adversary for a mere perversion of an old one.

The all-too-real embarrassment of Brother Thomas invited him to do so. What is it Thomas says of existence? *"Quasi constituitur per principia essentiae."* What does this *quasi* mean? If it means that existence is not really constituted by the principles of essence, he has said nothing; but, if it means that the principles of essence really constitute existence, then, since what matter and form actually constitute is substance, existence is bound to be its accident. And there is no way out, which means that, however long we turn it over and over or wander through it in all directions, there is no room for existence in the metaphysical universe of Aristotle, which is a world, not of existents, but of things. And this, at least, is what Siger has clearly seen. Granting to Brother Thomas that the constitutive principles of reality make up the whole cause of its existence, it necessarily follows that existence is a meaningless word. For, indeed, what is actually constituted by the principles of any conceivable thing is that very thing: *"Constitutum per principia essentiae est ipsa res,"*[23] and, once the thing is there, fully constituted by its principles, why should we bother further about its existence? If the thing is there, then it is; the existence of reality is identical with reality.

In such a metaphysics, essence, substance, thing and being are just so many points of view on reality itself. *Ens*, or being, designates what actually is. *Res*, or thing, designates the habitual possession of being: a thing is that which is. In this sense, Avicenna was right in saying that "being" and "thing" are not synonymous, but the fact that their significations are not the same implies by no means that they do not signify one and the same thing. It is the thing which is being, just as any being is a thing. Technically speaking, the mistake of all those who, with Avicenna, attempt to distinguish between beings and their being is to ascribe a distinct essence to what is but a mode of signification.[24] In fact, we should never forget that essence (*essentia*) primarily means the possession of being or the reality which belongs to being inasmuch as it actually is. What else could existence be, in Siger's doctrine, if

[23] *Ibid.*, p. 136.
[24] *Ibid.* This argument is borrowed from Averroes, *In IV Metaph.*, c. III, *ed. cit.*, f. 32ʳ: *"Et iste homo ratiocinatur ad suam opinionem . . .,"* which, for Averroes, it was a crime to do.

not essence itself in its supreme degree of actuality? *"Esse significat essentiam per modum actus maximi,"* that is to say, any fully constituted essence exists in its own right.[25]

Siger's metaphysics of being thus remains, on the whole, the same as that of Aristotle, and this is why, even after the decisive intervention of Thomas Aquinas, his philosophy rejects it as a mere verbal illusion. Yet, like those of Averroes and Aristotle, his metaphysics deals with actually real and concrete being. The point is noteworthy because, were it not so, a very large section of history would not make sense. I am here alluding to the fact that so many Christian theologies, during the Middle Ages and after, have expressed both themselves and their philosophies in the language of Aristotle. This is eminently true of the doctrine of Thomas Aquinas, so much so that, deceived by what is an irresistibly misleading appearance, too many of his historians have mistaken him for an Aristotelian. Radically speaking, he was not, but it is true that he has, so to speak, absorbed Aristotelianism, then digested it and finally assimilated its substance within his own personal thought.

What allowed him to do so, and what accounts for the fact that between the Averroists and himself conversation and discussion were at least possible, is precisely that they were all concerned with the same concrete reality. What Aristotle had said about it was not the whole truth, yet it was true, and it always was Thomas' conviction that no already acquired truth should be allowed to perish. His attitude on this point can best be understood by referring to the problem of creation. The world of Aristotle and of Averroes is what it is as it has always been and always will be. Wholly innocent of existence, no question can arise about its beginning or its end, or even about the question of knowing how it is that such a world actually is. It is, and there is nothing more to be said. Obviously, it would be a foolish thing to speak of creation on the occasion of such a world, and, to the best of my knowledge, Thomas Aquinas has never spoken of the Aristotelian cosmos as of a created world; on the other hand, Averroes and his disciples have always maintained that, in the doctrine of Aristotle, God is not merely the Prime Mover of the world, but that he also is its Prime Maker.

Nothing could have been better calculated than this subtle distinction between Mover, Maker and Creator, to help us in ascertaining the true nature of Aristotelian being. If the God of Aristotle were nothing more than·the Prime Mover of the

[25] Siger of Brabant, *op. cit.*, p. 137.

world, He would, in no sense of the word "being," be the cause of its being. A merely physical cause, such as God, would not be a metaphysical cause. If, as Averroes, Thomas Aquinas and many Averroists have said,[26] the God of Aristotle is the Maker of the world, the reason for it is that He actually is, for all beings, the cause of their very being. They owe Him, not only to move if they move, to live if they live and to know if they know, but to be. If men really were what Aristotle thought them to be, they would be very far from feeling free never to think of God. True enough, they would have very little, if anything, to expect from Him, since He Himself would not even be aware of their existence: species, at the utmost, not individuals, are worth being included in His own self-contemplation. Nevertheless, mediaeval texts are there to prove that there is such a thing as Averroistic piety. [27] To pray to the God of Aristotle would be pointless, in so far, at least, as prayer includes asking, but there would be very good ground to praise and to worship Him in Whom all men should recognize the Supreme Cause by which they act, they live and they are.

Still this is not yet a created universe. There still remains, in its beings, something which the God of Aristotle could not give them, because He Himself did not possess it. As a World-Maker, the God of Aristotle can insure the permanence of substances, but nothing else, because He Himself is an eternally subsisting substance, that is, a substantial act, but nothing else. His actuality is a self-contained one. He is an act to Himself alone, and this is why what happens outside Himself is not due to the fact that He loves, for He loves Himself only, but to the fact that He is loved. He has only to be what He is, in order to foster in other Pure Acts, inferior to Him yet no less eternal than He is, a permanent love for His own perfection and a permanent desire to be united with Him. Such are the divine Intelligences, and, as their desire of the First eternally reaches matter, a matter no less eternal than is the First Himself, everything eternally falls into place and eternally moves in virtue of that love which, in the words of the

[26] "*Ad quaestionem jam motam breviter, dico quod profundi philosophi, et majores eorum et maxime Averrois in tractatu* De substantia orbis *et in libro* Destructio destructionum *respondent quod Primum abstractum non tantum dat motum corpori caelesti, sed dat sibi esse et permanentiam aeternam in sua substantia.*" Helias Hebraeus, *Utrum mundus sit effectus*, in Joannes de Janduno, *De physico auditu* (Bergamo, 1501), f. 131ᵛ. Cf. Thomas Aquinas, *In VI Metaph.*, lect. 1, ed. Cathala, n. 1164.

[27] M. Grabmann, *Die Opuscula de Summo Bono . . . und de Sompniis des Boetius von Dacien*, in *Archives d'histoire doctrinale et littéraire du moyen âge* (Paris, J. Vrin, 1931), pp. 306-307.

altissimo poeta, "moves the sun and the other stars." Where there is motion, there is life. Divine intelligences and heavenly bodies immutably subsist by themselves; like the First, they are gods and the life they live is divine. Below them, in immediate contact with this sublunary world and even engaged in it, are those intelligible realities which, too weak to subsist and endure by themselves, stand, so to speak, in need of some material support. They are the species. Intelligible forms, and therefore no less eternal than the gods, they nevertheless are not by themselves, but they run, so to speak, through an infinite number of individuals, which eternally succeed and replace one another in order to maintain the species to which they owe their forms. This is why individuals do not matter in themselves; their species uses them in order to endure, so that, for each of them, not the individual, but the species is the true reality. In such a world, everything is indebted to the First for all that it is. From the heavenly beings, whose very substance it is to be pure acts of contemplation and love of the First down to the humblest corporeal being whose very substance it is to share, while it lasts, in the intelligible form of its species, nothing can be found which is not indebted to the First for all that which it is, inasmuch as it is. The world of Aristotle owes its divine maker everything, except its existence. And this is why it has no history, not even in history. Hermetically sealed against any kind of novelty, the existenceless world of Aristotle has crossed century after century, wholly unaware of the fact that the world of philosophy and of science was constantly changing around it. Whether you look at it in the thirteenth, fourteenth, fifteenth or sixteenth century, the world of Averroes remains substantially the same, and the Averroists could do little more than eternally repeat themselves, because the world of Aristotle was an eternally self-repeating world. It has opposed Christian theologians when they taught that God could have made another world than the one He has made. It has resisted Christian theologians when they maintained that, in this God-made world, there take place such events as are the work of freedom and escape necessity. Because theology was, before anything else, a history full of unpredictable events, it has branded theology as a myth, and science itself has felt the weight of its hostility. Itself scientifically sterile, there is not a single scientific discovery against which, so long as it lasted, it did not raise an indignant protest. And no wonder, for, since the world of Aristotle has no history, it never changes and it is no one's business to change it. No newness, no development, no history, what a dead lump of being the world of substance is! Yet, there certainly seems to be some newness, some development, some history in the actual world in which we live. It is now beginning to look as though we made some mistake in carelessly discounting existence. But we have not yet exhausted the list of its metaphysical substitutes. Indeed, one of them, namely, "essence," has played such a part in shaping the history of modern philosophy that, before turning to existence, we must single it out for detailed consideration.

Chapter III

Essence and Existence

IN AN individual being conceived according to the doctrine of Aristotle, what truly is, is the form by which it is a substance. Yet, in any genuinely Aristotelian metaphysics, the form of corporeal individuals does not subsist apart from the matter to which it owes its individuation. This is why, according to Aristotle, even in this world of sense, actual reality is "substance." It can then be said of the form that it is "what truly is in that which actually is." Were we to deny that, in corporeal beings, actual reality is the compound of matter and form, we would turn Aristotle's forms into so many self-subsisting intelligible realities, that is, into so many Platonic Ideas. But there is a subtler way to reinforce what is left of Platonism in Aristotle's metaphysics of being without going back to Plato's self-subsistent Ideas. Working on the assumption that, in actual corporeal beings, what is truly real is the form, a philosopher can decide to make the form in itself be the proper object of metaphysical speculation.

Aristotle himself provides ample justification for an experiment of that kind. In his own doctrine, the form is οὐσία, a term which means reality, or a "beingness," when it points out the actual reality of the thing, but which also means that which, in the thing, is truly real, namely, its intelligible form. Now, as has been said, just as the form is "nature" when taken as the innermost principle of the operations of the thing, so it is "essence" when taken as the possible object of an intelligible definition.[1] Now, philosophy is knowledge, and, even though it may feel compelled to recognize that there is some unintelligible element in concrete reality, such as matter, for instance, its proper object of study must need be that which in reality is intelligible. If, in any given thing, what truly is is its essence, then let us say that essence itself is being. If we do so, there then arises a metaphysics of essence, wherein the actually given world, while it remains the substantial world

[1] See Ch. II, pp. 43-44, 46-47.

74

of Aristotle, can safely be dealt with as if it were the ideal world of Plato.

Now, to do so was an almost irresistible temptation. In the course of its centuries-long history, Platonism has found itself engaged in countless hybrid philosophical combinations, but, like all pure philosophical positions, it has always exhibited a tendency to disengage itself from contaminating elements foreign to its own essence and thus to recover its original purity. This is what happened in Avicenna's philosophy when he conceived his carefully worked-out doctrine of essences. He probably had some predecessors, and one of them may have been Alfarabi, but, in so far as our own problem is concerned, Avicenna himself is the real starting point, because the influence of his doctrine can clearly be seen in many philosophies of essence, mediaeval or modern.

Essences, Avicenna says, are either in things themselves or in the intellect. For this reason, they can be envisaged under three different aspects. A first aspect is that of the essence taken in itself, that is, as unrelated to either any thing or to any intellect. A second one is that of the essence as engaged in individual things. The third is that of the same essence as present within an intellect, in which it receives various accidents such as predication, universality, particularity and other similar ones.[2]

At first sight, this seems to be a very clear and exhaustive division of all the possible conditions in which an essence can be found. On closer inspection, it is a very curious one, for the very first thing Avicenna tells us is that essences are either in things themselves or in the mind, yet he goes on to say that essences can be considered either in things or in the mind or in themselves. Now, if they exist solely when they are in things or in a mind, where are they when they are in themselves? This is a very simple question, but one for which no one has yet been able to find an answer. From the very wording of the problem, it appears that it is not susceptible of solution. Yet, Avicenna himself has posited essences in themselves, as if they were some neutral realities, floating, so to speak, between things and minds, now engaged in the reality of individual beings, then conceived by intellects, and always without losing their own privilege of being just what they are. How can such a position be really understood?

I am afraid that, to the extent that it is possible, its explanation has to be more psychological than metaphysical. Obviously, Avicenna does not mean to say that, taken in themselves, essences actually exist. On the contrary, when he first tells us that essences

[2] Avicenna, *Logica*, I, l, in *Avicennae . . . opera* (Venetiis, 1508), f. 1ᵛ. Cf. f. 2ʳ.

are to be found either in things or else in minds, what he wants to make clear is that they are not to be found anywhere else. This, at least, is a philosophical statement. But what comes next seems to have little to do with philosophy, and I fancy that this is the explanation. Here is an essence, *stone*, for instance, which I now find in an intellect and then in particular stones. It is existing according to two different modes and therefore in two different ways. Yet, when I think of it, it is the same essence. It is the same, at least, from the point of view of its definition. If there were no stones, the essence of "stoneness" would still exist, provided only there still be a mind to conceive it, even as a mere possible. On the other hand, if there were stones and no minds to know them, stoneness would still exist in the stones. Consequently, stoneness is in itself wholly unrelated to either minds or things. Hence an almost irresistible psychological illusion to which, in fact, Avicenna falls victim. He has simply imagined as existing in themselves essences which, according to what he himself has just said, never exist in themselves. In other words, after saying that they exist only in minds or in things, he considers as essences in themselves what those essences would be if there were neither minds nor things.

What nevertheless gives sense to this illusion is that Platonism answers one of the fundamental aspirations of the human mind. The essences of Avicenna are so many ghosts of Plato's Ideas. Their whole being consists in their abstract necessity. Endowed with an intelligible resistance of their own, they victoriously resist all effort of our intellect to change them. Then they are immutable, and what is being, if not selfhood, immutability? What we are now witnessing, in Avicenna's philosophy, is the rise of a curious type of being, the *esse essentiae* of Henry of Ghent and of so many other scholastic philosophers. It is not a being of existence (*esse existentiae*), yet it is some sort of a being, namely, the very one which belongs to essence as such, irrespective of the fact that it is or that it is not actualized in any knowing subject or in any individually existing thing.

Supposing that there be such essences, what should be their main characteristics? First of all, when taken in themselves, essences are their very own selves. Each of them is in itself exclusively what it is. As such, they cannot enter in composition with each other. To quote one instructive example, Avicenna will never admit that the human intellect is the substantial form of its body. To say that it is would be to suppose a dreadful confusion of essences, each of which, because it is one with itself and other than all the rest, is bound everywhere to remain exactly what it is. Not only essence itself, but its essential properties are incommunicable. Laughter, for instance, is such a property of man: we can accordingly be sure to find it everywhere the essence of man is, and nowhere else. In short, each essence is an unbreakable block of self-identical intelligibility.

This is why essences in themselves must needs be and always remain strictly neutral with respect to all their possible determinations. Out of itself, an essence is neither singular nor universal, but indifferent to both. When it is the form of an individual, it is singular; when it is in the intellect of a knowing subject, it can be posited as either singular or universal, but, taken in itself, it is neither one. To borrow an instance from the order of the genus, we will say that *animal* is in itself something, and that it remains the same, whether we speak of it as of an animal given in the world of sense or of an animal given as an intelligible in the soul. Out of itself, *animal* is neither universal nor singular. Indeed, if, out of itself, it were universal, so that animality were universal *qua* animality, there could be no singular animals, but each and every animal would be a universal. If, on the contrary, *animal* were singular *qua* animal, there could be no more than a single animal, namely, the very singular to which animality belongs, and no other singular could be an animal. Thus, when taken in itself, *animal* is nothing more than this intellection in thought: *animal*; "and, inasmuch as it is conceived as being *animal*, it is but animal, and nothing else: *et secundum hoc quod intelligitur esse animal, non est nisi animal tantum;*" "but, if, moreover, it is conceived as being universal or singular, or whatever else that may be, we are thereby conceiving, in addition to that which *animal* is, something accidental to animality."[1]

This is what Avicenna says in his *Logic*, and, lest we imagine that these are the words of a mere logician, it will be safer to read what he had said on the same question in his *Metaphysics*. Besides, the text is of historical interest, because it introduced, for the first time, a certain horse that was destined to become a battle-horse later to be ridden by no less a rider than Duns Scotus: "The definition of *equinity* lies outside the definition of universality, nor is universality contained in the definition of *equinity*. For, indeed, *equinity* has a definition which does require universality; consequently, *equinity* itself is nothing else than *equinity* solely: *unde ipsa equinitas non est aliquid nisi equinitas tantum.*" Out of itself, it is neither many nor single, neither is it existing in those

[1] *Ibid.*, P. III, f. 12ʳ.

sensible things of ours nor in the soul, and there is not one of those determinations which it could be said to be either in potency or in act, so that they be contained in the essence of *equinity*. Such is, as will be seen later, the root of the famous doctrine of the accidentality of unity and of existence with respect to essence in the metaphysics of Avicenna: "Because it is *equinity* only, oneness is a property which, when superadded to *equinity*, makes *equinity* be one in virtue of this very property. But, besides this property, *equinity* has many other properties that are accidental to it. Thus, because many beings answer its definition, *equinity* is common, but inasmuch as it is taken with determinate accidents and properties, it is singular: *equinity* in itself then is just *equinity*."[4]

Let us carefully commit this formula to memory: *Equinitas ergo in se est equinitas tantum*. If there ever was in history such a thing as an existentially neutral essence, here it is, and we should now feel able to understand why, to the disgust of Averroes, Avicenna upheld a world of things which, while being necessary through their Cause, still remained, within themselves, so many pure possibles. An actualized possible is an essence to which it happens that it exists. Even while it is, it remains true to say that, *qua* essence, it is not. Just as nothing forbids it to become either universal or singular,[5] so also nothing forbids it to become an existent or to remain a mere possible; what happens to it in no way alters that which it is, and we know that, as an essence, it is nothing else. But it is not enough to say that, out of themselves, essences are not. The truth about them is that, however we look at them, there is nothing in any one of them that calls for its existence. The First alone is necessary, hence He *is*, and He is *truly*, and, since truth is a property of being, the First is truth in virtue of His own necessity. But what about the rest? Since no possible essence is endowed with the slightest determination to existence, it has neither being nor truth. "As you know," Avicenna says, "the other essences do not deserve to be; considered in themselves and apart from their relation to the Necessary Being, they deserve privation of being, and this is why, inasmuch as they are in themselves, they are all false. To Him alone they owe what there is in them of certainty. It is in the sight of Him who knows, that they are, and for this reason every thing perishes, unless His face be turned towards it."[6] Obviously, Avicenna is here remembering the Koran: "There is no other God but Him. Everything is perishable, except His

---

[4] Avicenna, *Metaphysica*, tr. V, cap. I, *ed. cit.*, f. 86ᵛ. Cf. f. 86ᵇ.
[5] *Ibid.*, tr. V, cap. I.   [6] *Ibid.*, tr. VIII, cap. 6.

face."[7] No Mohammedan reader could miss the allusion. At any rate, it was not lost on Averroes, and it is no wonder that he reproached Avicenna with mixing philosophy with religion.

We now find ourselves in a better position to understand the famous Avicennian doctrine, so severely criticized by Averroes and so often discussed by Thomas Aquinas, of the accidentality of oneness and of existence with respect to essence. Oneness is a property which inseparably follows substance, and which cannot therefore exist in itself apart from the being which is said to be *one*. Yet, whatever substance we may happen to define, oneness does not enter the definition of its essence. Every thing has to be defined by its genus and its specific difference; now, oneness is neither the genus nor the specific difference of any substance; it does not therefore enter the definition of any substance, and, since it is neither its genus nor its specific difference, it is one of its accidents. A very peculiar kind of accident, however. Taken in itself, oneness is nothing more than the substance considered in its undividedness with respect to itself. Oneness, then, is inseparable from substance, but, as the notion of unity, by which this fact is expressed, is an addition to the notion of substance, oneness remains, though inseparable from it, yet an accident.[8] One could hardly wish for a more thorough substitution, for the concrete unity of being, of a multiplicity of distinct concepts, each of which represents a distinct being. So many concepts, as many essences; so many essences, as many things.

What is true of oneness applies to existence. The analysis of any given being will always fail to detect in it the presence of being. Being is not the genus of that which is, nor is it its difference, and this is why, as has been said, it can be found in many. What we called "man" is a "common" essence, which happens to have being in Plato, in Socrates and in Hippocrates. Let us say, then: "To the nature of 'man' *qua* 'man,' *to be* is an accident: *naturae hominis ex hoc quod est homo accidit ut habeat esse.*"[9] In other words, it is not inasmuch as he happens to have being that man has his human nature, nor is it inasmuch as he has his human nature that man happens to have being. To be is something that needs to be superadded to "manness" in order to constitute an existing man, while universality must be superadded to "manness" in order to produce, in a mind which conceives it as predicable of all men, the universal notion of man. This exteriority of being

[7] Surat XXVIII, 88.
[8] Avicenna, *Metaphysica*, tr. III, cap. 3, f. 79^r. Cf. tr. V, cap. 1, f. 87^r.
[9] *Ibid.*, tr. V, cap. 2, f. 87^v.

with respect to essence is what Avicenna means by saying that *to be* is an accident.

Let us now consider, in a more concrete way, the relation of existence to essences. After hearing Avicenna by way of Averroes' criticisim, it is only just to let him freely state his own case. The whole argument of Averroes against Avicenna's doctrine of the accidentality of being rests on the assumption that what cannot correctly be said in the language of Aristotle cannot possibly be true. The hardest reproach he can direct against Avicenna is that this man is now simply trying to think for himself, whereas, the true duty of any philosopher is to think exactly as Aristotle did. Now, if Averroes is right in this, there is no doubt that Avicenna was wrong. Not a commentator, but an original thinker, he really was trying to say something that was both new and true. Existence was there before his eyes, and he knew it, but he did not know what to do with it. In any actualized possible, existence appeared to him as an inseparable concomitant of the essence. Actual being can no more be without its existence than it can be without its unity. Yet, since actual being is primarily its essence, even while a being actually is it *has* its existence, it *is* not it. It *is* not it because, were it its existence, then it would have no essence. Here again the notionalism of Avicenna is at work, playing havoc with the constituent elements of concrete being.

He himself cannot help it. At least, he cannot if it is true to say that, once excluded from being, existence can never find a way to re-enter it. Since Avicenna parcels out reality into abstract notions, he can no longer admit that even an existing essence actually *is*. For, indeed, if what it is is existence, then it cannot be essence, whereas, if it is essence, it cannot possibly be existence. This is so true in Avicenna's doctrine that the Necessary Being, Who alone is in virtue of His own necessity, is also the only one to be His own existence. Hence, the Necessary Being of Avicenna has no essence: *"Primus igitur non habet quidditatem."*[10] In point of fact, on the strength of Avicenna's principles, we cannot have it both ways. If God is existence, He cannot have an essence. Had God an essence, then His essence would have existence, so He Himself would exist—not as Existence, but merely as having it. Nowhere does the absolute primacy of essence in the created world of Avicenna more clearly reveal itself than in this crowning piece of his metaphysics. His God is pure existence, but He keeps it to Himself; as to essences, they may have it on loan, and nothing more. The radical impossibility there is in "being an essence" is so

[10] *Ibid.*, tr. V, cap. 4, f. 99^r.

80

insuperable that, though God Himself had an essence, He could not possibly be it.

If this be true, the doctrine of Avicenna concerning being might possibly appear as a prefiguration of Thomism, but what it really did announce was something rather different. In a sense, Avicenna not only does not devaluate existence, he does not devaluate even existents. The First, the Necessary Being, that is, God Himself, is the pure act of existence, and nothing can be considered as superior to it. As to finite things, it is also true that, in this philosophy, each of them has an existence of its own, that it is a compound of essence and existence and, consequently, that there is a distinction of essence and existence in Avicenna's metaphysics of being. Yet, there is a difference between the two doctrines, and it is of such nature that, when confronted with Thomism, Avicenna's disciples will feel bound in conscience to fight it.

To account for this difference, I see no other way than to ask if, after all, what Avicenna called the Necessary Being really was existence. I know that Avicenna himself says He is, but our own point is, in what sense is it true? First of all, it is true in this sense, that the Necessary Being cannot not be. Then, it is true in this further sense that the Necessary Being is the whole cause of existence for all the rest, that is, for all that which happens to be through the will of the First. For, indeed, the First is will; He *is* will rather than having it. But the First is not blind; just as He is will, He is thought, and all the possibles are, so to speak, gathered together in the unity of His existence. It is only later, in the first Intelligence which flows from the First, that duality begins and, with duality, multiplicity. Since it exists only in virtue of the First, the first Intelligence knows itself as both possible in itself and as necessary in virtue of its cause. Hence an incipient gap between essence and existence, and yet an already unbridgeable one, since it shows us that essence coincides with pure possibility. Essences, then, are adequately measured by their very lack of existence or, rather, they are it. Now, here is a first Being Who is existence with essence and Whose existence is both the unity of will and thought, that is, of what we would call will and thought in a finite essence. In the First, all that we call by such names simply melts in the fire of true existence. Yet, and for this very reason, since thought and existence are in Him strictly one, He is absolute necessity. The Necessary Being necessarily is, and all that which is in addition to Him, necessarily is, because it is through His own necessity. Each actual existence is but a particular moment of

81

the necessity of the First, and this is precisely why a mere possible essence cannot possibly be its own existence. For essence to be its existence, possibility would have to be at one and the same time its very necessity. Yet, while it exists, any actualized possible is necessary through the necessity of the First, Who is Himself eternally bound by His own necessity. In this sense, the necessary Being is, *qua* being, necessity. To the question, "Is the God of Avicenna existence?" the answer is, "Yes, He is, but to be existence for him means to be necessity." Of such a God it can truly be said that He is *bound* to exist, and, just as He cannot help being, so everything else cannot help being while He is, nor can the Necessary Being do anything about it. How could He, since each and every actual existence is but a delegation of His own necessity? In both God and things, existence *is* necessity.

If what precedes is true, the relation of essence to existence in such a doctrine must needs be a very peculiar one. True existence is innocent of essence, and true essence is innocent of existence. Now, even without judging the doctrine in itself, it can at least be said that such a decision finally succeeds in completely dissociating essence from existence. An entirely new situation is here arising, and it is one which we know full well, because we still are engaged in it. Ever since the days of Plato, whatever "to be" might mean, essence at least had always meant: "to be that which *to be* means." In all philosophical language, be it Greek or Latin, the word "essence" had seldom broken loose from its root, which is the verb "to be." When a Greek said that a thing was οὐσία, he meant that the thing was real. When a Latin said that a certain thing was *essentia*, he too was pointing to the reality of that thing. Not so today. When we speak of an "essence," the very first connotation of the word which occurs to our mind is that what it designates may exist and as easily may not. Modern essences are pure possibles, of which it can truly be said that, metaphysically speaking, "they do not deserve to be." They would be existences, if they really deserved to be, and this is why, henceforth, there will always be philosophers in whose minds, paradoxically enough, *essentia* will not connote *esse*, but the mere capability of receiving *esse*. True enough, in the world of Avicenna, there is an absolute certainty that each and every possible shall eventually materialize; what is eventual there is by no means contingent. Yet, in such a world, essences always remain, in themselves, pure possibles, and no wonder, since the very essence of essence is possibility.

Clearly enough, Christian theology could not tolerate such a philosophy, by which I simply mean that Avicenna's metaphysics of being could not appear, to any Christian, as a philosophically acceptable interpretation of reality. Unless he resigned himself to living as a Christian in a world different from the world he lived in as a philosopher, he would have to turn down the metaphysics of Avicenna as incompatible with his own view of the world. The famous condemnation of Averroistic and Avicennian theses in 1277 has no other meaning. The very spirit of that famous ecclesiastical pronouncement is the solemn refusal it opposes to Greco-Arabic determinism and the claim it lays to liberty. When he signed that document, Bishop Etienne Tempier was simply asking, in the name of the Christian Faith, for a free world under a free God. And what he clearly understood by a free world was a world in which there is freedom wherever there is knowledge: a world in which there is room for real contingency even within the frame of its necessary laws: a world in which unexpected things may happen at any time, because, in the last analysis, the very fact that it is was, in so far as it itself is concerned, an unpredictable happening. There should be freedom in the world because the Christian God has eternally been free with respect to the world. Free with respect to *what* the world is, He is no less free with respect to the fact that the world *is*. But, where there is no existence, how could there still be liberty? The radical newness of truly free acts, that fundamental character which Bergson has so remarkably brought to light in his analysis of free will, has its original source much less in duration itself than in the very act of existing, by which enduring things themselves endure. Things are not because they last; they last because they are, and, because they are, they act. Everything is free in a Christian universe, since even what is binding law to matter is freedom to God. But there is nothing in this world of sense to compare with man in this respect. From the point of view of his body, man's freedom is but God's own freedom, while, as a mind, man has access within the limits of his essence to a freedom that is truly *his*. Each and every man, then, in order both to be and freely to act, must needs be a being which *is*. And how could he be that if he were but an existentially neutral essence, indifferent in itself to the very fact that it is?

It is, indeed, no wonder that almost all those Christian theologies whose authors were young enough to profit by its message seem to have taken it as the very charter and program of their own world. What fourteenth-century Christian speculation tried to do was to blow up the solid block of Greco-Arabic determinism, and this was mainly the work of the Franciscan School. Ockham, for instance, was going to do it by simply annihilating all essences, and by annihilating them in God first so as to be quite sure that none of them would ever be found in beings. If there are no essences, God is free. Between bare individuals and the all-powerful will of God, nothing remains that might set any limits to divine omnipotence. After all, what is the first article of the Christian creed, if not: "I believe in God the Father Almighty?" Would God still be almighty if there were essences? *Delenda est essentia!* There is what Ockham has done, and he has made a thorough job of it. But Duns Scotus also wanted to break up Greco-Arabic necessity, and he did it in a very different way: not through annihilating Avicenna's essences but, on the contrary, through taking fullest advantage of their existential neutrality.

The Scotist definition of essence is none other than that of Avicenna. According to Duns Scotus, Avicenna had been wrong on many points, but not on this one. Yet, from the very beginning, we should notice a slight difference in terminology, because it is indicative of the trend to metaphysical realism which characterizes Scotism. Where Avicenna had used the word "essence," Scotus not infrequently uses the word "nature." Out of itself, this nature is neither universal nor singular, but it is indifferent to both universality and singularity. It becomes universal when, present within an intellect, it receives universal predicability; it becomes, if not exactly singular, at least particular, when it is united with matter, and it becomes even singular when it receives its ultimate determination, the "thisness" (*hecceitas*) which, though not itself a form, gives individuality. The structure of Scotist being is much more complex than that of Avicenna's, but the core remains the same in both doctrines, and it is essence or nature. Out of itself, Scotus says, "equinity" is neither the concept of horse, nor is it a horse; it is simply a common essence which can indifferently become either one; whereupon, quoting Avicenna in support of his own position, he adds: "Equinity is equinity only."[11]

What do we know concerning that nature, and where is it to be found? If our question is about the kind of being which it possesses, then it is necessary to distinguish between the various conditions in which it can be found. At its very origin, it has no other being than that of an object of the divine mind. Of course, such an object should not be understood as subsisting by itself apart from God. This is in no way true; in God, the divine Ideas

---

[11] Duns Scotus, *Opus Oxoniense*, lib. II, dis. 3, q. 1, n. 7.

are nothing but God. Yet, since they are conceived by Duns as objects of the divine mind, they must needs have, in God Himself, the being that belongs to such objects, that is, the sort of being which consists in being an object in a mind; in short, what Duns himself calls a "being of object." Such a being is purely intelligible, and the infinity of all the intelligibles which are conceivable by an infinite mind is eternally present to the divine mind.

Let us now examine one of these intelligible natures. It can be turned by God into an actually existing creature. If God does it, it will be an effect of His will, which is an infinitely free will. Here, of course, the block of Greco-Arabic necessity disintegrates under the pressure of two charges of theological explosive: the absolute infinity of the divine essence and the absolute freedom of God's will. God is infinite, His Ideas are eternally with Him and, by as much as they are His, they are not even possibles. Their existence in Him is His own existence, and there is in Him no law which binds Him to create anything.

If God creates, then, He does so freely and out of pure love. His will, so to speak, singles out the Ideas which shall enter the structure of the world. As producible by His power, those Ideas become the "creables" (*creabilia*). This time they are so many possibles, but they are such only because they are related to their eventual creation by God. In Scotism, the will of God is in no way bound by the intrinsic necessity of essences; so, unlike that of Avicenna, the God of Duns Scotus is free because the very possibility of actual existences hangs on His free will. Presented by the will of God to His mind as "creable things," those intelligible natures have a being of their own, an *esse* which is their being *qua* possibles. Let us take an example: man as conceived by the divine mind. It is an object of divine knowledge which may, if God so wills, be endowed with actual existence. It is not yet *a* man, but it is not nothing. It cannot be nothing, since it is a possible. Let us say then that it has a sort of "abridged being," an *ens diminutum*, that is, such a being as is required for it to be at least a possibility. This possible is nothing else than the very common nature which we began to describe. It is the essence of Avicenna, equally indifferent to both universality and singularity, but able to receive either one. As to creation, it is the very act whereby such an essence is posited in actual existence, which is a free act of the divine will.

The question then arises to know what *esse* (to be) means in such a doctrine. It may mean existence, but it may also mean something else, since it cannot possibly mean existence in the two

85

first cases we have just mentioned. The divine Ideas are in God, and they are God. Yet, inasmuch as they are Ideas, they must have their being *qua* Ideas. At any rate, they are what they are, and consequently they are. This is so true that, under the pressure of his own mode of thought, Duns Scotus has gone so far as to say that, although they be God, the divine Ideas are God *secundum quid*, that is, relatively and comparatively. In other words, each of them is God, but it is not God *qua* God. Were it God *qua* God, it would not be an Idea, it would be the Divine Word Himself. Thus, verifying a law which has already been stated in the course of this inquiry, the infinitesimal distinction which Duns Scotus introduces between God and the divine Ideas is exactly proportional to the amount of Platonism which enters his own notion of being. Because there is an *esse* of Ideas *qua* Ideas, they cannot purely and simply be God.

What is true of the divine Ideas is still more obviously true of the "creables," of the "possibles" and, finally, of the "natures." For each and every condition of the essence, there is a corresponding degree of being (*esse*), which is exactly proportional to it. In other and perhaps better words, being (*esse*) is nothing else than the intrinsic reality of essence itself, in each one of the various conditions in which it is to be found. This is why, wherever there is essence there is being, and what we call existence is simply the definite mode of being which is that of an essence when it has received the complete series of its determinations. It is nothing new for it to be. Essence always is. An actually existing essence is, meaning by "is" that it exists, as soon as it is fully constituted by its genus, its species, its own individual "thisness," as well as by all the accidents which go to make up its being. Here is Socrates, for instance, all complete in all his details up to his snub nose. Obviously enough, he is Socrates, therefore he *is*, and what more do we want him to have so that we may say that he exists?

There is no room in Scotism for any distinction of essence and existence, because, as Scotus himself says, being is univocal, that is, being is always said in the same sense and always means the same thing. It means exactly this, that being is always determined by the actual condition of its essence. Such as is the essence, such is its being. In the words of one of his best-known commentators: "It is simply contradictory for any essence to have its being (*esse*) of possible, and not to have the existence of its being of possible, just as essence cannot have its actual being of essence and not have existence in 'actual being.'"[12] This is to say

[12] Lychetus, commentary in *Opus Oxoniense*, lib. II, dis. 3, q. 1, n. 7; in the

that the determinations of existence strictly follow those of essence, since existence is nothing but the definite modality of essence itself. An essence exists just as much as it is, and its existence is exactly defined by the mode of being which belongs to that essence. Such, at least, is the interpretation of the Scotist metaphysics of being that is put forward by the same authorized commentator: "Just as the essence of *man* in real and actual being finds itself posited in time, so also existence in real and actual being belongs to the essence of *man* taken precisely in such a real and actual condition. It is therefore simply impossible for the essence of *man* in real and actual being to be really distinct from its existence taken precisely in real and actual being." Then Lychetus goes on to say: "The essence of *man* in real and actual being is prior to its actual existence. This is evident, for a thing is naturally prior to its intrinsic mode; now, such an existence belongs to the essence by the intrinsic necessity of that essence itself, since it is through the definition of a thing that its existence can be proved. In whatever being, then, essence be posited, it is always posited there before existence and as its intrinsic cause."[13]

We can feel reasonably sure that Lychetus has not here betrayed his master, for Duns Scotus has availed himself of the problem of individuation to state his opinion on this point. A certain Doctor, whom Scotus does not quote and who is certainly not Thomas Aquinas, had maintained that material substance was individuated by its *esse*, that is to say, in the technical language of Duns Scotus, by the ultimate act, which, in this case, is the *esse existentiae*. This is rejected by Duns Scotus on the ground that, being itself neither distinct nor determined, the "being of existence" cannot be a principle of determination or of distinction. What gives to his argument its true Scotist force is that existence cannot possibly be the principle of individuation, since it itself is already determined by the essence. In point of fact, it would be impossible to conceive a hierarchical series of existences unless we first conceived a corresponding hierarchical series of essences. In such a case, what is determining and what is determined? Obviously, the determining element is the essence. If the existence of God is above the existence of any given thing, the reason for it is that God's essence is above the essence of any given thing.

But there is more. If the hierarchy of essences determines that of existences, the hierarchy of essences is ontologically self-sufficient. The whole series of its determinations is in itself

Wadding edition of Duns Scotus (Lyon, 1639), Vol. VI, p. 359, n. 5.
    [13] *Ibid.*, p. 359, n. 4.

complete, and there is no need for us to resort to existence in order to establish it. From the most universal genus, it goes down through a series of specific differences, until at last it reaches the most special species and ends in the individual which its own "thisness" determines. True enough, we cannot thus reach individuals without at the same time reaching actual existence, but this is so only because to be a thus fully determined individual is precisely to have the essence of man in the actual and real condition which is that of existence. An essence which has all that is required for it to be, thereby is, and it is in virtue of what it is.

Actual existence thus appears as inseparable from the essence when essence is taken in its complete determination. Yet the question still remains to know what relation there is between existence and the determining conditions. Strictly speaking, I think that Duns Scotus could and perhaps should have turned the question down as irrelevant. If essence is identical with being, and if every being has just as much *esse* as it has essence, then existence is merely another word by which to say being. Yet, Duns Scotus does not do it. In one of the very few texts in which he expresses himself on this subject, he says that there nevertheless remains a distinction between essence and existence. It is, Scotus says, a distinction "which is accidental in a way, though it be not truly accidental: *quae est aliquo modo accidentalis, licet non sit vere accidentalis.*"[14]

The very wording of this formula closely resembles those of Avicenna. Even when he said that existence was an accident, Avicenna never imagined that it had to be considered as an eleventh category. In point of fact, all he was saying was that existence happens (*accidit*) to the substance. But, when Scotus says that existence is not truly accident, he means something else. If existence merely expresses the definite mode and condition of its essence, it accompanies it as its corresponding degree. In other words, existence is so one with essence that it cannot even be said to be its accident.

The widespread influence exercised by Duns Scotus through his school has done much to generalize the opposition of mediaeval philosophers to the real distinction of essence and existence as Thomas Aquinas understood it. Scotus himself has on several occasions expressed his disapproval of the distinction at issue: "It

---

[14] Duns Scotus, *Opus Oxoniense*, lib. II, dis. 3, q. 3, n. 2. Cf. "*Praecise determinatur existentia ex determinatione essentiae.*" D. de Basley, O.F.M., *Scotus docens* (Paris, La France Franciscaine, 1934), p. 25.

is simply false [he says] that *esse* is other than essence: *simpliciter falsum est quod esse sit aliud ab essentia;*[15] and again: "I do not understand how something can be a being posited out of its cause without having its own *esse: non capio quod aliquid sit ens extra causam suam quin habeat esse proprium.*"[16] The notion of *esse* so completely absorbs both essence and existence in his doctrine that it correctly applies to both, and in the same sense. Any essence claims an existence of its own, which is for it nothing else than to be. There is an *esse existentiae* (being of existence) for substance, which is that of the substance as such; and there is a being of existence for accidents, which is their being of accidents as such, that is, independently of the substance which supports them. Matter has it own *esse* in the composite, independent of that of its form.

There is more. Within any given thing, as many forms as there are, so many *esse* there are, each form having its own being of form. Hence the famous Scotist "formalities." They were unavoidable in such a metaphysics of being. If the form as such enjoys its own being of form; as many forms there are in any actual being, so many beings of form there necessarily are in it. The only trouble we havedn understanding Scotist formalities originates in the fact that, to most of his readers, existence naturally means actual existence, whereas, in Scotus himself, it merely means the reality that belongs to any being *qua* such being. No Scotist being is made up of a plurality of separate actual existences, but each actual Scotist being is made up of a plurality of formally distinct essences, each of which enjoys the very existence which fits its own being; and actual existence appears only when an essence is, so to speak, bedecked with the complete series of its determinations.

It seems clear that, in such a doctrine, essence reigns supreme. The Christian God of Duns Scotus triumphantly overcomes the necessity of the Avicennian possibles. Since His free choice is the cause why some of the divine Ideas become "creables," whereby they become so many possibles, the divine will is the cause of their very possibility. How then could His will still be bound by their necessity? As has already been said, in the doctrine of Duns Scotus even possibility is contingent, so that the freedom of God is perfectly safe. What is remarkable, however, is that, while thus submitting being to the free will of God, Duns Scotus has not radically altered the Avicennian notion of being.

[15] Duns Scotus, *Opus Oxoniense*, lib. IV, dis. 13, q. 1, n. 38.
[16] *Ibid.*, lib. IV, dis. 43, q. 1, n. 7.

His own horse is still the same as that of Avicenna; only it has been broken in.

Two examples of its concrete applications will perhaps best help in realizing the meaning of Duns Scotus' doctrine.

In his *Summa Theologica*, having asked the question whether God alone can create, Thomas Aquinas had answered in the affirmative, on the ground that for God thus to cause a finite effect required an infinite power, since what then had to be caused was the very *esse*, that is, the actual existence of the being at stake. Now, God alone, Who is pure act of existence, can cause an act of existence. Since the first and the most universal of all effects is existence (*esse*) itself, it can be effected only by the first and most universal of all causes, which is God.[17]

On this precise point, and obviously with the position of Thomas Aquinas in mind, Scotus argues along entirely different lines. Of course, he too agrees that God alone can create, but not for the reason that God alone can give *esse*. In point of fact, Scotus could not well accept such a principle without giving up his own notion of being. What is it, according to him, to be an actually existing being? As has been said, it is to be an actually complete essence. Now, every time any efficient cause produces a compound of matter and form, all complete with all its individual determinations, since what it produces is a real essence, it also produces a real existence.[18] When two animals beget a third animal, all that enters the essence of an actual animal is actually given, and so what they beget is an actually existing animal. Hence, any efficient causality is productive of *esse*, and it cannot be said that God alone can do it.

But what about Thomas' argument that the production of even a finite *esse* requires an infinite power, because, between existence and nothingness, there is an infinite chasm which only such an infinite power can bridge? Here indeed we cannot fail to realize what is at stake. If actual existence is what posits being out of nothing, then the power that creates it can expect no cooperation whatsoever from its effect, and such a power must needs be infinite. Not so with Duns Scotus. To him as to Thomas Aquinas, the ontological distance between God and His creatures is infinite; but the Scotist reason for this is that God's *essence* is infinite, whereas the essences of things are finite. There is then an infinite distance between any finite being and the being of God, but this by no means implies that the distance between a finite being and nothingness is also infinite. Quite the reverse. Since the being

---

[17] Thomas Aquinas, *Summa Theologica*, I. 45, 5, Resp., and ad 3^m.
[18] Duns Scotus, *Opus Oxoniense*, lib. IV, dis. 1, q. 1, n. 7.

in question is finite, its remoteness from nothingness cannot be greater than what it itself is. In fact, the distance we are now trying to calculate is exactly measured by the essence of the thing. In other words, the distance there is between any finite being and nothingness is not infinite; on the contrary, it is strictly proportional to the quantity of being which its essence represents and, consequently, it is bound to be as finite as that essence itself is. In Scotus' own cryptic yet excellent formula, *"non plus deficit nihil ab ente quam ens illud ponat,"* which can be, if not translated, at least decoded as follows: the distance from nothing to being is no greater than being itself makes it.

Here are two unmistakably different metaphysics of being. In Thomas' doctrine, the fact that God produces finite beings does not prove His all-powerfulness. If to create were nothing more, then Thomas would fully agree with Scotus. Only, Thomas adds, "although to create a finite effect does not point to an infinite power, to create it out of nothing does point to an infinite power." And indeed it must be so, if what is at stake is existence, because, between to be and not to be, the distance is infinite. If, on the contrary, for any given being, to be is to be its own essence, then the distance from God to nothingness is indeed infinite, but the distance there is from any finite being to its own nothingness is bound to be just as finite as its own being. Clearly enough, we are here in a metaphysical world in which essence is identical with being.

If we look more closely at such a notion of being, it appears that, according to Scotus, existence is but an intrinsic modality of essence or, as some of his disciples will be fond of saying, a "degree" (*gradus*) of essence. And it is truly so, if existence is but essence in its ultimate degree of determination. But, if it is so, we still are in the world of Avicenna, in which an existent was a possible in its state of ultimate actualization. Seen from the point of view of God, there is no necessity that such a being should be, but, if a being actually is, its actual existence is but an intrinsic mode of its essence. As the Scotist Anthony of Brindisi has it, it can be said, with Avicenna, that existence is an accident of essence, since it is an intrinsic mode of that essence, and therefore is not included within its quiddity. "Accident," though, should not here be taken in the proper sense of something that is in another thing as in its subject; what it means in the present case is that existence is "foreign" (*extraneum*) to essence, because it is foreign to its quiddity.[19]

[19] Fr. Ant. de Brindisi, *Scotus dilucidatus in II Sent.* (Naples, 1607), p. 54:

Let us now consider, as a second example, the problem of the existence of God. Before entering it, we should carefully remember that, if Scotism be right, essence has precedence over existence. Here again, Anthony of Brindisi can help in clarifying the data of the problem. First, essence is a nature in itself, whereas existence is a mode which happens to created nature. Secondly, existence is a created nature, and, consequently, whether existence happens to a nature or not, that nature is by no means altered. The rose, for instance, has the same definition, whether it exists or not. Thus, as it is an intrinsic mode, existence does not alter the nature of the thing.

Thirdly, between the real being of essence and the real being of existence there is but a priority of nature, and what here comes first is essence. For, indeed, though it be true that nature cannot have actual existence outside individuals, yet the being of a common nature remains anterior in itself to really existing individuals, since any subject has precedence over its modes, and common nature is here a subject whose existence is a mode.

Last, but not least, between the real being of essence and the real being of existence, there is an order of perfection, and this is proved by the fact that the being of essence is more perfect than the being of existence, since the being of existence is something accidental which happens to nature: "*Inter esse essentiae reale et existentiae est ordo perfectionis, et probatur, quia esse essentiae est perfectius esse existentiae, quia esse existentiae est quoddam accidentale adveniens naturae.*"[20] This is a bit like letting the cat out of the bag, and Duns Scotus should not be held responsible for what he himself has not written. Yet, what Anthony of Brindisi here so clearly says looks like straight Scotism, and it may help in understanding the position of the problem of God's existence both in Duns Scotus himself and in his own school.

There is in the *Opus Oxoniense* a famous passage in which Scotus says that existence is *de quidditate essentiae divinae*, that is, belongs to or in the divine essence. This is why he himself further says that, to him who could conceive the divine essence such as it is, the proposition "God is" would appear as self-evident. The proposition would then be evident, not *secundo modo*, as if

---

"*Accidens accipitur dupliciter, uno modo proprie, alio modo pro.* extraneo; *quando Avicenna inquit quod existentia accidit essentiae, ly* accidit *accipitur pro* extraneo, *non alio modo, id est non est de quidditate essentiae.*"

[20] *Ibid.*, p. 274. According to the same author, existence is distinct from essence, *formaliter privative*, that is, in so far as I can judge, though the very lack of a form of its own whereby existence could distinguish itself from essence. And the title of the book is, *Scotus dilucidatus* . . .

the predicate could be deduced from its subject, but *primo modo*, because the predicate is seen as included within the subject. As Scotus himself says, to know the essence of God is to know Him as *this* God, that is, as *this* divine essence, which it eminently befits to exist: *"quia esse nulli perfectius convenit quam huic essentiae."*[21] This is what Scotus elsewhere repeats in different words: "In the Divinity existence belongs in the concept of the essence: *In divinis existentia est de conceptu essentiae."* In so far as God Himself is concerned, Scotus' position thus appears as diametrically opposed to that of Avicenna, but it is so because even in God it makes existence a modality of essence. The God of Avicenna has no essence, because, had He one, He would thereby be possible, not necessary. The God of Duns Scotus is essence, *this essence which God is*, and, because His essence is such as it is, it necessarily exists. By *this* essence, we must understand divine essence itself, taken with all the determinations which make it to be *this one*, namely, the very essence of God.

Unfortunately, we human beings do not have such a distinct concept of God, and this is why, in order to know His existence, we have to demonstrate it. Yet, even for us, there is no other starting point than God's essence. In other words, we have to look for existence among the intrinsic modes of the divine essence and to prove that it necessarily belongs to its quiddity. The subtle and wonderfully elaborate technical process whereby Scotus himself achieves this result does not matter here. The method of the demonstration alone is at stake, and here is how it works. Existence belongs to the divine essence, because it is *this designated* essence. What makes it to be *this one* and consequently unique? It is the fact that, whatever order of being we may investigate, we find it depending upon a First, Who, being First in all orders, is bound to be the same First. Then comes the next step. He who reigns supreme in all orders of being transcends all limits, which means that He is infinite. What makes God's essence to be *this one* essence, then, is its primacy in being and its infinity in being. Since, by considering the necessary properties of being in general, argumentation can build up the notion of such a being, its essence is at least possible. Now, in this unique case in which the possible at stake is the essence of a First and infinite being, its possibility is one with its necessity. A being that is both first and infinite in the order of being is, out of its very essence, the actual totality of being. Then such an essence

---

[21] Duns Scotus, *Opus Oxoniense*, lib. I, dis. 2, q. 1 and 2, sect. 1, n. 4.

93

is a necessary being, and, if it is necessary, it necessarily exists. In short, if God is possible, God exists.

The order of the divine modes must then be the following one. First of all comes essence, which is not a mode, but the source of all its modes. Then that essence is first in the order of essence. Then that first essence is infinite. Then that first and infinite essence is "this one" essence as determined by its two previous modes. And we should be careful to note that infinity comes here before "thisness." It is, Scotus says, as though infinity had, so to speak, to be understood as a mode of the entity in question before we could understand that entity as "this one" entity.[22] As soon as we realize the implications of this statement, the unity of the Scotist metaphysics of being appears in full light. We have said that each essence is entitled to an existence proportional to its very being, and we have added that each and every essence enjoys actual existence as soon as it has received all its determinations. God Himself is no exception to the rule. He is essence, He is first and He is infinite; as infinite, He is "this one" essence, the like of which cannot be found anywhere else, because there is no else. What then is God's existence? It is the very way He is, namely, the intrinsic mode according to which a first, infinite and thereby individualized essence is exactly as it is. The decisive part which is played by "thisness" cannot be here overlooked. In Scotism, as in Thomism, there is an act of even the form in concrete reality, and, in both doctrines, that act of the form is not itself a form. In the metaphysics of Thomas Aquinas, it is existence; in that of Duns Scotus, it is "thisness" (*hecceitas*) that is *ultima actualitas formae*. The Scotist "thisness" is not the cause of existence, but it is the unmistakable sign that the essence under consideration is now fit to exist; then, as a matter of fact, it does exist. Be it in God or in finite things, existence is that modality of being which belongs to a completely individualized essence. Whether they be such by themselves, which is the case of God alone, or they be such by another one, which is the case of all creatures, fully individualized essences exist in their own right.

A study of the Scotist school would not fail, I think, to confirm this conclusion. Francis of Mayronnes, *Scotistarum princeps*, when speaking of what he calls the "mode of reality or existence," puts it third among the modalities of the divine essence. *"Er scheut sich nicht es zu sagen!"*[23] his excellent but horrified German

[22] *Ibid.*, lib. I, dis. 8, q. 3, a. 3, n. 28.
[23] Bart. Roth, *Franz von Mayronis, O.F.M., Sein Leben, seine Werke, seine Lehre von Formal Unterschied in Gott* (Werl in Westfalen, 1936), p. 413. Here,

historian exclaims. But why should Francis feel ashamed to say so? At any rate, he does not: "My first conclusion," he says in one of his *Disputed Questions*, "is that God's infinity precedes His existence and His actuality . . . The second conclusion is that God's infinity precedes His thisness [*hecceitas*] . . . The third conclusion is that the divine singularity precedes His existence and His actuality."[24] Nor was he the only Scotist to say so. As late as the sixteenth century Antonio Trombetta will find still more remarkable formulas in his famous treatise *On Formalities*. For, indeed, Trombetta seems to have been one of those Scotists who were more Scotist than Duns Scotus himself cared to be. However he himself understood it, Duns Scotus had at least written that existence belongs to the quiddity of the divine nature, and he was too great a theologian to miss that point. It was true to Duns Scotus because it is undoubtedly true of the Christian God. But, if you compromise with a metaphysical principle, you must be ready for its consequences. Sooner or later, they will come out, and they did with Trombetta. If essence is just what it is, then it cannot be its own existence. Himself a Christian, Trombetta cannot possibly grant to Avicenna that God was not an essence; for the same reason, if he posits God as an essence, he cannot refuse Him existence; but, if the Avicennian notion of an existentially neutral essence still holds good in his mind, then he is bound to deny that God's existence is included in the quiddity of His essence. In fact, he denies it. There are people, Trombetta says, who maintain that in God existence belongs to the quiddity of His essence, "*cum quibus minime convenio:*[25] but I don't at all agree with them." For those who see God face to face, existence is included in the concept of His essence, because being a mere mode of the essence, existence cannot be conceived apart from that essence; yet, even while God is known as both essence and existence, that is, while both are grasped at once in the unity of a single concept, it still remains true to say that, in God Himself, His existence is modally distinct from the quiddity of the divine essence. Trombetta himself feels by no means ashamed to say so and, in his own opinion, the very principles of Duns Scotus make it impossible to avoid this conclusion. According to Duns Scotus, infinity itself is a mode. Now, "if infinity, which is more

---

however, the order of the modes is inverted: essence, thisness, infinity, existence. As will presently be seen, Francis of Mayronnes has given the right one in another text.

[24] Fr. de Mayronnes, *Quodlibet.* III, art. 7.

[25] Ant. Trombetta, *Aureae formalitatum lucubrationes* (Paris, Kernet, 1576), p. 37.

BEING AND SOME PHILOSOPHERS

interior to essence than existence, is itself an intrinsic mode and does not belong in the quiddity of the essence, the same should hold good, and with still greater reason, in the case of something still farther removed from the essence, as Scotus himself admits that existence is."[26]

Coming from so famous a theologian, this is a remarkable statement indeed. It is not for us to settle theological controversies, but this one is of the highest interest for the discussion of our own problem. If there is a God Whose very essence it is to be, it is the Christian God. Now, here is a Christian theologian who is careless enough to grant Avicenna that essence as such is, out of itself, foreign to all its possible determinations, including even existence. Moreover, he allows the Avicennian essence to invade the whole field of being, including even God, Whom Avicenna himself had carefully kept out of it. Having done this, our theologian starts wondering how his God can possibly, at one and the same time, be essence and yet exist. The only way out is obviously for him to exclude existence from the divine essence as such, that is, to refuse it to its quiddity, and to posit it as one of its modes. If, against Avicenna's own opinion, God is an Avicennian essence, actual existence happens to Him as some sort of accident which is not quite an accident. We have by now reached such a state of affairs, according to which *essentia*, which means *esse*, has grown entirely foreign to actual existence. When concepts, instead of being made in the image of reality, begin to make reality in their own image, there is something rotten in the kingdom of metaphysics.

Francis Suarez was no man to share in such metaphysical adventures. A sober, well-ordered and uncommonly clear mind, he had been teaching theology for years, when, while he was engaged in writing out the substance of his lectures, it occurred to him that, as a theologian, he had been constantly using philosophical principles without going to the trouble of explaining them, at least to his own satisfaction. He then interrupted his theological work for some time and wrote down the bulky philosophical interlude which bears the title *Metaphysical Debates* (*Metaphysicae Disputationes*).

These *Metaphysicae Disputationes* occupy a very peculiar place in the history of philosophy. As *disputationes*, they still belong in the Middle Ages. Suarez has kept the mediaeval habit of never settling a philosophical dispute without first relating, comparing and criticizing the most famous opinions expressed

[26] *Ibid.*, pp. 37^v-38^r.

96

by his predecessors on the difficulty at hand. On the other hand, the *Disputationes* of Suarez already resemble a modern philosophical work, not only in that they are purely philosophical in their content, but also because they break away from the order, or disorder, of the Aristotelian *Metaphysics*. As Suarez himself says, not far from the beginning of his book, the subject matter of the *Disputationes* is not the text of Aristotle's *Metaphysics*, but the very things (*res ipsas*) with which metaphysical knowledge is concerned.[27]

Among those things the very first one is, of course, being. What is the meaning of that word? We should first distinguish between being (*ens*) as a present participle and being as a noun. *Ens* (being) is derived from *sum* (I am). *Sum*, as *existing*, is derived from *I exist*. As to *sum* itself, it is a verb which always signifies actual existence and of which it can be said that it always includes its own present participle. *Sum* (I am) always means *sum ens* (I am being), just as *quidam est* (someone is) actually means *quidam est ens* (someone is being). This is why, in its primary acceptation, the word *ens* (being) seems to have signified any thing that was endowed with actual existence, that is, with that very existence which the verb *sum* (I am) signifies. Only, owing to a spontaneous extension of this primary meaning, *ens* has later come to point out, besides such subjects as actually possess existence, those that are merely capable of it.[28] When understood in this second sense, being (*ens*) becomes a noun which signifies what Suarez himself calls a "real essence" (*essentia realis*). By this formula, which still plays a very important part in large sections of modern Scholasticism, Suarez means to designate such essences as are not arbitrary products of thought, that is, such essences as are neither self-contradictory nor chimerical nor fancied by some play of our imagination, but are true in themselves and thereby susceptible of actual realization.[29] In a doctrine in which the realness of essences is defined by their fitness for existence, the Avicennian divorce between essence and existence needs no longer to be feared. If essences are "real" as *aptae ad realiter existendum*, the very nature of possibility is the possibility to exist. *Essentia* therefore regains with Suarez its intrinsic

[27] Fr. Suarez, *Metaphysicae disputationes*, disp. II, Prooemium (Coloniae, 1614), Vol. I, p. 31.

[28] *Ibid.*, II, 4, 3, p. 42A.

[29] *Ibid.*, II, 4, 4, p. 42F: "*Si ens sumatur prout est significatum hujus vocis in vi nominis sumptae, ejus ratio consistit in hoc, quod sit habens essentiam realem, id est non fictam nec chymericam, sed veram et aptam ad realiter existendum.*" Cf. II, 4, 8, p. 43B.

relation to *esse*. At least, it looks so; but we still have to ascertain up to what point it is really so.

There is no reason to worry about this twofold meaning of the word "being." The fact that it signifies at one and the same time both actual being and possible being does not make it an equivocal term. For, indeed, the word "being" does not signify two distinct concepts, that of existent being and that of possible being. It does not even signify a common concept of being wherein those two other ones would be included and, as it were, blended together. What we are now dealing with is a single concept, but taken in two different degrees of precision. And, indeed, "used as a noun, *ens* signifies what has a real essence (*essentia realis*), prescinding from actual existence, that is to say, neither excluding it nor denying it, but merely leaving it out of account by mode of abstraction (*praecisive tantum abstrahendo*); on the contrary, taken as a participle (namely, as a verb) *ens* signifies real being itself, that is, such a being as has both real essence and actual existence, and, in this sense, it signifies being as more contracted."[30]

What Suarez means by this last expression is that actually existing being represents a restricted area of being in general which, as has just been said, includes both possible and actual being. This is a statement which necessarily implies that both possible and actual being are the same being and, furthermore, that actual being is a particular case of being at large. Exactly: actual being is being in general, taken in one of the cases when it actually exists.

Such are the Suarezian data of the problem, and, since actuality is there posited as a particular case of possibility, the Suarezian solution can easily be foreseen. We can at least foresee that the nature of the "real essence" is called upon to play a decisive part in determining that solution. What is essence? It certainly does not come first in the order of origin. God alone excepted, it is not in the essence of things that we can hope to discover the origin of their being. On the other hand, in the order of dignity and of primacy, essence is certainly first among the objects of the mind. For, indeed, the essence of a thing is that which belongs to that thing in the very first place, and, consequently, it is what makes it to be, not only a being, but that very being which it is.[31] Inasmuch as it provides an answer to the question, "*quid sit res?* (*What* is the thing?)," essence assumes the name of "quiddity," that is, of "whatness" (*quid*, meaning "what"). Inasmuch as it is what actual existence confers upon actual being,

[30] *Ibid.*, II, 4, 8, p. 43B.   [31] *Ibid.*, II, 4, 14, p. 44EG.

it assumes the name of "essence" (from *esse:* to be). Thus, real being is an essence actualized by its cause and drawn from possibility to actuality. Lastly, inasmuch as essence is envisaged from the point of view of its effects, it remains what it already was to Aristotle, namely, a "nature," that is, the innermost principle of all its operations.[32] Our own problem then becomes one of defining the relation of such an essence to its existence, especially in the case of actually existing finite beings.

In the Preface to his *Metaphysical Debates* Suarez modestly introduces himself as a theologian who, to facilitate his own work, has felt it advisable to lay down, once and for all, the philosophical principles of which he makes use in his theological teaching. In fact, Suarez enjoys such a knowledge of mediaeval philosophy as to put to shame any modern historian of mediaeval thought. On each and every question he seems to know everybody and everything, and to read his book is like attending the Last Judgment of four centuries of Christian speculation by a dispassionate judge, always willing to give everyone a chance, supremely apt at summing up a case and, unfortunately, so anxious not to hurt equity that a moderate verdict is most likely to be considered a true verdict. Rather than judge, Suarez arbitrates, with the consequence that he never wanders very far from the truth and frequently hits upon it, but, out of pure moderation of mind, sometimes contents himself with a "near miss."

In so far as our own problem is concerned, Suarez observes that it has received three different solutions. Either there is a real distinction between essence and existence, or there is a modal distinction, or there is a mere distinction of reason. Some of his modern disciples do not hesitate to maintain that Thomas Aquinas himself has never taught the real distinction of essence and existence, but, in this at least, they are not good Suarezians, for Suarez himself asserts that the real distinction "is commonly assumed to have been the opinion of St. Thomas, and almost all the ancient Thomists have subscribed to it."[33] This last part of his statement is almost tautological, since one can scarcely reject the actual distinction of essence and existence and yet be a Thomist. I say "actual" distinction, but Suarez himself says "real," and he means it. When defining the Thomistic distinction of essence and existence, he does not use the words of Thomas Aquinas, but those of Giles of Rome whose personal terminology had done

[32] *Ibid.*, II, 4, 5, p. 42H.
[33] *Ibid.*, XXXI, 1, 3, p. 115G. Suarez here mentions Avicenna, Giles of Rome (*latissime de ente et essentia*), Cajetan, etc.

much to obscure the genuine meaning of the doctrine. According to its supporters, Suarez says, the real distinction of essence and existence means that "existence is a certain *thing* wholly and really distinct from the entity of created essence."[34] Without unduly pressing the fact, one may well wonder if this detail has not had something to do with Suarez' own ultimate decision.

In point of fact, his whole discussion of the Thomistic distinction of essence and existence revolves around this difficulty: it cannot be said of the created essence, once it is posited in act out of its causes, that it still is distinct from its existence, "as if essence and existence were two distinct entities, two distinct things: *ita ut sint duae res seu duae entitates distinctae.*"[35] And, indeed, if this is the correct formula of the problem, all that Suarez can do is to answer *no*, because, as both Aristotle and Averroes agree in saying, there is no difference whatsoever between "being man" and "man." Of course, in a purely philosophical question such as this, Aristotle and Averroes were bound to weigh more in the mind of Suarez than Avicenna and Thomas Aquinas, but he had his own personal reason for making such a choice. And that reason was such that it requires careful consideration for the light it sheds on the true nature of our problem.

At first sight the endless controversies between supporters and opponents of the distinction between essence and existence have the appearance of a purely dialectical game, with each party trying to prove to the other that he is making some logical mistake and to show him where he is doing it. Even today, adversaries who come to grips on this problem are still trying to catch each other in the very act of committing some logical blunder. This is to forget that, in so far as logic is concerned, one may be faultlessly wrong as well as faultlessly right. No philosopher can expect a fellow philosopher to draw from being, through logic alone, more than his philosophy puts into it.

Now, I have often thought that the endless debate between Thomists and Suarezians, when it is more than a mere juggling of texts, is partly obscured by that illusion. Much more than dialectical arguments, what matters here is the notion of being. What does Suarez call being? If it is really actual being, then it is that being which belongs to an essence when, once a mere possible, it has become actual owing to the efficacy of its causes. It then enjoys the being of actual essence (*esse actualis essentiae*).

[34] *Ibid.*, XXXI, 1, 3, p. 115G. Cf. "*nam si essentia et existentia sunt* res *diversae* ...," XXXI, 3, 7, p. 120C.

[35] *Ibid.*, XXXI, 6, 1, p. 124B

Having said this, Suarez asks himself whether, in order to be actually, such a being as that of actual essence still requires the supplement which Thomists call existence. And, of course, his answer is, *no*. Let us posit any essence whatever, for instance, "man." Since it is not contradictory nor fancied by imagination, it is a "real essence." Again, it is a real essence because it is, if not actual, at least possible. If it is only possible, it still lacks actuality, and consequently it does not exist; but, if it is an actual possible, that is, if that essence has the being of an "actual essence," what could it still lack in order to exist? Nothing. Essence can be but actual or possible, and the only difference between these two conditions is that what is actual is, whereas what is only possible is not. To say that an essence is a true actual being (*verum actuale ens*) is therefore to say that such an essence actually is, or exists.

What is going on in the mind of Suarez seems pretty clear. He begins by identifying being with essence. Accordingly, he conceives all actual beings as simply many fully actualized essences. He then wonders what actual existence could well add to an already existing being. The question is the more absurd as, from the very definition of its terms, existence itself is here conceived as a thing, so that, in order to exist, an already existing thing should include, over and above what it is, another thing. All this does not make sense, and it is no wonder that Suarez parted company with Thomas Aquinas on this most fundamental of all philosophical problems.

But let us look more closely at his own position. Like all philosophers, and, I suppose, like practically all men who understand the meaning of those terms, Suarez realizes that what makes an actual essence to be different from a merely possible one is existence. Like all *Christian* philosophers, Suarez moreover admits, and indeed expressly teaches, that no finite essence exists out of itself but owes its existence to the divine act of creation. Existence then is to him, as he readily acknowledges that it is to all men, the supreme mark of reality. He accordingly declares that existence is a formal and intrinsic constituent of reality properly so called. "Existence," Suarez says, "is that whereby, formally and intrinsically, a thing is actually existing;" whereupon he adds that "although existence be not a formal cause strictly and properly said, it nevertheless is an intrinsic and formal constituent of what it constitutes."[36] Obviously, Suarez is not existence-blind. He knows that real things do exist; what he does not know is where

[36] *Ibid., XXXI.* 5, 1, p. 122.

101

existence can fit in such a philosophical interpretation of reality as his own is.

The very example offered by Suarez in support of his statement is enough to arouse suspicion. Existence, he says, is a formal constituent of actual essence, as personality is a formal and intrinsic constituent of the person. If this is really what he means, it is no wonder that he refuses to consider existence as a truly formal cause; for, indeed, personality is not a cause of the person in any sense of the word. There is not a person where there is personality; there is personality where there is a person. So, too, existence is not the formal cause whereby an existent actually exists, rather, existence is the property of actually given existents. What puzzles Suarez at this juncture is, that existence seems to add so much to essence, and yet is itself nothing. Here is a possible essence, then God creates it; what has God created? Obviously, God has created that essence. And, as we already know, for that essence to be actualized by God and to exist are one and the same thing. What Suarez fails to see, unless, perhaps, his adversary is himself suffering from double vision, is that, when God creates an essence, He does not give it its actuality of essence, which any possible essence enjoys in its own right; what God gives it is another actuality, which is that of existence. Taken in itself, the essence of man is fully actual *qua* essence. For a theologian like Suarez, the "real essence" of the humblest possible being must needs be eternally and eternally completely determined in the mind of God, so that it can lack no actuality *qua* essence. What it is still lacking is existence. Creation thus does not actualize the essentiality of the essence, but it actualizes that essence in another order than that of essence, by granting it existence. Now, this is precisely what the philosophical essentialism of Suarez forbids him to see. *"Ens actu,"* Suarez says, *"idem est quod existens:* A being in act is an existing being."[37] True, but the whole question is to know if a being in act is but its own essence, which is an entirely different proposition. In a mind, an essence is in act through the existence of that mind; in a thing, an essence is in act through the existence of that thing. In no case is it true to say that an essence is in act through its actualization *qua* essence. Yet, this is what Suarez forcefully asserts, and this is why he finally decides that between an actualized essence and its existence there is no real distinction, but a mere distinction of reason.[38]

It is noteworthy that Suarez is here going even beyond Duns Scotus in his reduction of being to essentiality. We have seen how

[37] Suarez, *Met. Disp.*, XXXI, 1, 13, p. 117.   [38] *Ibid.*

thin the distinction between essence and its existential modality
was in the doctrine of Duns Scotus. Yet, Suarez considers the
Scotists to be so many supporters of some sort of real distinction,
because, like Avicenna, they make existence an appendix of the
essence. To him, this is still too much. According to Suarez, it is
the same for an essence to be *in actu exercito*, that is, actually to
exercise its act of essence, and to exist. Of course, we can *think* of
the essence as not yet exercising its act; then it is a pure abstraction of the mind; and it is true that we can thus abstractly
distinguish an existing essence from its existence, but this mental
distinction does not affect the thing itself. Between actual existence and an actual, existing essence, there really is no distinction.

I wish I knew of a way to make clear what Suarez says, without
myself saying what I think he does not see, but we are now reaching absolutely primitive positions and, so to speak, primitive
philosophical options. To contrast them is the best way to realize
their true import. Besides, this is what Suarez himself does when
he dares the supporters of the distinction of essence and existence
to define its meaning.

First, Suarez says, what can the proposition, "an essence is,"
mean, unless it means that that essence exists? If a man says
that a thing is, he thereby thinks that that thing exists. Now,
to what can the word "exists" apply in such a case, if not to the
thing itself? It does not apply to existence, for, when I say: this
rose exists, I am not saying that its existence itself exists. Then
it must needs apply to the essence; now, if it does, it necessarily
means that the essence of the rose no longer is a mere possible,
but has become an actual being. In short, there now "is a rose,"
and, if its essence now is, what can it still lack in order to exist?
Such is the first argument of Suarez, and it is, as he himself says,
an *a priori* argument. What it proves for us is at least this, that
in his own notion of being Suarez has no room for existence as
such. The whole question is to know if the actuality of the "real
essence" does not require an existential act in order to become an
existential actuality; but this is a point which Suarez cannot see,
because essence is for him identical with being.

His second argument, which he introduces *tam simpliciter
quam ad hominem*, aims to prove that the reasons why his adversaries posit the distinction of essence and existence are futile,
since the being of the real essence, such as he himself understands
it, already exhibits all the properties which they ascribe to existence. Now, the reasons which he refutes are actually foreign to
the problem at hand. For instance, Suarez shows that the dis-

BEING AND SOME PHILOSOPHERS

tinction of essence and existence is not necessarily required to save the distinction between the Creator and His creatures, which is true. If created beings were nothing but essences actualized *qua* essences, they still would be creatures. But this is irrelevant to the question. The real question is to know what the metaphysical structure of concrete being is; when we know what it is, whatever it may be, then we will know what sort of a being God has actually created. What is noteworthy, however, in this objection of Suarez is his remark that he himself does not ascribe an eternal being to possible essences, since, as mere possibles, they are nothing real. I cannot help wondering how he himself has not seen what followed from this obvious truth for his own doctrine. If, out of itself, an essence is a mere possible, and if a mere possible is nothing, what will be the result of its actualization? Nothing. This existential nothingness of the possible essence is precisely what compels us to look outside the order of essence for an intrinsic cause of its actual reality.

My opponents, Suarez goes on to say, assert that existence belongs to finite essences in a contingent way only, and that, consequently, essence is really distinct from existence. Now, the actualized essence would be just as contingent, since the cause of its actualization would still be God. Hence the contingency of created beings can be saved without resorting to the distinction of essence and existence. And there again Suarez is right. No one pretends that, if being is what he says, the contingency of finite being would not be safe. But, once more, that is not at all the question. The point which Suarez is trying to make is this. If you reject my doctrine of being because it cannot answer these two last difficulties, you are wrong, because my actualized essence answers them as well as your being of existence.[39] And Suarez is still right: his possible essences are not eternal beings, and his actualized essences are truly created beings. But the question at stake is to know, of these two possible notions of created being, which is true and which is not. Equally acceptable to Christian theologians, they can nevertheless both be philosophically wrong, but they cannot both be philosophically true.

There would be no point in protracting a discussion which is obviously marking time. It now resembles one of those conversations in which one man says to another: "Don't you see it?" "No." "Well, have a better look. Do you see it now?" "No." Then what? All that is left to do is for the man who thinks he sees to account for the fact that the other does not. And this is

[39] *Ibid.*, XXXI, 4, 4, p. 121CF.

just what we are now trying to do. We are not refuting Suarez, but giving an intelligible account of his own position of the question. His complete intellectual honesty is beyond even the shadow of a suspicion; he is absolutely sure he is right, and he clearly sees why his adversaries are wrong, which makes him doubly sure he is right. Their fundamental mistake, Suarez says, is that they are begging the question.[40] When he asks them: "How can you know what existence is?" they answer by positing the distinction of essence and existence as a condition for such knowledge. But how can we distinguish essence from existence, unless we already know what existence is?

This last argument probably is the most enlightening of all, in so far as the personal position of Suarez is concerned. What he would like to know is *quid existentia sit:* what is existence, as if existence could be a *what*. Having himself identified being with its essence, he could not possibly find in it an *is* which, if it is, is neither an essence nor a thing. This is why Suarez does not know existence when he sees it. Hence his strange metaphysical notion of being. If we take an essence, Suarez says, "abstractly conceived and precisely in itself, that is, as being in potency, it is distinguished from actual existence as non-being is distinguished from being."[41] In his doctrine, the actualization of non-being as such is the very origin and philosophical explanation of being.

The influence of Suarez on the development of modern metaphysics has been much deeper and wider than is commonly known. It has naturally reached in the first place those seventeenth-century scholastic philosophers who find very few readers today, yet have themselves exerted a perceptible influence on the development of metaphysical thought. Through them, Suarez has become responsible for the spreading of a metaphysics of essences which makes profession of disregarding existences as irrelevant to its own object. This is the more remarkable as, after all, Suarez himself had never discarded existences as irrelevant to metaphysical speculation; but he had identified existences with actual essences, so that his disciples were quite excusable in ruling existence out of metaphysics.

This is what they were still doing yesterday and what they are still doing today. "Real being" is to them the proper object of metaphysics, but, if you ask one of them, Kleutgen, for instance, what *ens reale* means for him, he will tell you, with explicit reference to the authority of Suarez, that it means exactly the same thing as *ens*, not, however, *ens* as a present participle of the verb

[40] *Ibid.*, XXXI, 4, 5, p. 121A.   [41] *Ibid.*, XXXI, 1, 13, p. 117.

esse, but as the noun which derives from it. *Ens* then signifies something that has an essence and is therefore a being. As to the essence itself, it is a "real essence," that is to say, "the root, or the innermost bottom and the first principle of all the activity as well as of all the properties of the things;" in short, it is what "is most excellent in things and what grants to our whole knowledge of things both its basis and its perfection." And, as if afraid of not being understood, Kleutgen goes on to say: "It follows from the preceding considerations that, among the Scholastics, the *real* is not confused with what is *actual* or *existing*, nor is it opposed to the possible. The real may be possible as well as existing;" and this, Kleutgen adds, "is what Suarez has expressly stated." God save us from our disciples, for, even though this be more or less what Suarez had said, he had at least common sense enough not to say it in that way. But nothing could stop Kleutgen; he not only says it, he emphasizes it: "When we conceive a being as real, we do not think of it as merely possible, by excluding existence, nor yet do we think of it as existing, but we leave existence out of consideration." Whereupon he triumphantly concludes: "Thus, and only thus, can those finite and created things, to which existence is not essential, become objects of science."[42]

There is a weird beauty in the perfect self-consistency of philosophical principles. Unless he live under some sort of metaphysical spell, how could a man write such things? The possible is here just as real as the actual, which means that possible reality is just as actual as actual reality. When we think of a being as real, we do not think of it as existing, and we do not even think of it as merely possible, because, in order to think of it as possible, we should have to exclude existence, a thing not to be mentioned in metaphysics. A metaphysician should never pollute his mind with the impure thought of existence, not even to exclude it! Last, but not least, the first and most necessary condition for things to become objects of scientific knowledge is to be purified of the slightest trace of existence. A perfect case of conceptual imperialism, if there ever was one! And all this owing to Avicenna, who begot Scotus, who begot Suarez, who begot Kleutgen; and the list still remains open.

But the main responsibility for this strange metaphysical adventure might well not be Avicenna. The rebellion of human reason against what of reality remains impervious to its abstract

[42] J. Kleutgen, *La Philosophie scolastique*, Vol. II, pp. 89-92, as quoted in P. Descoqs, *Institutiones metaphysicae generalis, Eléments d'ontologie* (Paris, G. Beauchesne, 1925), Vol. I, pp. 100-101. P. Descoqs himself fully agrees with both Kleutgen and Suarez

concepts has probably more to do with it than any single philosopher we might quote. For reason has only one means to account
for what does not come from itself, E. Meyerson says, and it is to
reduce it to nothingness.[43] This is what essentialism, at least,
has done on an exceptionally large scale, by reducing to nothingness the very act in virtue of which being actually is.

[43] E. Meyerson, *La Déduction relativiste*, p. 258, art. 186.

Chapter IV

Existence Versus Being

We are now reaching what will be, though the continuation of the same story, a distinctly new episode in the metaphysical adventures of being. Modern philosophy is currently described as a decisive breaking away from the old Scholastic mentality. At least this is what it is supposed to have been in its very beginning, for, now that Scholastic philosophy has been dead for nearly five centuries, philosophers don't even care to remember how it died.

Nevertheless, there was something queer about its death. Scholastic philosophy actually died to the whole extent to which its *philosophy* of nature had been mistaken, by both itself and its adversaries, for a *science* of nature. The rise of mathematical physics did not necessarily entail the giving up of the notion of substantial forms. In point of fact, Leibniz has always upheld the contrary position. Yet, the reduction of matter to quantity was the easiest way to turn the world of sense into a fitting subject for mathematical speculation, and, since a physical universe of pure extension was what modern science needed, modern philosophers decided that the physical universe was indeed nothing else than pure extension. Having taken this step, they did not very much bother about metaphysics itself, except in order to show that this new conception of the world of sense did not make it impossible for them still to prove the existence of God, and of a God who was really the same as the Christian God of mediaeval Scholasticism. In so far as metaphysics is concerned, the dividing line between mediaeval and modern philosophy does not run through the works of Francis Bacon or of Descartes; I am not even sure that is runs through the *Ethics* of Spinoza, but it is beyond doubt that, by the time of Hume, readers of philosophy had entered a new philosophical world.

What the great seventeenth-century metaphysicians actually did was, rather than to destroy mediaeval metaphysics, to save all that could still be saved of it and, in so doing, they took a great many things philosophically for granted. Descartes, for instance, raised a strong protest against the bad habit, which then obtained among Scholastics, of obscuring what was self-evident by defining, explaining and eventually proving it. When I say, "I think, therefore I am," why should I bother about explaining what existence is? Such notions as that of existence are in themselves quite simple and, besides, "they don't help us in acquiring the knowledge of any existing thing."[1] And this is true, at least in so far as physical science is concerned; but Descartes' meaningful remark merely proves that what he himself was aiming at was not primarily metaphysics, but physics.

This is why, when he happened to meet the problem of being and existence, Descartes simply held it for an already settled question. Himself a pupil of the Jesuits, he had learned metaphysics according to Suarez, and, though I would not bet that he had read the whole *Metaphysicae Disputationes*, there are positive reasons to feel sure that he knew the work, and I even believe that, for a time at least, he personally owned a copy of it. To Descartes, Scholastic philosophy was Suarez, and this is why, when confronted with the problem of existence, he flatly denied its distinction from essence.

This is a point on which we should not allow ourselves to be misled by what Descartes says in his *Fifth Meditation* concerning the existence of God. The point he is trying to make in that passage is that the notion of God necessarily involves His existence, which the notion of a finite being never does.[2] But now is the time for us to remember what has already been said on the subject. All Christian philosophers agree that no creature exists in its own right: in order to be, a creature stands in need of receiving existence. Where Christian philosophers begin to disagree is on this entirely different question: when a creature has received existence, is existence actually distinct from its essence? We have seen Suarez answering that question in the negative, and Descartes himself agrees that Suarez was right.

According to Descartes, a Scholastic philosopher looks somewhat like a tipsy man who sees double, or more, when he sees in corporeal beings a matter and a form, plus any number of accidents; but he acknowledges that Scholastics do not make that mistake about essence and existence, between which they

[1] Descartes, *Principia philosophiae*, Pars I, cap. 10, ed. by Adam-Tannery, Vol. VIII, p. 8.
[2] Descartes, *Meditatio V. ed. cit.*, Vol. VII, p. 66.

usually do not see more distinction than there actually is.[3] In point of fact, according to Descartes himself, there actually is no distinction whatever. For, indeed, "to conceive the essence of a thing apart from its existence or non-existence, is another way to conceive it than when it is conceived as existing, but the thing itself cannot be outside our thought without its existence." There is then no real distinction between essence and existence. And it is true that there is a "modal" distinction between my two ways of conceiving the thing, according as I conceive it as an existent or as a non-existent; but even this does not imply that there is any "modal" distinction between the essence of the thing itself and its existence. The only distinction there is between them is a distinction of reason, which means that essence is by no means and in no way distinct from existence in reality: *"In quo manifestum mihi videtur essentiam et existentiam nullo modo distingui."*[4] And what is true of existence, Descartes concludes, holds good for all the universals.

Descartes could not well think differently since, according to his own principles, there are as many things as there are clear and distinct concepts. If there is no definable concept of existence, then existence is nothing. Now, in this at least Spinoza kept faith with Descartes, just as Descartes himself had kept faith with Suarez. I am not saying that Suarez, Descartes and Spinoza have taught the same metaphysics; my only point is that their attitude towards existence as such has been substantially the same. To all of them, existence is but the complete actuality of essence, and nothing else.

In his *Cogitata Metaphysica* (*Metaphysical Thoughts*), Spinoza declares his intention "briefly to explain the more difficult questions that occur in metaphysics, general as well as special, concerning being and its properties, God and His attributes and the human mind." Among the difficulties which Spinoza examines, some are of immediate interest for our own problem. Unfortunately, no more than Descartes, in whose footsteps he is here treading, does Spinoza deem it necessary to define exactly all the notions which he uses. Some of them, Spinoza says, are in themselves so clear that we cannot attempt to throw light on their meaning without getting them involved in more obscurity. Such are, partic-

---

[3] Descartes, Letter to X***, August 1641, *ed. cit.*, Vol. III, p. 435.
[4] Descartes, Letter to X***, 1645 or 1646, *ed. cit.*, Vol. IV, pp. 349-350. It is to be noted, however, that Descartes himself seems to have mistaken the distinction between God and creatures for that of essence and existence: *Med.* V, Vol. VII, p. 66; *III*[ae] *Objectiones*, Vol. III, p. 194; *V*[ae] *Responsiones*, Vol. VII, p. 383; *II*[ae] *Responsiones*, Axioma X, Vol. VII, p. 166.

ularly, the two notions of "essence" and of "existence."[5] According to Spinoza, the being of essence is "the mode under which created things are comprised in the attributes of God;" as to the being of existence, it is "the very essence of things outside God, and considered in itself, namely, that being which we ascribe to things after their creation by God." Of course, since finite beings can be conceived apart from their existence, essence is in them distinct from existence, with two reservations, however. First, there is no use in trying to explain what essence is, what existence is; since we can form no definition of them without resorting to them, any attempt to clarify them will succeed only in making them more obscure than they actually are. If anyone wants to learn the difference between essence and existence, let him go to a sculptor; he will see the difference there is between the notion of a statue that does not yet exist and that statue after it exists because it has been made. Secondly, this distinction merely means that, for any finite being, the cause of its existence lies outside its essence; it by no means implies that, in an actually existing essence, existence is distinct from it. According to the definition of existence which has just been given, existence is nothing else than "the very essence of things outside God and considered in itself: *ipsa rerum essentia extra Deum et in se considerata.*" As has been aptly said by one of his interpreters, this definition entails the real identity of essence and existence in finite beings, since the being of actual existence is the being of essence as found outside God, namely, in things after they have been created by God.[6]

It seems then to be a fact that, in seventeenth-century classical metaphysics, essence reigns supreme. No two philosophers would then agree on their definitions of God, but they all agree that God exists in virtue of His own essence. It is so with Descartes, for whom the essence of God necessarily entails existence; so much so that, as he himself says in his *Fifth Meditation,* God is "cause of Himself." It is so with Fénelon, who writes in his treatise *On the Existence of God,* Part Two, that God's essence "entails His actual existence." It is so with Leibniz, who says in his *Monadology,* n. 44, that, in the Necessary Being, "essence involves

---

[5] Spinoza, *Cogitata metaphysica,* Pars I, cap. 2. For an interpretation of this work, see J. Freudenthal, *Spinoza und die Scholastik,* in *Philosophische Aufsätze Eduard Zeller . . . gewidmet* (Leipzig, 1887), pp. 94-106. Also Julius Lewkowitz, Spinoza's *Cogitata metaphysica und ihr Verhältnis zu Descartes und zur Scholastik* (Breslau, 1902), pp. 5-15, 78-79.

[6] *Ibid.* See A. Rivaud, *Les Notions d'essence et d'existence dans la philosophie de Spinoza* (Paris, Alcan, 1905), pp. 29, note, and 32.

existence," so that it is enough for God to be possible in order that He be actual. And again, in *Monadology*, n. 45: "The Necessary Being has in Himself the reason for His own existence." It is so with Spinoza, who, taking up the "God, cause of Himself" of Descartes, says in the very first of the definitions which open his *Ethics:* "By cause of itself, I understand that whose essence involves its existence." The God Essence of the Middle Ages is everywhere carried shoulder high, and every philosopher of note pays him unrestricted homage. As to that other God of Whom it had been said that He was, not a God Whose essence entailed existence, but a God in Whom what in finite beings is called essence, *is to exist*, He now seems to lie in a state of complete oblivion. *Deus est id cujus essentia est esse:* this proposition no longer makes sense, and, because they have lost sight of Him Who Is, philosophers have also lost sight of the fact that finite things themselves are. The times are now ripe for some systematic science of "being *qua* being," as completely free from existence as being itself actually is.

And then Suarez begot Wolff. But his birth had been announced by signs.

One might have seen it coming as early as the middle of the seventeenth century. In the prolegomena to his *Elementa philosophiae sive Ontosophiae* (1647), J. Clauberg remarks: "Since the science which is about God calls itself *Theosophy* or *Theology*, it would seem fitting to call *Ontosophy* or *Ontology* that science which does not deal with this and that being, as distinct from the others owing to its special name or' properties, but with being in general." This text may be held, in the present state of historical knowledge, for the birth certificate of ontology as a science conceived after the pattern of theology, yet radically distinct from it, since being *qua* being is held there as indifferent to all its conceivable determinations. "There is," Clauberg says, "a certain science which envisages being inasmuch as it is being, that is, inasmuch as it is understood to have a certain common nature or degree of being, a degree which is to be found in both corporeal and incorporeal beings, in God and in creatures, in each and every singular being according to its own mode." Leibniz will later praise Clauberg for such an undertaking, but he will regret that it had not been a more successful one. The very word "ontology" occurs at least once in an undated fragment of Leibniz,[7] and one can expect accidentally to meet it later in various places,[8] but it is not until

---

[7] Couturat, *Opuscules et fragments inédits de Leibniz* (Paris, 1903), p. 512.
[8] For instance, in J. B. Duhamel, *Philosophia vetus et nova*, 2nd ed., 1681,

1729 that it finally comes into its own with the *Ontologia* of Christian Wolff.

An extremely versatile mind, and perhaps the most accomplished professor of philosophy of all times—although his professorial career was not exactly a smooth one—Wolff has published his complete course of lectures, including a *Prime Philosophy, or Ontology, treated after a scientific method and containing the principles of all human knowledge.*[9] He was a very remarkable man and a good example of what an honest pedagogue can achieve for the benefit of mankind. Wolff reminds one of Quintillian, not a great man, but a great master, whose proper job it was to keep a certain discipline alive, pending the arrival of greater men. I don't know if I will create scandal by saying that, apart from Spinoza, there was something amateurish in even the greatest of seventeenth- and eighteenth-century philosophers. Their work no longer was that of professional teachers, and what it gained in freedom and in originality, it lost in accurate technicality. What I mean will perhaps become more apparent if I mention Kant as the first philosopher who, after a long interlude of brilliant amateurs, has claimed for philosophy the right to a "scholastic" method of exposition. Whether we agree with their philosophy or not, we certainly agree that, technically speaking, the doctrines of Kant, of Fichte and of Hegel belong in the same class as the most perfectly elaborated Scholastic philosophies and theologies of the Middle Ages. Such has been one of the main reasons for the world-wide influence of nineteenth-century German philosophies. Even those who did not want to learn from them what to think have felt that they could at least learn from them how to think. There is a standard of philosophical thinking which should in no case be allowed to perish, and, if Kant was able to restore it, it was because Professor Wolff had obstinately maintained it. We know that Kant himself was aware of the fact. But, if Wolff had been able to maintain that standard it was because, before his own time, Suarez had resolutely maintained it. And Wolff, too, was fully aware of the fact. Kant always felt convinced that real philosophy should be "serious," and genius is no fitting matter for school teaching, but seriousness is, inasmuch as "serious" philosophy is "Scholastic" by definition.

---

according to P. Gény, *Questions d'enseignement de philosophie scolastique* (Paris, 1913), p. 48.

[9] Chr. Wolff, *Philosophia prima sive Ontologia methodo scientifica pertractata ua omnis cognitionis humanae principia continentur*, edit. nova (Veronae, 1789).

It is not my intention here to express personal opinions and, still less, personal feelings. Unless I be greatly mistaken, I am stating straight historical facts. Let us open Wolff's *Ontology* and read his Preface: "Prime Philosophy (namely, metaphysics) was first laden by the Scholastics with enviable praise, but, ever after the success of Cartesian philosophy, it fell into disrepute and has become a laughing stock to all."[10] What Wolff clearly sees then is that, since the time when Descartes "grew weary of metaphysics," there still may have been metaphysicians, *but there has been no metaphysics.* As a distinct science, metaphysics has simply ceased to be. And Kant himself was only echoing Wolff when he wrote in his Preface to the first edition of *The Critique of Pure Reason:* "There was a time when metaphysics used to be called the queen of sciences . . . Now, in our own century, it is quite fashionable to show contempt for it." *Our own century* here is the eighteenth century, which was the century of both Wolff and Kant.

When he made up his mind to put a stop to that technical decadence in the field of philosophy, Wolff was keenly conscious of carrying on the work of the great Scholastics. What they had done was not perfect, but that was the thing to do, and, since it could be done better, Wolff himself was going to do it all over again. Let us be as precise as possible. Wolff did not wish to be reproached with bringing back a Scholastic philosophy that was dead. In point of fact, that was not what he wanted to do. But he was claiming the right to retain at least Scholastic terminology, for all there was to be done about it was, keeping the same terms, to build up better definitions and more exactly determined propositions.[11]

This is what Wolff set about doing first with the term "being," and it is typical of his attitude that he can reach it only through the notion of possibility. "Being," Wolff says, "is what can exist and, consequently, that with which existence is not incompatible: *Ens dicitur quod existere potest, consequenter cui existentia non repugnat.*"[12] In other words, what is possible is a being: *Quod possible est, ens est.*[13] Besides, Wolff adds, this is a metaphysical notion which is accepted by all, and which exactly tallies with common language. "Being," "something," "possible;" here are so many words that are practically synonymous, and meta-

[10] Wolff, *Ontologia*, beginning of the Preface. Cf.: *"Si Cartesius non fastidio philosophiae primae correptus fuisset . . ."*

[11] Wolff, *Ontologia*, n. 12, pp. 4-5. [12] *Ibid.*, n. 134, p. 60.

[13] *Ibid.*, n. 135, p. 60.

physics does nothing more than bring their implicit meanings out in the open. True enough, what is commonly called a "being" is something that exists, but he who understands that a A is being because it exists will as easily understand that, if A exists, it is because it can exist.[14] Possibility then is the very root of existence, and this is why the possibles are commonly called beings. The proof of it is that we commonly speak of beings past or future, that is, of beings that no longer exist or that do not yet exist. In any case, their being has nothing to do with actual existence; it is, though a merely possible being, yet a being.

In order to probe more deeply into the knowledge of being, what we have to do is to inquire into the causes of its possibility. The first one is, of course, the one we have already mentioned, namely, the absence of inner contradiction; but this is not enough. In order to posit a being, one must ascribe to its notion such constituent parts as are not only compatible among themselves, but are its *primary* constituent parts. The primary constituents of a being are those which are neither determined by some element foreign to that being, nor determined by any one of the other constituent elements of the same being. If an element supposedly foreign to some being were determining with respect to any one of those elements which enter its constitution, then it would not be foreign to it; it would be one of its constituent elements. On the other hand, if some of the constituent elements of a being determine each other, then we must retain only the determining elements as constituent parts of that being.[15] In short, every being is made up of such elements as are both compatible and prime. Such elements shall be called the "essentials" of being (*essentialia*), because they constitute the very essence. Hence this conclusion, whose full significance it is superfluous to stress: Essence is what is conceived of being in the first place and, without it, being cannot be.[16] Thus, the essence of the equilateral triangle is made up of the number three and of the equality of its sides; again, the essence of virtue is made up of a habit (*habitus*) of the will and of the conformity with natural law of the acts which follow from that habit. Let any one of those conditions be altered, there is left neither equilateral triangle nor virtue; let them be all posited, then there is equilateral triangle and virtue. The presence of the "essentials" of the thing is therefore both necessary and sufficient to define its essence. Those "essentials" always entail certain properties which are inseparable from them and, since a thing

[14] *Ibid.*, n. 139, p. 61.   [15] *Ibid.*, n. 142, p. 62.
[16] *Ibid.*, n. 144, p. 63.

never is without its "essentials," it is also inseparable from the thing. Such properties are called the "attributes" of being. As to its "modes," they are such ulterior determinations which are neither determined by the essence nor contradictory with it. The attributes of a being are always given with it, but not its modes, which are what the Scholastics used to call "accidents."

In a being so conceived, the "essentials" obviously are the very core of reality. Taken as non-contradictory, they ensure the possibility of being. It is through its "essentials" that a being is possible: *Per essentialia ens possibile est.* Now, since the essence of being is one with its possibility, he who acknowledges the intrinsic possibility of a thing knows also its essence. We are saying "acknowledges," and rightly so, for it is possible to account for the attributes of being from the "essentials" of that being, but there is no accounting for the fact that those "essentials" belong to it. Since they are prime, there is nothing above them from which they could be deduced. As to the modes, they cannot be deduced from their essence either. For, what makes up an essence accounts for the fact that such and such a mode *may* belong to a certain being; it does not account for the fact that such a mode actually does belong to it. The reason for the actual presence of modes in a given being must always be looked for outside that being. We call "external" those beings which constitute the sufficient reason for the actual presence, in a given being, of modes which cannot be sufficiently accounted for by its essence alone. The essence then is for any being the sufficient reason for the actual presence of its attributes and of the possible presence of its modes.[17] Hence its nominal definition: "Essence is that which is conceived of a being in the first place, and in which is to be found the sufficient reason why all the rest either actually belongs to it or else may belong to it: *Essentia definiri potest per id quod primum de ente concipitur et in quo ratio continetur sufficiens, cur caetera vel actu insint, vel inesse possint.*"[18]

The scrupulously exacting method which Wolff was using in his determination of being was entirely his own, but the results achieved by that method had really nothing new. And Wolff himself was clearly aware of it.

"This notion of *essence*—namely, that it is the first thing that we conceive about being, and that it contains the explanation of whatever else is present or can be present within it—is in agreement with the philosophers' notion [of essence].

[17] *Ibid.*, n. 167, p. 71
[18] *Ibid.*, n. 168, p. 72.

"Certainly, Francis Suarez, of the Society of Jesus, who among Scholastics has pondered metaphysical realities with particular penetration, as it is known, says that the essence of a thing is the first and basic and innermost principle of all the activities and properties which befit a thing. And, although he proves, through the testimony of Aristotle and St. Thomas, that essence so understood is the same as the nature of each thing, nevertheless he immediately adds that, according to a second acceptation in St. Thomas, the essence of a thing is what is made manifest by the definition, and, to this extent, as he infers therefrom, the essence of a thing is what we conceive as first to befit a thing and as first to be established in the reality (esse) of a thing, or of such a thing. Suarez further goes on to say that a real essence is one which contains no contradiction within itself, and which is not one that is merely manufactured by the intellect; and also that it is the principle and source of all a thing's real operations or effects.

"Therefore, if you look more to the idea which the Metaphician [Suarez] had before his mind, rather than to the words by which he expressed what he was observing (#920, Log.), you will easily see that anyone who sets out to conceive the essence of being

(1) must posit within being, when it is conceived as absolutely without determination, something as a prime factor; that

(2) it [the essence of being] contains within itself only such elements as do not oppose one another or involve any contradiction, and as are not determined by other elements that are present along with them, since otherwise these determining elements would be prior to them; and that

(3) it [the essence of being] contains the explanation of whatever else is constantly present, or can be present, since otherwise it could not be called the root of the properties and the activities, i.e., whence they take their origin.

"Consequently, the notion of essence which St. Thomas and Suarez had in mind is the same as the one which we have deduced a priori, and which we have refined in distinctness and precision. Descartes retained the notion of essence which he had derived, in the schools of the Jesuits, from Scholastic philosophy. Indeed, he says in his Principles of Philosophy, Part I, #53, that there is in each substance a principal character which makes up its nature and essence, and to which all the other characteristics are referred. And his interpreter, the excellent Clauberg, says, in his Metaphysics of Being, #560, p.m. 13, that among all the attributes of

117

a thing there is one which we are accustomed to consider as what is prime and principal and most intimate in a thing, which in a way gathers the other attributes to itself, or which certainly is as their root and foundation. This is what we call the *essence* of a thing; and in relation to the properties and operations that flow from it, we also call it *nature.*"[19]

What a text! No commentary could exhaust its contents. Let us at least stress its main implications. First of all, the genuine meaning of the Thomistic notion of being is, around 1729, completely and absolutely forgotten. To Wolff, Thomas Aquinas and Suarez are of one mind concerning the nature of being, and it is not Suarez who agrees with Thomas Aquinas, but Thomas Aquinas who agrees with Suarez. In short, Suarezianism has consumed Thomism. Next, Wolff knows that his own notion of being is fundamentally the same as that of Suarez, whom he has not only read, but analyzed, and whom he proclaims as the deepest among Scholastic metaphysicians. Last but not least, the very notion of being on which he agrees with Suarez is that of the "real essence," which he conceives at one and the same time as the very stuff beings are made of and the ultimate source of all their operations. In drawing up the balance sheet of Scholastic metaphysics, one should never forget that Christian philosophers have not been able to entrust their modern successors with the greatest metaphysical discovery which any one of them had ever made. One cannot even help wondering how many among them had even understood it.

It is hardly possible to guess what would have happened to modern philosophy if, instead of teaching with Suarez that *operatio sequitur essentiam*, Wolff had taught with Thomas Aquinas that *operatio sequitur esse*. But this was the very last thing he could have undertaken to do. When he finally turns to locating existence, Wolff readily acknowledges that it is something else than mere possibility. When an artisan conceives a certain machine, the thus-conceived machine is but a possible, and, what is more, there is nothing in its possibility that can make it to exist. This is why the cause of existence always lies outside the possible itself, and this is why, in a justly famous formula, Wolff has nominally defined existence as the complement of possibility: *"Hinc existentiam definio per complementum possibilitatis."*[20] This "com-

[19] Wolff, *Philosophia prima sive Ontologia*, Part I, sect. 2, cap. 3, art. 169, pp. 72-73. Wolff often refers not only to Suarez and to St. Thomas Aquinas, but also to Dominic of Flanders, whom he calls "The Prince of Thomists."

[20] Wolff, *Ontologia*, n. 174, p. 76.

plement" closely resembles Avicenna's "accident," but it still more closely resembles the existential "mode" of Scotism, for, if actual existence does not necessarily follow from the "essentials" of being, not only is it not one of them, but it cannot even be an attribute; it can only be a mode. In short, the sufficient reason for the actual existence of any finite being is never to be found in that being itself; it always is to be found in another one. Of course, once it has received this modest complement, which costs so little yet yields so much, the Wolffian being actually is, or exists. Nevertheless, even then, and however one looks at it, existence still remains wholly foreign to its own essence; which means that existence remains wholly foreign to being.

And this is why, in the philosophy of Wolff, existence is completely excluded from the field of ontology. There are special sciences to deal with all the problems related to existence, and none of them is ontology. Are we interested in finding out the sufficient reason for the existence of God or for that of the world? Natural theology will give the answer. Do we want to know how those beings which make up the material world are, though contingent, yet determined? Cosmology will inform us about it. Are we wondering how, in the human mind, the possibles are drawn from potency to act? Psychology holds the key to that problem. When today we make use of the term "ontology," what it means to us is just the same as "metaphysics." Not so in the philosophy of Wolff, who needed a new word to designate a new thing. Strictly speaking, an ontology is a metaphysics without natural theology, because it is *a metaphysics without existence*. The extraordinary readiness of so many modern textbooks in Scholastic philosophy to welcome, together with the Wolffian notion of ontology, the breaking up of the science of being into several distinct sciences is a sure sign that, to the extent to which it does so, modern Scholasticism has lost the sense of its own message. But spoiling a few textbooks is a minor accident in the long history of the Wolffian tradition. Nothing can now give us an idea of the authority which his doctrine enjoyed throughout the schools of Europe, and especially in Germany. To innumerable professors and students of philosophy, metaphysics was Wolff and what Wolff had said was metaphysics. To Immanuel Kant, in particular, it never was to be anything else, so that the whole *Critique of Pure Reason* ultimately rests upon the assumption that the bankruptcy of the metaphysics of Wolff had been the very bankruptcy of metaphysics.

119

Students of Kant cannot read without a smile what he himself once wrote of "the celebrated Wolff, the greatest of all dogmatic philosophers." Thus, Wolff has been to Kant what Suarez had been to Wolff himself, and this is why the *Critique of Pure Reason* has been conceived as a work to be treated, "not popularly, but scholastically." The spirit of profundity which Kant praises in German philosophy goes back through Wolff to Suarez.[21] Everything is justified in this eulogy, except one praise. Had Kant written something like "the estimable," "the respectable" or even "the venerable Wolff," we still might understand; but, when he rates that exceptionally fine professor above such philosophers as Spinoza, Leibniz or Descartes, one cannot help feeling that he is paying him a rather high compliment.

Yet, Kant usually is in earnest, and he never was more so than on this occasion. Wolffism had been his philosophical fatherland. The doctrine of Christian Wolff had taken root in the university of Koenigsberg through the teaching of that same Franz Albert Schultz of whose teaching Wolff himself had once said: "If anyone ever understood me, it is Schultz, in Koenigsberg."[22] Now, Kant had been a pupil of Schultz. He had thus become acquainted with that abstract ontology of Wolff which was wholly focused on "entity" as such, and for which, as one of Kant's historians has aptly remarked, the world, the soul and God were but so many particular objects to which the ontological categories had to be applied by cosmology, pneumatology (that is, the science of the soul) and theology in as many particular sciences.[23] Now, what was to lie at the bottom of Kant's *Critique of Pure Reason*, if not the fundamental objection that *dogmatic metaphysics is ontological in its own right?* And, if Wolffism is metaphysics itself, this is absolutely true. It is a widely discussed point to know if Kant was right in saying that *all* demonstrations of the existence of God involve in their texture the ontological argument. In point of fact, they do, at least if being is what Wolff has said that it is. Where being is identified with the pure possibility of its essence, metaphysics finds itself confronted with the impossible task of finding a sufficient reason for actual existence in a world in which being as such, taken in itself, is essentially foreign to it. Not only the Anselmian argument, which can then

---

[21] Kant, *Critique of Pure Reason*, trans. by J. M. D. Meiklejohn, 2nd ed. (London, 1893), p. xxxviii.

[22] Fr. Wilh. Schubert, *Immanuel Kants Biographie*, in *I. Kants Sämtliche Werke*, ed. by K. Rosenkranz and Fr. W. Schubert (Leipzig, 1842), Vol. XI, 2nd part, p. 28.

[23] K. Rosenkranz, *Geschichte der Kant'schen Philosophie, ed. cit.*, Vol. XII, p. 44.

rightly be termed "ontological," but any proof of God's existence, nay, any demonstration of any actual existence is bound to be "ontological" in such a philosophy. The whole doctrine of Wolff was ontological because it was suspended from an ontology which had defined itself as the science of being *qua* possible. A proof is "ontological" whenever it looks at existentially neutral essence for the existential complement of its own possibility.

This important fact should be kept in mind, at least if one wants to understand in what sense the discovery of Hume by Kant has been for him a decisive event. When Kant wrote that Hume had "aroused him from his dogmatic slumber,"[24] what he really meant to say was that Hume had aroused him from his Wolffian sleep. To him, the dogmatism of the greatest among all dogmatic philosophers naturally was dogmatism itself, and this is why Kant brought the full weight of his own *Critique* to bear on a metaphysics whose very notion he had not even dreamed of criticizing. In order to make sure that we ourselves are not constructing a Kant suitable to our own dogmatic purpose, we had better let it be said by some historian entirely favorable to his philosophy: "It was a thus-understood metaphysics [that is, as a science of pure possibles] which became preponderant in Germany, and it exercised upon Kant a deep influence. It took the childish simplicity with which Wolff had handled the ontological categories directly to oppose the skepticism of Hume. But Kant himself had been, up to the very time of his own maturity, so deeply immersed in that simplicity; he has, on the whole, so well persevered in it that he has finally welcomed it in his own system with his *forms of understanding*. This trustfulness has often since been a subject of reproach to him, as being a lack of critical spirit."[25] Leaving this discussion to the critics of his *Critique*, we will content ourselves with observing the reaction of a thus-made mind to the philosophical message of Hume.

As straight empiricism, the doctrine of David Hume was an existential reaction against abstract metaphysical dreaming. There exist, in concrete reality, such elements as cannot possibly be deduced *a priori* by any method of analytical reasoning. This, of course, is eminently the case with what philosophers usually call "efficient causality," and it is very remarkable that Kant did at once realize the full import of the problem. There is nothing surprising in the fact that, from a given idea, another idea happens to follow, but physical causality is entirely different from abstract causality. It no longer is a relation between two possible beings,

[24] Kant, *Prolegomena*, Preface.　　　　[25] K. Rosenkranz, *op. cit.*, p. 44.

but between two actually existing beings. · Abstract causality raises no problem, because no actual existence is involved in it. Not so in the case of physical causality. As Kant himself was to write after reading Hume: "It is absolutely impossible to see why, because a certain thing exists, something else should also necessarily exist, nor does one see how the concept of such a connection could be deduced *a priori.*"[26]

Nothing could be more true, for, if you allow existence to get a foothold in philosophy, essentialism immediately goes to pieces. What Kant himself had discovered in Hume's analysis of causality was the irreducibility of actually given causal relations to the analytical properties of abstract essences. In short, he had discovered the radical "givenness" of existence, and indeed no honest reader of Hume could well fail to realize it: "There are two principles which I cannot render consistent," Hume says in the Appendix to his *Treatise of Human Nature,* "nor is it in my power to renounce either of them, namely, *that all our distinct perceptions are distinct existences,* and *that the mind never perceives any real connection among distinct existences.*" We do not know with certainty what, exactly, Kant had read of Hume, but there is little doubt that this sentence was the very one that aroused him from his dogmatic slumber. It shows at least what a tremendous charge of existential explosive was introduced by Hume into the Wolffian universe of nicely concatenated essences in which Kant himself was slumbering. The ontological world of Wolff was at once blown to pieces in the mind of Kant, and it almost immediately dawned upon him that his own philosophical problem was going to be: What are we to do with existence, if all our perceptions are distinct existences, and if the mind never perceives any real connection between them? To this question, his own answer was finally to be: The mind does not *perceive* such connections, it *prescribes* them. But in 1755 Kant was still a long way off from what was to be his ultimate conclusion.[27]

In 1763, three important treatises attest how deeply the empirical existentialism of Hume has already marked his personal reflections. In his *Essay towards Introducing into Cosmology the Concept of Negative Quantities,* Kant accepts full responsibility for the fundamental distinction which Hume had made between relations of ideas and matters of fact, but he himself gives it a

[26] Kant, *Prolegomena*, Preface.
[27] On Kant's philosophical evolution, see the excellent pages of R. Verneaux, *Les Sources Cartésiennes et Kantiennes de l'idéalisme français* (Paris, G. Beauchesne, 1936), pp. 224-241.

more precise formulation by distinguishing between two kinds of philosophical foundations, the "logical foundation" (*den logischen Grund*), which ultimately lies in the principle of identity, and the "real foundation" (*den Realgrund*), of which he says that "though such a relation belongs to my true concepts, its very nature renders it irreducible to any kind of judgment." Obviously, Kant has not yet discovered the class of the synthetic *a priori* judgments. Hence, for him, the question asked by Hume is still waiting for an answer: "*Wie soll ich es verstehen, das weil etwas ist, etwas anderes sei?*" How am I to understand that, because something is, something else should be?"[28] This time we are sure that Kant has read at least the Appendix to Hume's *Treatise*,[29] and that its lesson has not been lost on him.

In order to solve the problem, Kant begins by transposing it from epistemology to metaphysics. What had made it impossible for both Leibniz and Wolff to discover any really "sufficient reason" for the existence of the world was that they were looking for it in the order of abstract essences. Now, even if we know that there is a God, that there are ideas in the mind of God, and that among His ideas there is one which is the idea of the best possible world, we may well have found the sufficient reason for the choice which God has made of the proper world to create, but we still do not have the sufficient reason why God should create any world. The foundation for the existence of the world then cannot be a logical one, that is, a concept; it must needs be a real one, that is, a thing, such as, for instance, the will of God. But then Hume's problem again arises: "The will of God is the sole real foundation for the existence of the world. The divine will is something. The existing world is something *quite different*. Yet the one is posited by the other."[30] How can such a relation be conceived?

Things would perhaps clear up a bit if, before trying to understand the relation of existing creatures to God, we first tried to understand the relation of God's existence to His own essence. Wolff had found no difficulty in solving that problem, since he could do it by merely following the public highway of essentialism. To Wolff, God is an essence which possesses in itself the sufficient reason for its own existence. We are not now concerned with the elaborate deduction of God's existence in Wolff's *Natural Theology;*

[28] Kant, *Versuch den Begriff der negativen Grossen in die Weltweisheit einzuführen*, III, Allgemeine Bemerkung.
[29] D. Hume, *A Treatise of Human Nature*, ed. by G. A. Selby Bigge (Oxford, 1896), pp. 635-636.
[30] Kant, *Versuch, loc. cit.*

123

let it suffice for our own purpose to note that his God is such a being as has in His essence the reason for His existence: *"Ens a se rationem existentiae in essentia sua habet."* And again, a being is said to be *a se* if its existence necessarily follows from its essence: *"Dicendum erit, ens a se esse illud ex cujus essentia necessario fluit existentia."* [31] In the light of Hume's principles, such an argument is far from convincing, for, if the order of existence is radically *other* than that of essence, no essence can entail its own existence, not only in things, but even in God. Had any one of these philosophers remembered what another philosopher, now lost in the darkness of the Dark Ages, had said on the question, it might have altered their whole outlook on the problem. But they could not remember that, while no essence entails its existence, there might well be such an existence as is both its own essence and the source of all other essences and existences. They could not remember it because the very men who were supposed to hold that truth in trust had themselves very long ago forgotten it.

This is what makes the treatise written by Kant in 1763 on *The Only Possible Foundation for a Demonstration of God's Existence* so interesting for us. The problem constitutes in itself a metaphysical crucial test. If there is a case in which existence can be deduced from an essence, it should be the case of God. But what do we mean by existence (*Dasein*)? To this precise question, Kant naturally answers by saying what existence is not. And the very first thing which existence is not is a predicate, that is to say, existence is not a logical determination of a subject. Let us consider any *possible* subject, Julius Caesar, for instance, and let us suppose it as posited in the mind of God. If it is there, it must be there with all the determinations, including even those of space and time, which go into the making of its complete notion. Should we alter any one of those determinations, however trifling it may seem to be, that essence will no longer be Julius Caesar's; it will be the essence of another man. Thus, inasmuch as it is a pure possible, the essence of Julius Caesar includes all those predicates that are required for its complete determination. Yet, *qua* possible, Julius Caesar does not exist. His notion then can be completely determined without including his existence; whence it follows that existence is not a predicate. Common language is here greatly misleading. When we say that some regular hexagons exist in nature, it might look as though we were ascribing existence to such things; but common language can easily be corrected as

[31] Wolff, *Theologia naturalis* I, 31, (Verona, 1779), Vol. I, p. 15 (the Preface is dated March 31, 1736). Cf. *Ontologia*, n. 309, p. 132.

follows: to certain natural objects, such as bee cells or rock crystals, for instance, belong the predicates included in the concept of hexagon. Thus, instead of ascribing existence to some possible, we correctly ascribe all the predicates of the possible to something that is an existent.[32]

Thus to put existence outside the order of predication was to put it outside the order of logical relations, in which the verb "is" always plays the part of a copula. In this sense, "is" in no way implies existence. Whence it follows that, where "is" signifies existence, what it designates cannot be a relation. If I say: *"Julius Caesar is,"* I am not ascribing a new predicate to an already fully determined notion; I am positing Julius Caesar absolutely, including all his determinations. And it is the same with the notion of God. Everybody agrees that, if God is, He is all-powerful, since this predicate is necessarily included in the notion of a possible God; but, if I say: *"God is,"* or *"exists,"* I am positing God Himself at once and absolutely, taken with the totality of His attributes.[33]

This, of course, raises a very embarrassing question. Does existence add something to possibility, and supposing that it does, what is it? In Kant's own words: "Can I well say that, in existence (*im Dasein*), there is more than pure possibility?" Then was for Kant, if ever, the time to reinstate existence in its metaphysical right. But we have long ago ceased to feel optimistic with respect to such possibilities. What Kant answers to his own question is that one should carefully distinguish between *what* one posits and *how* one posits it. *What* is posited is identically the same in both cases: it is the essence of Julius Caesar or the essence of God. But that essence is not posited in the same way when it is posited *qua* essence as when it is posited *qua* existence. In the first case, we posit the relations of all its determinations to a certain subject; in the second case, we posit the subject itself together with all the determinations which constituted it as a possible. What existence adds to the possible is therefore the subject itself taken in its absolute reality.

The words used by Kant are quite clear, but it is hard to see in what sense they solve the problem. They are a very good answer to the question: How do I *signify* existence? But, to the question—*What* do I add to the possible when I assert its existence? —they bring no answer. Yet this was the very question which

[32] Kant, *Der einzig mögliche Beweisgrund zu einer Demonstration des Daseins Gottes,* I Abb., 1 Betr., 1.
[33] *Ibid.,* I, 1, 2.

Kant himself had asked. If *what* I then add to the essence is but the *how* I posit it, the obvious conclusion is that I have added nothing to it. And, of course, this is exactly what Kant holds to be true. When I posit a possible as real, I am not positing something else, but the same thing; only *what* is posited as existing is "more posited" (*mehr gesetzt*).

I am very far from thinking that Kant's answer does not make sense. It does, indeed, and he is much nearer than he himself imagines to his final philosophy, in which existence will be a mere modality of judgment. What is interesting to observe in his answer is how it shies at the existential obstacle raised by Hume. The great lesson taught by Hume was that no existence can ever be deduced from any essence. Kant then begins to wonder what happens to essence when I ascribe existence to it, and his answer is: Nothing. But, then, if existence really adds nothing to essence, how is it that I posit *more* by positing an existing essence than by positing essences alone? My own way of positing it cannot give it existence, and, if existence lies neither in my judgment nor in the very essence to which it is ascribed by my judgment, where is it? Obviously, the meaning of Hume's message is already lost. Existences are given—that was the main point—and to account for their bare givenness by our own way of positing the subject of their essences was to retreat from Hume, indeed, to retreat from Hume as far as possible, and towards old Professor Wolff as much as was still possible.

Yet, a complete return to Wolff had by then become an impossibility. Wolff had said that existence was the complement of possibility, but, says Kant, this is very vague, for, if we don't know beforehand what it is that can be ascribed to a thing over and above its possibility, to call it a "complement" will not teach us anything. Baumgarten, a disciple of Wolff, had said that existence was the complete determination of the object,[34] but since, as has been seen, each object is completely determined by its predicates, it could not receive existence as a complementary determination. As to the "celebrated Crusius," he thought that the "sometime" and the "somewhere" were sufficient marks of existence; but any possible man includes in his notion all the places and times where and when he would be, did he but exist. The Wandering Jew certainly is a possible man, yet he does not exist.[35]

[34] "*Existentia est complexus affectionum in aliquo compossibilium, id est complementum possibilitatis internae, quatenus haec tantum ut complexus determinationum spectatur.*" Al. Gottlieb Baumgarten, *Metaphysica*, P. I, c. I, s.3, n. 55, 4th ed. (Hallae Magdeburgicae, 1757). pp. 15-16.
[35] Kant, *op. cit.*, I, 1, 3.

Obviously, when confronted with the explanations of existence given by others, Kant realizes that they do not do justice to its irreducible givenness. He himself now knows that existence is never included in an essence,[36] but he does not seem to imagine that it might be a constituent element of concrete reality.

In point of fact, Kant never was to speculate on existence as such, but he never was either to deny it or even to forget it. Rather, he was to bracket it, so that it would always be present where there was real knowledge, yet would in no way limit the spontaneity of human understanding. In this sense, at least, the actual "givenness" of existence, so forcefully stressed by Hume, has not been lost on Kant. As he himself says at the end of his *Introduction to the Critique of Pure Reason*, "There are two sources of human knowledge (which probably spring from a common, but to us unknown, root), namely, sense and understanding. By the former, objects are *given* to us, by the latter, thought."[37] This empirical moment in Kant's doctrine will remain as a standing legacy from Hume and, to this extent the *Critique of Pure Reason* is really a vindication of the rights of existence against the essentialism of Wolff.

This is why, though a critical idealism, the philosophy of Kant remains a realism of the sensible world, and much more so than it is sometimes supposed to be. After the transcendental analysis has revealed the pure *a priori* elements which sensibility and understanding contribute to real knowledge, it still remains to mention sensible intuition. Now, in sensible intuition as such our sensibility is merely passive. Located, as it were, below even the forms of space and time, it is pure receptivity, and all the attempts of Leibniz, as well as those of Wolff, to explain it away by making it a confused intelligibility can safely be considered as so many failures. At any rate, Kant resolutely turns them down, so much so that, when he finds himself taxed with idealism, he can answer in all sincerity: "What I have called idealism was not concerned with the existence of things; now, to doubt their existence is what constitutes idealism properly so called, according to the usual meaning of the term, and it never occurred to my mind to doubt it."[38]

The critical idealism of Kant thus includes a realism of existence, and such a one as can rightly be called a perfectly candid realism. Kant naturally rejects the straight idealism of Berkeley,

---

[36] *Ibid.*, III, 2, init.
[37] Kant, *Critique of Pure Reason, ed. cit.*, p. 18.
[38] Kant, *Prolegomena*, Der transzendentale Hauptfrage, I Teil, Amm. 3.

according to whom the world of matter does not exist, but he also reject what he very aptly calls the "problematic idealism" of Descartes, according to whom the existence of the external world, though demonstrable, needed at least to be proven. There is no such thing in Kantism as a demonstration of the existence of the world, because it is not even a problem. "Things are" is to him no less immediately evident a proposition than "I think," and these two evidences are not only equal, they are of the same nature: The reality of material phenomena is just as immediately perceived in the *a priori* form of space as the spiritual reality of the thinking subject is immediately perceived in the *a priori* form of time. What directly strikes our sensibility in sensible intuition is, precisely, existence. But what is philosophy going to do with it?

The whole effort of Kant's philosophy, in so far at least as existence was concerned, has been to keep it out of philosophy. Human knowledge needs it in order to have something to know, but that is all. The sole business of existence is to be, after which it has nothing more to say. That things are is a fact to be accepted as such, but *what* they are is something for which the human understanding alone is responsible. If, as Hume had said, reality itself refuses to say how it is that, because a certain thing is, another thing should also be, it merely proves that intelligibility does not belong to things in themselves, but has to be put into them by the human mind. This is the "Copernican revolution" attempted by Kant in philosophy: Henceforward, the mind shall not revolve around things; things themselves shall revolve around the mind as around a sun which sheds on them its own intelligibility. How firmly resolved Kant himself is not to let raw reality interfere with the work of philosophy is best seen from the threatening language he uses when speaking of it: "Reason must approach nature with the view, indeed, of receiving information from it, not, however, in the character of a pupil, who listens to all that his master chooses to tell him, but in that of a judge, who compels the witnesses to reply to those questions which he himself thinks fit to propose."[39] Such has been the method which, in the past, has conducted science into the path of progress; such also must be the method of a scientific metaphysics. Thus summoned before the court of human understanding, existence shall not be permitted to speak, save only to answer its questions.

As was to be expected, Kant himself never asked it any question. The technically elaborate system of the *Critique* resembles one of

[39] Kant, *Critique of Pure Reason*, Preface to the 2nd edition, *ed. cit.*, p. xxvii.

those power plants that pipe water power at its source and compel it to serve without ever allowing it to be seen. Existence is not given to us in space, since even space is an *a priori* form of our own sensibility. The very exteriority of material things is thus internal to the mind, and, when we speak of a given reality, we are wrong, because what is given to us in sensible intuition, inasmuch as it is only given, is not yet a reality. Let us strip reality of what it owes to the categories of understanding and to the forms of sensibility, and what is left will be an I know not what, neither intelligible nor even perceivable, since it will be out of both space and time. In short, it will be an x, an unknown quantity.

Such is existence in the final philosophy of Kant. All we can do about it is either to feel it or else to affirm it, and, if we affirm it, its affirmation must in no way add anything to the notion of what it affirms. Even in the *Critique of Pure Reason* it remains true to say that existence can be added to or subtracted from the concept of any object without altering it in the least. Now, among the various functions of judgment, there is one which exhibits this remarkable character, that it in no way affects the very contents of our judgments. It is the function of modality. The various modalities of judgment answer the various values which the mind ascribes to its copula, according as it posits an affirmation (or negation) as problematical (possibility), assertive (reality), or apodictical (necessity). There are thus three categories of modality; six, if their contraries are added to them. The category which answers to existence is obviously the second one, the assertive category, whose proper function it is to assert reality.

But in what exactly does "reality" consist? In such a doctrine it is bound to be both given in sensible intuition and known by understanding. Unless it be given in sensible intuition, it cannot be known by understanding, while, on the other hand, where thought does not agree with sensible intuition, there still may be thinking, but no knowledge. It can therefore be posited as a postulate: "What agrees with the material conditions of experience (that is, of sensation), is real." Existence then appears where the assertive judgment, "x is," happens to posit as real such an object of thought as answers to a sensible intuition, that is, a "given." Thus, the *Critique of Pure Reason* has kept faith with the main conclusion of the dissertation of 1763: Existence is not the *what* which I posit, but the *how* I posit it. Moreover, though essence has now become what is conceived of being through the *a priori* forms of understanding, it still does not involve existence, so that, following an old law which has by now grown familiar to us, existence can be but a "mode" of the essence, namely, something which pertains to it without altering "what" it is. Thirdly, since existence can be grasped only in a reality which is the work of the mind (since both the *a priori* forms of sensibility and the *a priori* categories of the understanding cooperate in its making), existence can no longer be a mode of essence itself, but a modality of judgment.

Kant himself has summed up his doctrine of existence in the three following postulates: (1) "That which agrees with the formal conditions (intuition and conception) of experience is *possible;*" it is possible because, in such cases, the two conditions that are required for eventual assertions of existence are both hypothetically fulfilled. (2) "That which coheres with the material conditions of experience (sensation) is *real;*" it is real, because, in such cases, the two conditions required by Postulate I happen to be actually fulfilled. (3) "That whose coherence with the real is determined according to universal conditions of experience is (exists) *necessary;*" it is necessary because judgment determines that, in this case, the universal conditions required for reality are actually fulfilled. But, whatever the modality of our judgments, whose *a priori* conditions here replace the intrinsic necessity of the late essences, it still respects the existential neutrality which had always belonged to essences. In critical idealism, the categories of modality fall heir to the privileges of the Scotist "modes" of being; they determine it without changing it. Only, what had once been a privilege of being has now become a privilege of thought: "The categories of modality possess this peculiarity, that they do not in the least determine the object, or enlarge the conception to which they are annexed as predicates, but only express its relation to the faculty of cognition."[40]

If it is so, where nothing is given, there is no knowledge; yet that which is given is an *x* that is not even existence, but is that to which existence is ascribed by the assertive modality of judgment. Of that *x*, taken in itself, we know nothing, save only that it is. And how could we know it? Inasmuch as it is known, or even simply perceived, what is either perceived or known is its phenomenon, that is, its appearance through the *a priori* conditions that are required for both its intellectual knowledge and its sensory perception. In short, "all those properties which constitute the intuition of a material thing belong solely to its appearance." Whereupon Kant adds: "For the existence of the

[40] Kant, *Critique of Pure Reason*, Transcendental Analytik, II, 4, The Postulates of Empirical Thought, *ed. cit.*, p. 161.

thing which appears is not thereby suppressed, as it is in straight idealism, but it is thereby only shown that, through sense, we absolutely cannot know that thing such as it is in itself."[41] Since what is true of sense is still more true of the understanding, there must be existence in order that there be knowledge, but the fact that reality exists, though a necessary condition, does not enter our scientific knowledge of reality. Which was indeed perfectly true, for, if there is such a thing as a knowledge of existence, it cannot be a physical, but a *meta*physical, one. Science as such has no use for existence. By consigning it to the unknowable realm of the "thing in itself," Kant has maintained it as a necessary condition for real knowledge, but he has also made it that fundamental condition for knowledge of which nothing is or can be known. Never, not even in his *Opus Posthumum*, has Kant consented to suppress that "thing in itself" which divides critical idealism from straight idealism. Never, not even in his *Critique of Practical Reason*, has Kant consented to posit the "thing in itself" as something that is "known." Practical reason may well teach us something concerning what the "thing in itself" postulates, but such postulates entail no "knowledge" of what it is. The knowledge of what a thing is inasmuch as it is not known is a flat contradiction in Kant's doctrine. Existence, then, is an *x* which Kant never eliminates because he never completely betrays Hume, and that *x* remains an *x* because Kant never completely betrays Wolff.

Kant could indeed do it on the strength of his own initial bold stroke: "Understanding does not derive its *a priori* laws from nature, it *prescribes* them to it."[42] But, then, if what is at stake is the very "possibility of nature," and if nature is what understanding makes it to be, why should understanding not prescribe existence? Because, Kant says, that would be idealism. But, if idealism is true, why not idealism? Everything points to the fact that, in spite of its precarious revival under the influence of Hume, existence is not there to stay. Kant could still afford to maintain it, because what he was building up was a *Critique* of human knowledge, which, to him, was one with "scientific" knowledge. Now, obviously, where there *is* nothing to be known, there can be no knowledge at all, but, if both physics itself and its Critique are well founded in taking existence for granted, a metaphysics of that Critique has no right to do so. That common root from which sensibility and understanding both spring, and

[41] Kant, *Prolegomena*, Transcendentale Hauptfrage, I Teil, Amm. II.
[42] *Ibid.*, II Teil, *Wie is Natur selbst möglich?*

of which Kant says that it exists, but that we don't know what it is, should at last be dug out and brought to light. In short, if it is not to remain like a foreign body arbitrarily inserted in the intelligible world of understanding, existence has either to be flatly denied, or else to be deduced *a priori* like all the rest. In point of fact, both choices have been made by post-Kantian philosophers. Kantism has thus normally resulted in either phenomenalism or straight idealism, and both cases might prove fruitful subjects of investigation for our own problem, but no one can even compare in importance with the *a priori* deduction of existence by Hegel.

Hegel was not a philosopher; he was a world, a self-creating world, whose inner trouble it was to realize that, while it could not exist without exteriorizing itself through concepts, it could not do so without spreading far and wide its innermost depth at the very risk of losing it.[43] Yet, according to Hegel, philosophy *is* such a risk and, after all, the world itself *is* such a risk, since it is nothing more than the progressive self-determination, through the many steps of a patient dialectic, of the inner unity of a self-subsisting Mind.

What is most remarkable in the world of Hegel is that, for it to be wholly intelligible, everything in it has to be susceptible of an exhaustive justification. This is to say that a philosophical interpretation of reality should account for the whole reality, including nature, geography, law, history and the history of history, philosophy together with the history of philosophy and the philosophy of that history, including even Hegel's own philosophy. Such an ambition of exhaustive intelligibility necessarily entailed two important consequences. On the one hand, if each and every thing can be rationally accounted for, all that which is real is rational, which means that it is just what it should be. As such, each and every thing is rationally justifiable, because, in point of fact, it is rationally justified. On the other hand, while each thing is what it should be when seen from its own point of view, it does not seem to be what it should be when envisaged from the point of view of another thing. The most superficial glance at nature will show that certain things manage to exist only by destroying other ones. Even in the order of abstract thinking you cannot affirm something without at one and the same time denying something else. Now, if we look at it more closely, this is exactly what has until now prevented philosophy

---

[43] Hegel, *The Phenomenology of Mind*, Preface, trans. by J. B. Baillie, 2nd ed. (London and New York, 1931).

from giving an exhaustive account of reality. Philosophers could not welcome in their doctrines any conceivable element of reality without turning down another one. Their very notion of rational knowledge stands therefore in need of being revised.

What philosophy does Hegel have in mind while thus criticizing his predecessors? He is not thinking of what Kant himself had called "dogmatic philosophy," that is, "any procedure of pure reason without previous criticism of its own powers."[44] Hegel is more particularly thinking of Wolff, and what he reproaches Wolffianism for is something else than its lack of criticism. "Taken in its most completely determined and most recent form, that manner of philosophizing was the metaphysics of the past, such as it had become established in our own country. Nevertheless, that metaphysics is of the past for history of philosophy only, for, indeed, taken in itself, it remains something wholly present, viz., the simple consideration by understanding of the objects of reason."[45]

Now, Hegel sees nothing fundamentally wrong in assuming that, from the very fact that something is being thought, it is being known in itself. Far from taking ancient dogmatism to task for implicitly trusting the cognitive powers of reason, he holds it much superior to the critical idealism of Kant, which had intended to supersede it. What was wrong with ancient dogmatism was something else, namely, the illusion which it always entertained that to know the absolute consisted in ascribing to it predicates, without worrying about their content or their value, and without determining the absolute itself through the very attribution of those predicates. In other words, dogmatic philosophers had been right in assuming that absolute reality can be known, exactly such as it is in itself, by means of concepts, but they had been wrong in their method of handling concepts. Theirs was a truly candid and unsophisticated dogmatism, not indeed because it had not occurred to them to criticize the powers of reason—with what would we criticize them, if not with reason itself?—but because it was a mere ontology, that is, a science of the abstract determinations of essences. Now, as Hegel himself aptly says, when it is understood as a simple presentation of an essence to the mind, a concept contains nothing more than "the empty abstraction of indeterminate essence, of the pure reality or

[44] Kant, *Critique of Pure Reason*, Preface to the 2nd edition, *ed. cit.*, p. xxxviii.
[45] Hegel, *Encyclopädie der philosophischen Wissenschaften im Grundrisse*, 2nd ed., ed. by G. Lasson (Leipzig, Meiner, 1911), art. 27, p. 60.

positivity, the dead product of the modern Philosophy of Light."[46] Given such concepts, those philosophers merely wondered of what subjects they could be predicated, and their only rule was that any predication is true, provided only that it involves no contradiction, whereas, if it involves contradiction, then it is false. In short, such an ontology was but a logic, and this is why such philosophies have always failed to grasp reality.

Against the abstract conceptualism of Wolff, Hegel sets up the raw empiricism of Hume. The trouble facing dogmatism had been to get out of abstraction and to join concrete reality. The trouble facing Hume's empiricism is just the reverse, namely, to reach true generality. For, indeed, generality means something quite different from "a large number of similar cases," just as the notion of "necessary connexion" means something quite different from "changes regularly following each other in time, or juxta-position of objects in space." Hume himself knew this so well that he deemed it impossible to establish any universal and necessary proposition, because no one can be justified on the ground of experience alone. But the criticism of Kant was not so different from the empiricism of Hume as Kant himself imagined it to be. The very fact that Kantism posits a "given" at the origin of all real knowledge is enough in itself to burden it with all the shortcomings of empiricism. Kantism thus becomes such an empiricism as requires a "given," concerning which nothing can be known, since, as a prerequisite to all knowledge, it cannot fall under it. Such is the thing-in-itself, "the total abstract, the empty whole, without any further determination than that of a 'beyond.'"[47] True enough, and Hegel knew it, Kant himself had strongly protested against the accusation of idealism directed against his doctrine. Yet, it was nothing else: Not at all a "critical idealism," but the most vulgar type of idealism; for, indeed, the "given" maintained by Kant was such that everything took place for knowledge as if that "given" itself were not. Despite all that Kant himself could say, being was, in his own philosophy, just what it had been in Berkeley's idealism, in which *to be* was *to be perceived: esse est percipi.*

This argumentation is doubly interesting for us, in that it lends credibility to our own interpretation of Kant and opens for us a way to the correct interpretation of Hegel's own doctrine of being. There is too much existence in Kant's criticism, or not enough. Too much, because it is arbitrarily given, just as in the case of Hume; not enough, because it is so utterly unknowable

---

[46] Hegel, *Encyclopädie*, art. 36, p. 64. [47] *Ibid.*, art. 44, p. 70.

that there is practically no more of it in the critical idealism of Kant than there was in the absolute idealism of Berkeley. At the same time, since Hegel himself was resolved to trust essences and concepts as fitting *media* to reach absolute reality, he had no other choice than to achieve a complete reformation of both essence and concept. What he himself needed was "concrete universals," that is, concrete essences adequately grasped through concrete concepts. By the concreteness of an essence or of a concept we simply mean the totality of their interrelated and mutually determining constituent determinations.

As a first approach to the meaning of Hegelian concreteness, the refutation by Hegel of the Kantian refutation of the ontological argument may be conveniently taken into consideration. The main objection of Kant to that argument was, that from no essence and from no notion would the existence of God be validly deduced. To which Hegel rejoins that, although the existence of any finite being is indeed distinct from the concept of it, the concept of God involves its being: God expressly is *that which can be thought of only as existing*; that is, that whose concept includes within itself being. It is this unity of the concept and of being which makes up the concept of God.

Perfectly classical in its formulation, this time-honored answer nevertheless carries a new meaning in the metaphysics of Hegel. Inasmuch as it was directed against the ontological argument of Wolff, in which the concept of existence was *predicated* of the concept of God, the criticism of Kant was very much to the point. For, indeed, what has abstract predication in common with existence? What Kant should have seen, on the contrary, is that God's essence is in itself not only the most concrete of all essences, but the very fullness of reality. God is spirit itself in its innermost life, the "wholly concrete totality" of all possible determinations. When he was thinking of such an essence, Hegel could not help feeling slightly amused at Kant's critical scruples. For, Kant was always wondering whether or not he should "ascribe" existence to the essence of God, as if God had been waiting for Kant to ascribe existence to Him. God has it. The true problem is not to know if we can *ascribe* existence to the essence of God; it is rather to know if we can *refuse* to that essence an existence which it obviously includes among the infinite number of the other determinations.

The attitude of Kant looks still more strange if one considers what it is that he dares not ascribe to God. To predicate existence is to predicate being. Now, what is being? It is "the poorest and the most abstract of all notions." The very least thing that a being can do is to be. Being thus appears, in the philosophy of Hegel, as the most poverty-stricken of all concepts, and it is so because of its supreme abstractedness. There is nothing, Hegel says, which has less to exhibit to the mind than being, whereupon he nevertheless adds this enlightening remark: "There is only one thing whose contents can be still poorer, and it is what is sometimes mistaken for being, namely, an external sensible existence, like that of the paper which lies before me; but an external and sensible existence like that of a finite and passing thing should not here even be mentioned."[48] The essential indigence of being is therefore one with its abstractness. Being is what is left of the concreteness of an essence after all that which it is has been removed from it. On the contrary, the essence of God is both the most concrete and the fullest of all essences, because it is the unity of an infinite number of determinations. This is why the problem of the existence of God is, after all, of small importance: To say of the Supreme "I" that He is, is the very least that can be said of Him.

That Hegel is thereby reviving the old theology of the God-Essence is so obvious that it would be pointless to prove it. His essentialism is more sophisticated than that of Wolff and of the fourteenth-century Scotists, but it is fundamentally the same. The only difference is that, instead of coming third or fourth among the determinations of the divine essence, being comes last in the theology of Hegel. Being is so very little in itself that to posit it among the determinations of the absolute subject we call God is to pay Him rather poor homage. As to existence itself, it is wholly irrelevant to the question.

We now are in a better position to understand the place assigned by Hegel to being in his *Encyclopedia of the Philosophical Sciences.* It is the first one, because it is the lowest one in the progressive determination of Him Who is the fullness of reality. Taken in itself, being is the *immediate* indetermination, that is to say, not that already determined indetermination which comes before a further determination, but absolute indetermination. Being is the indetermination which precedes *all* determinations. And that total indetermination is the very stuff which being is. How can it be grasped by thought?

Since being is totally abstract, it cannot be perceived by any sensation; and, since it is completely void of content, it cannot become an object of any representation or of any intellectual

[48] *Ibid.*

136

intuition. Being is not even essence, for essence as such already entails many additional determinations of being. Now, if being is not perceived, nor represented, nor intuited, and yet is known, only one hypothesis still remains to be made about it, namely, that being is identical with thought. To think is to think being, or, if it seems clearer that way, being is thought when thought takes itself for its own object. This is why it can be said that the beginning of philosophy coincides with the beginning of the history of philosophy, for that history actually begins with Parmenides. By positing being as the absolute substance, Parmenides identified absolute reality with pure thought, which itself is thought about being; and for us, too, who after so many centuries are recommencing the ever-present experiment of Parmenides, to think being simply and solely is to think simply and solely.

Let us now proceed a little farther. This being, which is completely void of all determinations, is thereby absolute emptiness. Whatever else could be ascribed to it, we should have to deny it. In other words, since it is neither this nor that nor any other thing, it is nothing. Nothing is the absolute negative taken in its immediateness. That is, "nothing" is not a relative negation, such as those which presuppose some preceding affirmation (*a* is not *b*); it is that negation which comes before any other negation.[49] If it seems scandalous to say that being is nothingness, this is merely because we fail to realize that, since there is nothing which being is, being is nothing. Pure being and pure non-being are one, and no wonder, since "these two beginnings are but empty abstractions, and each of them is just as empty as the other one." In this extreme degree of indetermination the equivalence of these two terms appears evident.

This looks very much like marking time, but we have made more progress than may appear. To say that being *is* non-being is to unite these two terms in a third one. To unite them actually means to conceive that, just as being *is* non-being, so also non-being *is* being. In other words, if it is true to say that being is non-being, and conversely, then the truth of being *is in* non-being, and conversely. This very unity, which *consists in the passing of the one into the other and of the other into the one*, is a motion; properly, it is *becoming*.

The whole newness of Hegel's method thus appears in full from the very first step of his philosophical journey. As has already been said, dogmatic metaphysics always failed to make provision for the whole of reality. We are now beginning to see

[49] *Ibid.*, art. 87, p. 109.

137

why. Completely built upon the principle of contradiction, dogmatic metaphysics has always used it in order to divide and to exclude. In a logic entirely devoted to abstract concepts, it may be true that no thing can be, at one and the same time, itself and its contrary; but it is not so in reality, where things always are, at one and the same time, themselves and their very contraries. The principle of contradiction may well be the law for abstract concepts; contradiction itself is the law for reality. When Hegel says that his own universals are concrete, he means precisely that, contrary to the abstract logical notions used by Wolff, his own metaphysical notions include in their unity the dialectical becoming which begets them. Moreover, when Hegel says that his metaphysics is not "dogmatic," he means to say that, unlike those ancient metaphysics which were always making their choice between two contradictory terms, his own philosophy never makes any choice between two contradictory things. It takes them both, by uniting them in a third thing whose very concreteness is the reciprocal passing into one another of its contradictory constituents. For these constituents have to be two, in order that they may be one. Contradiction is the motive power which begets Hegelian dialectic and, since it is the same thing, Hegelian reality.

If we grant to Hegel his initial position of the philosophical problem, we must also grant him this unusual conception of the "real." What Hegel wanted was a reality made up of essences both concrete and yet knowable through concepts. If the "abstract" is the non-contradictory, then the "concrete" can be nothing else than the contradictory. And here again philosophy recapitulates history of philosophy. For, if philosophy began with Parmenides, it continued with Heraclitus. And they have both been right, for they have been two contradictory moments of the same dialectical becoming.

We have thus reached the first concrete object of thought, that is, the unity of the reciprocal notion whereby thought is constantly thinking of being as nothingness and nothingness as being. In Hegel's own forceful formula: "Becoming . . . is restlessness in itself: *Werden . . . ist die Unruhe in sich.*"[50] Yet, we can grasp this radical restlessness as constituting in itself an end. With it, thought for the first time finds a place of rest, which is becoming grasped as becoming. But, then, *qua* becoming, becoming itself has now become. It *is* becoming. It is a "given," which we call, in German, a *Dasein* (a "to be there"), because deter-

[50] *Ibid.*, art. 88, 4, p. 113.

138

mination in space can be used as a symbol for *any* immediate determination. "Givenness," then, is that determination of being which precedes *all* its other determinations; it is what makes the first of all concrete concepts a "to be there." In Hegel's own words: "Being, in becoming, that is, being as one with nothing, and nothing as one with being, are only vanishing away; becoming is swallowed up, owing to its self-contradiction, by that unity wherein they are both sublated (*aufgehoben*); becoming thus results in givenness (*Dasein:* to be there)."[51] Abstract logic was bound to hold contradiction as the typical token of impossibility; the logic of real being is bound to hold contradiction as the very concreteness of concrete reality. And it should not be said that, since being is nothing, concrete givenness is creating itself out of nothing. For, it is nothingness itself which appears in becoming as a *determined* nothing.[52] It is the "nothing of being." Such a nothing is the nothingness of that from which it results. This determined nothing then has a content of its own, and this is why "givenness" (*Dasein*) ultimately appears as the already overcome unity of its own inner contradiction.

Thus, the "given" is the first concrete notion, because it arises from the first immediate determination. As such, it itself has determination, and we call it a "quality."[53] Where there is a "given," then, there also is quality; but, where there is a "given" endowed with quality, the possibility arises to say *what* it is, which is "reality." As *real*, the given now is what it is. But, for any given reality to be that which it is, is relation. It is relation to its own self. Henceforth, any given reality will be both *an* itself and *in* itself, and this is to be "essence" (*Wesenheit*). Essence then is being in its simple relation to itself,[54] which means that, after justifying its own history up to Heraclitus, philosophy now justifies it up to Plato. Yet, let us be careful to observe that the two terms of this relation of self-identity are not themselves identical. In essence, being *appears as identical with self*. In other words, the being which essence includes is "that which appears in essence;" in short, it is "appearance," which itself, as mere appearance, is "unessential." Thus, inasmuch as it is an appearance of being to self, essence necessarily includes its own "unessential," and, since it includes it as being its own appearing

---

[51] *Ibid.*, art. 89, p. 114.
[52] Cf. Hegel's *Phenomenology*, Introduction, where non-being appears as a "nothingness of being," that is, a nothingness which is determined by the very being it denies.
[53] Hegel, *Encyclopädie*, art. 90, p. 115.
[54] *Ibid.*, art. 112, p. 126.

to self, it includes unessentiality, as it were, essentially. This mutual reflexion of two terms passing into one another is nothing new to us. Just as we could not think being without thinking non-being, and conversely, so also we cannot think of essence without thinking of appearance, and conversely, for the simple reason that essence is the very appearance of reality to its own self. The fecundity of contradiction here shows once more to the full. For, indeed, as the appearance of being to itself, essence is the proximate foundation for existence: *"Das Wesen als Grund der Existenz."*[65]

We rightly call it "existence" (*Ex-istenz*), precisely because there is a foundation (*Grund*) out of which it springs. In abstract metaphysics, the self-identity of an essence is but the formal identity of being as a subject with being as a predicate. Not so, here. Concrete essence, that is, real essence, is the unity of being *qua* being with its own appearance to itself. Now, between being *qua* being and being as appearance there is a difference, so that essence is difference from itself grasped as identity with itself. Essence is neither pure sameness nor pure otherness; rather, it is the mutual reflecting and passing of the one into the other. If essence is truly this, then, *qua* essence, it is "that which has its being in another."[66] This is why essence is the foundation, or basis, that is, the proximate reason, for something else. Essence is the proximate reason for existence, because, as concrete self-identity, it itself arises from that interrelation of being with its own appearance which essence itself is. Existence then is to essence as "givenness" (*Dasein*) is to being. In short, existence arises from the actual overcoming, by a concrete essence, of both appearance and reality. Now, let us suppose, for the sake of brevity, that a similar dialectical process had succeeded in overcoming the actual opposition there is between essence and its own existence; their unity will then be the thing (*das Ding*).

This indeed constitutes a decisive step in the Hegelian dialectic, in that it marks the triumph of concrete idealism over critical idealism. We now know what "the thing" is, and this is to know not at all what this and that particular thing is, but what it is to be a thing as such. To be a thing as such is to be the already overcome opposition of a concrete essence with its own existence, and to know that is at once to know what the "thing in itself" is. The celebrated "thing-in-itself" of Kant is not only here overtaken by Hegel in the course of his dialectical journey; it is known in itself and exactly such as it is. Indeed, there was

[65] *Ibid.*, art. 115, p. 128   [66] *Ibid.*, art. 121, p. 134.

no mystery in it; we see through it, and it is not much. Just as being was indeterminateness itself, the thing is nothing more in itself than its very "thingness," that is, its condition of complete and total indetermination and of open liability to all its ulterior determinations. In other words, instead of positing the thing-in-itself as the unknowable root of all appearances, that is, as the primitive fecundity wherein, could it only "appear such as it is," the source of all being and of all intelligibility would at once be found, Hegel posits it as the penurious condition which is that of the thing when as yet it is just "thing."

It could have been foreseen. Hegel never tires of attacking that logicism of abstract concepts which Wolff had mistaken for philosophical knowledge. But he himself has no objection to logic, provided only that it be the right sort of logic, his own logic, that is, the logic of concrete essences. This is so true that, in his own doctrine, all the problems discussed by Wolff under the title of ontology constitute for Hegel himself the very beginning of his logic. If possible readers are frightened away from the so-called *Great Logic* of Hegel by its bulk, nothing can be done about it; but, if what they are afraid of is formal logic, they should be under no apprehension about it. In Hegel's philosophy, logic is the concrete dialectic of being *qua* being, wherein it appears as progressively conquering all the determinations which belong to it as such. Actual reality itself (*die Wirklichkeit*) is simply the thing as the actualized unity of its essence and of its existence.[57] Thus understood, actual reality still belongs in the order of logic, whose limits are reached only with the determination of being as Idea. Then, that is to say, at that very moment when being as idea walks, so to speak, out of itself and thus posits itself under the form of "being other," as both the negative of and the external to itself, then does being become "nature"[58] Logic then comes to an end, and philosophy of nature begins, itself to be later followed by the philosophy of mind. Hegel himself has claimed for his own philosophy the title of "absolute idealism," and it surely deserves it, since, in it, even concreteness is ideality. Yet, when all is said, Hegel's absolute idealism is a thorough overhauling of ancient essentialism, and it appears as so triumphant a one that it buries itself under its own trophies. Logic has eaten up the whole of reality. After raising a helpless protest in the doctrine of Hume, existence had attempted at least to hide somewhere in the critical idealism of Kant. It had made itself so inconspicuous that it could reasonably hope to be there to stay.

[57] *Ibid.*, arts. 142 and 143, p. 145.   [58] *Ibid.*, art. 247, p. 207.

But now the brand new essence of Hegel has not only explained it *a priori;* it has explained it away. In the centuries-old process of "essence versus existence," essence has at last won its case; which means, of course, that the process of "existence versus essence" is about to begin again, and this time, owing to the complete victory of Hegel, if it is to be fought at all, it will have to be fought out to a finish.

As was to be expected, the attack on Hegel's absolute idealism came from religion. I say that it was to be expected, because it had already happened, and more than once. Four names will say it best: Bernard of Clairvaux against Abelard, Pascal against Descartes. And this will show us at once what is going to happen again, namely, that the reaction of existence against essence is bound to become a reaction of existence against philosophy. What matters, Bernard had said, is not to explain mysteries away, as Abelard was doing, but to believe them and thus actually to save one's soul. And Pascal had only been following suit when, having elsewhere branded Descartes as "useless and ineffectual," he had added that philosophy was not worth "an hour of trouble." Now, if there is any proposition that sums up the manifold message of Kirkegaard, it is that what matters is not to *know* Christianity, but *to be* a Christian.

That the question was at last raised under this form, and with such force, can be accounted for only by the passionate interest of Kirkegaard in religious problems. I am not here using the words "religious experience," because it is not proven that he ever had any, at least if those words are to be taken in their full meaning. The very core of his religious life is perhaps best expressed by his unwillingness to think that he deserved the title of *Christian*, not because Christianity was not good enough for him, but, on the contrary, because truly to be a Christian appeared to him as so difficult and so noble an undertaking that he himself would never boast of having achieved it.

Such is the authentic meaning of his whole work, as he himself early saw it; it was to be wholly dedicated to the service of Christianity. But this early dedication entailed that, even though he himself never succeeded in being a Christian, he would put his heart and soul into the service of God, so that at least he might throw full light upon the nature of Christianity as well as upon the point at which, in Christendom, confusion then prevailed.[59] And this confusion was mainly Hegelian confusion; it consisted

[59] Sören Kirkegaard, *Point de vue explicatif de mon oeuvre,* trans. by P. H. Tisseau (1940), p. 75, n. 1.

in believing that to be a Christian was to know Christianity, and that there was a system, a "speculation," that is, a "specular" knowledge, through which it was possible to "become Christian."

What really worried him was his own personal difficulty in being a Christian; but he was no less worried by the, to him, always surprising fact that he was almost alone in finding Christianity difficult. Christians were plentiful around him, and they all seemed to find it a very easy thing to be. *They*, at least, had no misgivings about their right to call themselves Christians. Now, why were they so sure of being Christians? Why were their ministers so sure of being Christians? Why was his bishop so sure of being a Christian? So many pertinent questions indeed, especially the last one, because Bishop Mynster was such a good theologian and such a learned Hegelian that he could explain everything away, including religion in general, Christianity in particular and, if given a chance, even God. Had Kirkegaard merely protested in the name of religion, it would have been nothing new in the history of Christianity and nothing at all in the history of philosophy. But Kirkegaard did something else. He laid hold of one of those raw evidences that are both so obvious and so massive that nobody knows what to do with them, and he spent his whole life in both teaching it and preaching it. Kirkegaard was haunted by the conviction that, if religion, which is life, is in constant danger of degenerating into abstract speculation, the reason for it is that one of the standing aims of philosophy is to eliminate existence. The very origin of contemporary existentialism is there, and one might even wonder if pure existentialism did not cease to be immediately after the death of Kirkegaard.

His whole argumentation rests upon a fundamental distinction between two types of cognition: objective knowledge and subjective knowledge. I am afraid the words "subjective knowledge" are rather misleading, but, if we want to understand Kirkegaard, we must accept them without discussion and progressively grow used to their meaning. Objective knowledge is such knowledge as, once acquired, does not require any special effort of appropriation on the part of the knowing subject. It is called "objective," not only because it aims towards grasping objects, but also, and still more, because it deals with them in a perfectly objective way. It is "specular;" it simply mirrors them. A sure sign enables us to identify such knowledge, and it is that, once acquired, it does not require the slightest effort of appropriation on the side of the knowing subject. This does not mean that no man can feel a passion for objective knowledge. One can be a passionate mathe-

143

matician or a passionate logician as well as a passionate entomologist; but, once the passionately desired knowledge is there, it is known, and all there is to do about it is to know it. Even though its acquisition may have cost an infinite amount of toil, the problem of its appropriation does not even arise: the knowledge of objective truth is one with its possession, or, in other words, to achieve such knowledge is to achieve its appropriation.

Not so with subjective knowledge. Let us take for an instance the case of philosophy. Were we to believe Hegelians and, for that matter, professors of philosophy in general, all one has to do to know philosophy is to learn it or, supposing there be no satisfactory philosophy at hand, to provide oneself with a new set of philosophical conclusions. This is at least how it looks, but is it truly so? It was not so in ancient times, when, while walking along the streets in Greek or in Roman cities, you would from time to time meet some strange-looking man and say: "Here comes a philosopher," just as we say today, "Here come a clergyman or a priest." Such men did not dress like everybody else, because they were not like everybody else. What they wanted was actually *to be* philosophers, that is, to be "lovers of wisdom" and not merely knowers or teachers of wisdom. Now this does not mean merely that in order to be a philosopher one should not feel satisfied with knowing philosophy without also loving it; it means that a philosopher *is a lover*, and do we call a lover a man who knows everything about love, but *is not in love?* Love's knowledge and *to be in love* are one and the same thing; the knowledge of philosophy is to be a philosopher, just as Socrates was— Socrates who never wrote a thing in all his life, but who was the very love of wisdom walking around the streets and places of Athens; so also is the knowledge of Christianity, for, indeed, there is no other way to know what it is than to be a Christian. Subjective knowledge is knowledge whose acquisition is its active appropriation by the subject.

Why such a distinction? Because the very nature of knowable reality requires it. Mathematical truth or physical truth is wholly unrelated to my own *Ego*, so that I can achieve mathematical or physical knowledge without getting myself involved in the process of its acquisition. Let us go further. In a way, there can be such a thing as an objective knowledge of philosophy or even of religions, and, what with history of philosophy, speculative theology, biblical exegesis and general and comparative history of religions, we have plenty of it indeed! But there is a radical difference. To know mathematics or physics is to know mathematical or physical reality just as it is, whereas, objectively to know religion is not to know it as it is. For, what is religion, if it is not *to be religious?* Now, if religion is that, it cannot be known from merely looking at religious men, because to know it that way is to know it as it looks, but not as it is. In Kirkegaard's own words: "To speak objectively is always to speak of the thing; to speak subjectively is to speak of the subject and of subjectivity, and it so happens that here it is the subjectivity which is the thing."[60]

Let us try to render precise this important conclusion. What is it to be, not only a religious man, but a Christian? Christianity's own goal and solemn promise is to give each man eternal beatitude. It *is* both that promise and the way to fulfill it. Such a promise is for man of a literally "infinite" interest, and the only way for him to welcome it is to experience an "infinite passion" for it. In terms of the religious life, this means that the only answer a man can give to God's message is a passionate will to achieve his own salvation, that is, to achieve his own infinite beatitude. A half-hearted effort to such an end would be quite out of proportion with it; it would not at all be a will to that end; it would not be that will at all. On the other hand, if such a will actually arises in any man, it has to be the will to *his own* salvation, because what God has promised him actually is to save *him.* Whether or not he was aware of the fact, Kirkegaard himself was merely repeating Bernard of Clairvaux, when he said: "This problem concerns no one but me." And such indeed is the case, if the problem actually is to know how *I myself* can share in that beatitude which Christianity promises. True enough, the same problem arises for each and every man, so that for an infinite number of men its solution, which is Christianity itself, is bound to be the same, but this does not mean that there is a general solution to the problem. Quite the reverse. Out of its own nature, this is such a problem as requires to be solved, an infinite number of times, once at a time;[61] to solve it differently is not to solve it at all.

This is what Kirkegaard intends to convey when he describes subjective knowledge as a knowledge which, in order to be knowledge, requires from the knowing subject a personal appropriation. "When it comes to some observation for which the observer must needs be in a determined condition, it is true to say, is it not,

[60] Kirkegaard, *Post-Scriptum aux miettes philosophiques*, trans. by Paul Petit (Paris, Gallimard, 1941), pp. 9-10.
[61] *Ibid.* Hence Kirkegaard's personal interest in the Christian monk, pp. 213-214, 271 and 273-283. Whether he does it well or not, the Christian monk is at least trying *to be* a Christian.

145

that, unless he be in such a condition, he knows nothing at all?"[62] Now, should we take it literally, as indeed we should, such a position would raise a fascinating metaphysical problem, and it is for having raised it that Kirkegaard himself has unwittingly become the father of a large family of philosophical illegitimates, our own modern existentialists. In the case of Wolff and Hegel, we had ontologies without existence, but in Kirkegaard's own speculation we seem to be left with an existence without ontology, that is to say, without any speculative metaphysics of being. Kirkegaard himself was by no means involved in this problem, precisely because, to him at least, the harder you try objectively to know, the less subjectively you are. He was a pure existentialist for this very reason, that his whole philosophical message consisted in imparting to his contemporaries his deeply rooted conviction that there can be no such thing as an objective philosophy of existence. The very expression is self-contradictory. Kirkegaard had Hegel in mind when he said: "There can be a logical system, but there can be no system of existence;"[63] and again, for it is the same problem, can we use becoming as a basis, for logic, "although logic itself cannot account for becoming?"[64] Or, still more explicity: "Existence is in itself a system for God; but it cannot be a system for an existing mind. To be a system is to be something closed, while existence is just the opposite. From an abstract point of view, system and existence cannot be conceived together, because, in order to think existence, systematic thought has to think it, not as existing, but as abolished. Existence is that which plays the part of an interval, it is what keeps things apart; whereas, the systematic is the interlocking and the perfect fastening of things."[65] One could hardly say better, and, to anyone who feels interested in existence, all this comes as a godsend; but it certainly does raise an extremely interesting question, namely, is an existentialist philosophy *possible?* In other words, while contemporary existentialism seemingly carries Kirkegaard's own message, does it not actually betray it? The only thing a true existentialist should do is to become silent, in order the better to be, for, indeed, one ceases to be as soon as one begins talking about it.

Now, this is the very last thing you could guess from looking, not only at Hegel, but at professors of philosophy in general. The universe which they teach is not the one whence they draw salaries for teaching it. Old Socrates *had* no philosophy, he *was* it, but the professors *are* not their own philosophies, they just

[62] *Ibid.*, p. 50, note 1.   [63] *Ibid.*, p. 72.
[64] *Ibid.*, p. 73.   [65] *Ibid.*, p. 79.

have them. To express it in Kirkegaard's own words, such men are comical, two-in-one, twofold beings: "On the one hand, an eery being that lives in the realm of pure abstraction, and, on the other, the sometimes sad figure of a professor, who is set aside by that abstract being, as one puts a walking stick in a corner."[66] Yet, and this is perhaps the main point in Kirkegaard's own argumentation, they themselves have no right to do so, because, willy-nilly, these thinkers do themselves exist. However abstract his own thinking may be, the abstract thinker actually *is*. Hegel himself must have felt it, or else he would not have raised so vigorous a protest against abstract philosophical thinking. Yet, Hegel's own "concreteness" still remains pure abstraction. The German philosopher had seen a decisive token of the metaphysical genius which permeated his mother tongue in the fact that the same German verb *aufhehen* (to sublate) indifferently means "to suppress" or "to preserve." And this indeed had done wonders in Hegel's own philosophy, in which contradictories could always be both suppressed and saved by merely "sublating" them. But this in no way solves our own problem, nor that of Hegel. Abstract contradiction is none the less abstract for having been "sublated." If you turn actual existence into a problem of logic, you certainly will logicize existence, but you will not existentialize logic. What you will then have will be, precisely, logic such as Hegel himself understood it, namely, a perpetual overcoming of abstract contradictions. And indeed nothing is easier to achieve. In the order of pure abstraction, everything is given together, and there is no reason why one should choose. No room is left, there, for any "either—or," precisely because, there, nothing exists. In short, abstraction itself drives out actual contradiction. Thus, Hegel overcame contradiction so easily because there is no contradiction at all in the order of abstraction.[67] Existence and existence alone is a necessary prerequisite for actual contradiction.

When this point was reached, it became more and more evident that Kirkegaard himself could not be expected to bequeath to his successors what we would call a philosophy, but his message was to remain for philosophy as a thorn in the flesh. "It is true of existence as it is true of motion: they are very difficult to deal with. If I think them, I abolish them, so that I don't think them. It then might seem correct to say that there is something that does not bear being thought, and this is existence. But, then, the difficulty remains, that, since he who thinks also exists, existence is posited as soon as thinking itself is."[68] And this indeed was the

[66] *Ibid.*, pp. 201-202. [67] *Ibid.*, pp. 203-204. [68] *Ibid.*, p. 206.

147

problem of problems for philosophy, such as Kirkegaard himself understood it. The only question is, can that philosophical problem be solved by philosophy?

Let us look at it a bit more closely. Objective knowledge, as such, is wholly unrelated to either existence or time; it is therefore eternal, and the objective thinker *par excellence*, Spinoza, was quite right in asking us to envisage everything *sub specie aeternitatis*. Yet, the knowing subject is himself engaged in both existence and time, so that, in him, eternity co-exists with time, and abstraction with existence. Now, we may well suppose that, in God, the synthesis of eternity and of something like what we call existence is actually achieved. We also know that, in man himself, the co-presence of eternity and of existence can at least be observed; but, because God is eternal, whereas man himself is not, their co-existence alone is possible in man, their synthesis is not. Their co-existence, then, is a fact, and that fact is a bare paradox. It is indeed the very paradox which accounts for that other one, namely, that objective human knowledge never succeeds in grasping existence or, what amounts to the same, that existence always disappears as soon as objective knowledge is concerned. And nothing shows this better than the classical definition of true knowledge as an *adaequatio intellectus et rei*. An obviously correct formula, indeed, but only because it is a tautology. For such an adequation to be possible, existence has first to be left out, and, since what then remains is the thing minus the existence, it is a pure abstraction, that is, thought. Where thought and thing are the same, the adequation of intellect and thing merely expresses the adequation of abstract identity with itself,[69] which ultimately means the adequation of thought with thought. However we look at it, whether in man himself or in human knowledge, the paradox simply refuses to be eliminated.

The only thing for us to do, then, is to accept it for what it is, but also to accept all the consequences it entails with respect to real knowledge. And the very first one it entails is indeed an important one. If objective knowledge fails to grasp existing reality, we have no other choice than to resort to subjective knowledge. From this it follows that "only ethical and ethico-religious knowledge is real knowledge," because such knowledge is the only one which is essentially related to the fact that the knowing subject exists."[70] This proposition claims to be taken in its full force. What makes ethico-religious knowledge subjective, and consequently real, is neither that it enriches our objective

[69] *Ibid.*, p. 126.   [70] *Ibid.*, p. 131.

knowledge of ethico-religious objects, nor that it enables us indirectly to know such objects in their actual existence. The truth of ethico-religious knowledge lies in its very appropriation by the knowing subject. Let us suppose, for instance, a theologian saying or writing only true things about the true God; he can unfold his story indefinitely without approaching more closely to a real knowledge of God. Subjectively speaking, that is to say, speaking of actual truth, the knowledge of God appears at the very moment when, beginning to behave as though God really meant something to him, the knower enters into relationship with God. The truth of subjective knowledge thus lies in its very subjectivity. It does not aim to know the object as such, neither does it aim to know the objective truth about its object; nor does it even aim to know that that with which it establishes relations is true: in subjective knowledge the relationship itself *is* the truth, which means that the subject itself *is* the truth.[71] In short, if ethico-religious knowledge is the sole real knowledge, it is because in it truth is one with existence and existence with truth.

One could hardly wish for a knowledge more free from all admixture of objectivity, and after such a devastating criticism the magnificently ordered world of Hegelian essences is a wreck. But there is a heavy bill to pay. Perfectly safe in the possession of subjective existence, will Kirkegaard be able to reach another existence than his own? In other words, to what can we rightly ascribe existence outside the only being which we experience from within? If what is at stake is existence in general, that is to say, existence as conceived in an abstract and objective way, we can safely ascribe it to many and various beings; but such knowledge is nothing more than a knowledge of being in general, and since, because of its very generality, it disregards the concrete reality of those beings to which it is ascribed, such knowledge grasps being as a mere possible. And indeed the only real existence we can grasp in its very reality, that is, otherwise than through an objectifying knowledge, is our own existence. Kirkegaard never tires of repeating it: "All knowledge concerning reality is possibility; the only reality which an existing being can know otherwise than through some abstract knowledge is his own, namely, the fact that he exists, and this reality constitutes his absolute interest."[72] To avoid all possible misunderstanding, it may not be useless to make precise the fact that Kirkegaard is by no means going back to the *Cogito* of Descartes. Quite the reverse, for it is not true to say that, if I think, I am. According

[71] *Ibid.*, pp. 131-132   [72] *Ibid.*, p. 211.

149

to Kirkegaard, if I think, I am not. And how could it be other-wise? To think is to disregard existence; so much so, that did we quite succeed in thinking, we would at once cease to exist. It is true that I am thinking and that I know it with complete evidence, but I am grasping my thought in my existence, not my existence in my thought. As soon as I make the slightest mistake about it, I am bound to wonder, like Descartes: but what am I? which leads me to conclude that I am a "thinking thing." Pure objectivity is thus reached at once, and actual existence is lost from view. The truth of the matter is that I am, and also that I think, but I am not a "thinking thing." Rather, the paradox here is that, in spite of the fact that I am, I also think. But we know that the co-presence in him of both thought and of existence is the very paradox which, in point of fact, man is.

If we cannot reach reality through the abstract notion of existence, can we at least compare between themselves two or more actually existing subjects? Scarcely. Inasmuch as they are subjects, that is, existents, they are non-comparable. Here again any attempt to grasp through knowledge the actual reality of another man necessarily results in objectifying him and reducing him to the condition of a mere possible. "Each particular man is alone,"[73] Kirkegaard says. The only case in which another subject can be directly grasped in its subjectivity is religious faith. But this is precisely why faith, too, is a paradox. It is so, because its object is "the reality of another." And, when we say its reality, we mean that other *himself*, not what he teaches, for, even though he may be a teacher, faith is not faith in what he says, but faith in him. In other words, "the object of faith is the very reality of him who teaches, namely, that he really exists."[74] And this is why faith is such a paradox, even an in-finite paradox; it is that incredible thing: the knowledge, by an existing subject, of an existent other than the subject.

This is not the place to discuss the theology of Kirkegaard, whose criticism would no doubt entail another discussion, that of the doctrine of faith in the theology of Karl Barth. Let it suffice to mention here the deep influence exercised by the exist-ential dialectic of Kirkegaard on the development of modern Protestant theology. What this notion of faith reveals to us as philosophers is that no normal knowledge of a subject by another subject is possible in the doctrine of Kirkegaard. But, if we turn at last to our own selves, in which each of us is alone, what can we say of that existence which we are?

[73] *Ibid.*, p. 216.   [74] *Ibid.*, pp. 211-219.

It would be very foolish of us to expect from Kirkegaard any definition or description of "what" it is. All that he can tell us about it is what it does. And here is where the paradoxical nature of man needs to be taken into careful consideration. Eternity, on the one hand, and time, on the other hand, find themselves juxtaposed in the unity of a single being, but they are not really there side by side. Their relations are a constant interplay, or, perhaps, rather a constant interference. To be a being engaged in time is to be in the present moment, and present being is nothing else than existence. This is why all objective knowledge, which is eternal in its own right, cannot possibly be brought into relationship with actual existence. This is so true that we cannot even imagine to what kind of being that eternal knowledge, which is for us a mere possible, could belong as actual. All objective knowledge is spontaneously relegated into the past, as is done in history, or projected into the future, as is done in the previsions of science; or else it is supposed to float in that atemporal kingdom of abstractions in which the speculations of metaphysics move so easily and so freely. The only place in which no one ever dreams of locating it is in the present, precisely because time coincides with actual existence; and this should at least lead us to a determination of the function of existence.

A purely abstract thought would be that in which there is no thinking subject; it would therefore be a thought without existence. A pure existence, like that of stones, for instance, would be an existence in which there is no thought. But, since man himself both exists and thinks, his thought finds itself, as it were, in the midst of surroundings that are foreign to its own essence; but it would be just as true to say that, in man, existence is constantly aiming to join thought, whose very essence is equally foreign to its own. As a consequence, human beings are both pathetic and comic, at one and the same time. They are pathetic because, at the price of an infinite toil, they are constantly trying to turn eternity, which they can only know, into their own actual existence. And they are comic because the battle they are so bravely fighting is nevertheless a losing battle, since what they are trying to achieve is in itself a contradictory task.[76] The proper function of existence is to exclude man from eternity, by creating a constant rupture between himself and that eternal aspect under which he thinks all that he can intellectually conceive. If man were that eternity, he would not have existence, but being. He would not possess that reflection of eternity in him, which his objective knowledge

[76] *Ibid.*, pp. 60-61.

of truth is. Man would then actually be what he now only thinks. Such, precisely, is the case of God: "God does not think, He creates. God does not *exist*, He is eternal. But man both thinks and exists, and existence separates thinking from being by keeping them apart from each other in duration."[76]

This identification of existence as a permanent rupture of being has become, since Kirkegaard, the starting point of contemporary existentialism. It is a well-known fact that modern existentialism is not exactly a gay affair, but there is no reason why it should be. If to be an existent is to have existence, and if existence is but a constant failure to be, coupled with a perpetual and futile effort to overcome that failure, human life can scarcely be a pleasant thing. When today's existentialism scrutinizes existence, all it can find in it, as its very core, is that ceaseless tottering of all existents to their own fall and their equally ceaseless effort to bridge the ontological chasm which separates any two of their successive instants. In doctrines in which existence is but a lack of being, unless, in Jean-Paul Sartre's own words, it be a disease of being, it is no wonder that the realization of one's own actual existence is achieved either in "anguish" or in "nausea," unless it coincide with the realization of its own "absurdity," finally to end in despair.[77]

But one should not attempt to write contemporary history, even though there be much less novelty in it than those who make it seem to believe. What is much more important for our own problem is to realize the full meaning of Kirkegaard's philosophical message. Acutely conscious of the all-importance of existence, as opposed to the mere possibility of abstract essences, he has turned existence itself into a new essence, the essence of that which has no essence. All its determinations are negative, yet it behaves as a true essence precisely in this, that it obstinately refuses to communicate with anything else in order to save its own purity and to remain exclusively that which it is. It is *not* possibility, but actual existence. It is *not* objective reality, but what cannot be expressed in terms of objective reality. It is *not* knowable from without, and it can *not* be known from without, but it can at least know itself, and, when it does so, what existence

---

[76] *Ibid.*, p. 222.

[77] These remarks do not apply to existentialism as such, but only to the illusions which it too often entertains concerning its value as a possible substitute for metaphysics. The proper task of existentialism is to work out a "phenomenology of existence," a task which it does very well indeed when, leaving pseudo-metaphysics aside, it addresses itself to it.

discovers in itself, as the ultimate ground, is that it is in itself a radical lack of being.

There is no inconsistency in such an undertaking—quite the reverse—and Kirkegaard has cleverly used his exceptional mastery of dialectic to lead his own thought to its normal conclusion. But we should not mistake the meaning of its work. It was, before anything else, the exasperated protest of a religious conscience against the centuries-old suppression of existence by abstract philosophical thinking. But it was the protest of existence against philosophy, not an effort to reopen philosophy to existence. Indeed, the deepest import of Kirkegaard's message was that, if existence is the only actual reality which man can grasp, and the only one that matters to him because it is the only one he has, then man's only business is to exist, and not philosophize. In so far as philosophy is objective knowledge, there should be no philosophy at all, and, less than any other, should there be such a monstrosity as a "philosophy of existence." Thus, after innumerable metaphysics of being in which no provision was made for actual existence, existence itself finds nothing better to do than to break away from being. It was exactly the same thing as breaking away from philosophy, and, if Kirkegaard himself has made this so clear, it is because this twofold result was exactly the task he had undertaken to achieve. If philosophy has no use for existence, why should existence have any use for philosophy? The divorce between existence and philosophy is then both open and absolute. But the main responsibility for it lies, not with Kirkegaard, but with that abstract speculation about possible essences which has so obstinately refused to unite essence and existence in the unity of being.

Chapter V
Being and Existence

IT MAY seem strange, and almost preposterous, to look back to the thirteenth century for a complete metaphysical interpretation of being, according to which neither essence nor existence is considered as irrelevant to it. Yet, such a return is unavoidable, since all other philosophies have advocated either a metaphysics of being minus existence, or a phenomenology of existence minus being. On the other hand, at least in the present state of historical knowledge, it would be vain for us to go farther back into the past than the time of Thomas Aquinas, because nobody that we know of has cared to posit existence *in* being, as a constituent element *of* being. And it would be no less vain to look in the more immediate past for a more modern expression of the same truth, because, paradoxically enough, what was perhaps deepest in the philosophical message of Thomas Aquinas seems to have remained practically forgotten since the very time of his death.

The better to recapture his message, we must first consider the essential transformation which the Aristotelian notion of metaphysics underwent in Thomas Aquinas' own doctrine.

For Aristotle, metaphysics was that science whose proper subject was being *qua* being.[1] Now, to know being as such may mean three somewhat different things: first, the abstract notion of being, conceived both in itself and with its inherent properties, such as, for instance, self-identity and resistance to contradiction. Thus understood, being would be what will be called by later Aristotelians the formal object of metaphysics. Next, metaphysics may deal with those beings which can truly be said to be because their being actually answers to the true definition of being. Such is, for instance, the First Act, as well as the other Pure Acts which we call gods. In this second sense, the science of being is Divinity, that is, theology.[2] In a third sense, inasmuch as it is a science,

---

[1] Aristotle, *Metaphysics*, K, 3, 1060 b 31, and Γ, 1, 1003 a 21-31.
[2] Aristotle, *Metaphysics*, E, 1, 1026 a 6-32; as such, metaphysics is the science of the ὀυσία ἀκίνητος, *op. cit.*, E, 1, 1026 a 29-30. Cf. *op. cit.*, K, 7, 1064 b 6-14.

154

metaphysics has to know its subject through its cause, and, since the subject at hand, namely, being, is the first of all subjects, metaphysics has to know everything that is through its first causes. As a commentator of Aristotle, Thomas Aquinas does little more than repeat Aristotle on this point, except that he clears up what was obscure in his text and puts some order into this complex problem.[3] True enough, the very order which he puts into it is not without significance from the point of view of his own thought; yet, had we nothing else to rely on than his Commentary on the *Metaphysics* of Aristotle, we would be reduced to conjectures concerning his own position on the question.[4]

The problem here is to know if those various determinations of the subject of metaphysics can be reduced to unity. And it is a very important problem indeed, for, if metaphysics is concerned with three different subjects, it is not a science, but a name for three distinct sciences, each of which has to deal with a different subject. True enough, those three subjects are all related to being and, to the whole extent to which they are, they are one. But to what extent are they?

In order to simplify the problem, let us leave aside the consideration of being in general as the "formal object" of a possible metaphysics. Although many things which have been said by Aristotle may bear such an interpretation of his thought, he himself has certainly not reduced the highest of all sciences to the abstract knowledge of a merely formal object. Nor, for that matter, has Thomas Aquinas himself ever done anything like it. We then find ourselves confronted with two possible points of view on being, that of the supreme beings, and that of the first causes of being. Obviously, if the supreme beings are the first causes of all that is, there is no problem. In such a case, the knowledge of the absolutely first being is one with that of the absolutely first cause. But it is not so in the metaphysics of Aristotle. It is not so and it cannot be, for the decisive reason which follows.

It is true that Aristotle himself had called metaphysics a "divine science,"[5] because, if there is a science which deals with things divine, it is metaphysics. It is also true that Aristotle has said that supreme beatitude lies for man in the contemplation of divine things,[6] but he does not seem to have inferred from these two propositions what anybody would hold as their necessary

[3] Thomas Aquinas, *In Metaph. Arist.*, Prooemium, ed. Cathala, p. 2.
[4] *Ibid.*
[5] Aristotle, *Metaphysics*, A, 2, 983 a 6-11.
[6] Aristotle, *Eth. Nic.*, X., 10.

155

consequence, namely, that, as a science of being *qua* being, metaphysics is wholly ordered to the knowledge of the first cause of being. And he could not well say it, because the very notion of a cause which is absolutely first in all the departments of being was lacking in his doctrine, or, at any rate, was absent from it.

In one of the very texts quoted by Thomas Aquinas in support of his own position, Aristotle had said this: "It is therefore manifest that the science here to be gained [namely, metaphysics] is that of the first causes, since we say of each thing that we know it only when we think that we know its first cause." Whereupon, Aristotle immediately proceeds to add: "Now, causes are said to be in a fourfold way."[7] And, indeed, among the celebrated four Aristotelian causes, there is at least one, namely, the material cause, which cannot possibly be reduced to the other three. That which is a "formal" cause can also be a "final" cause and, in its capacity as "final" cause, it can likewise be held as a "moving" cause, but it cannot well be that and, at the same time, be matter. Whence it follows that, in its own way, matter itself is a first cause in the metaphysics of Aristotle. It is so because it enters the structure of material substances as one of their irreducible constituent elements. Now, if it is so, you cannot say that metaphysics is both the science of true beings and the science of all beings through their causes, for there is at least one cause, that is, matter, which does not truly deserve the title of being. In short, because the God of Aristotle is one of the causes and one of the principles of all things,[8] but not *the* cause nor *the* principle of all things, there remains in the Aristotelian domain of being something which the God of Aristotle does not account for, which is matter, and for this reason the metaphysics of Aristotle cannot be reduced to unqualified unity.

The answer is quite clear in the doctrine of Thomas Aquinas, in which God is the cause of all that is, including even matter. The doctrine of creation is bound to modify the notion of metaphysics itself, in that it introduces into the realm of being a first cause to whose causality everything is strictly subjected. This is why, in his *Contra Gentiles*, in which he does not speak as a commentator of Aristotle, but in his own name, Thomas Aquinas can take over the very formulas of Aristotle, yet give them a distinctly new turn. For it still remains true to say that perfect knowledge is knowledge through causes, but metaphysical knowledge no longer is sufficiently defined as the science of being through

---

[7] Aristotle, *Metaphysics*, A, 3, 983 a 24-27.
[8] *Ibid.*, A, 2, 983, a 8-9.

its first causes; what metaphysics really is, is the science of being through its first "cause."

This is why, in Thomas Aquinas' own doctrine, inasmuch as he wants to know reality through its first cause, since God is that first cause, man naturally desires, as his ultimate end, to know God. Aristotle therefore was speaking better than he knew, when he said that metaphysics truly deserves the name of "divine science," for what it ultimately aims to achieve is to know God: the ultimate end of metaphysics is the same as the ultimate end of man. What deeply alters the Aristotelian notion of metaphysics in the doctrine of Thomas Aquinas is the presence, above natural theology, of a higher theology, which is the science of God as known through revelation. The very fact that the absolutely highest of all human sciences, namely, revealed theology, is in itself a knowledge of God, makes it impossible for us to define metaphysics as the science of being *qua* being, *and* the science of beings as known through their first causes, *and* the knowledge which man may have of the gods. Metaphysics, then, necessarily becomes that science which is the science of being both in itself and in its first cause, because it is the science of God as knowable to natural reason. This inner reordering of metaphysics by the final causality of its ultimate object confers upon the diversity of its aspects an organic unity. The science of being *qua* being passes into the science of the first causes, which itself passes into the science of the first cause, because God is, at one and the same time, both the First Cause and being *qua* being. This inner ordering is what Thomas Aquinas suggests when he says: "Prime philosophy itself is wholly directed towards the knowledge of God as towards its ultimate end; wherefore it is called divine science: *Ipsaque prima philosophia tota ordinatur ad Dei. cognitionem sicut ad ultimum finem, unde et scientia divina nominatur."* [9] By tearing ontology apart from natural theology Wolff was later to wreck that organic unity of metaphysics, and, if there is any consistency in the thought of both Thomas Aquinas and Wolff, this radical difference between their two notions of metaphysics should be to us a safe indication that there is a radical difference between their two conceptions of being.

What is being, according to Thomas Aquinas? In a first sense, it is what Aristotle had said it was, namely, substance. For, indeed,

[9] *Ibid.* On the distinction between natural theology, in which God is considered as cause of the subject of metaphysics (*viz.*, being), and revealed theology (*viz.*, Scripture), in which God Himself is the very subject of that science, see *In Boethium de Trinitate*, V, 4, Resp., ed. by P. Wyser (Fribourg, 1948), p. 48, ll. 28-33.

157

it is true that being is substance, although it may also be true that being entails something more, over and above mere substantiality. In other words, it may be that Aristotle has left something out while describing being, but what he has seen there, is there. The presence, in Thomism, of an Aristotelian level on which being is conceived as identical with οὐσία, is beyond doubt, and, because Aristotle is in Thomas Aquinas, there always is for his readers a temptation to reduce him to Aristotle. Texts without number could be quoted in support of such an interpretation, and there is no need to distort them in order to support it. All there is to do is to leave out all the other texts, a process, which, in fact, has never ceased among generation after generation of his interpreters.

For those who identify what Thomas calls being with what is commonly called substance, there can be no distinction between essence and existence, since being and οὐσία are one and the same thing. Each time Thomas Aquinas himself is looking at being as at a substance, he thereby reoccupies the position of Aristotle, and it is no wonder that, in such cases, the distinction between essence and existence does not occur to his own mind.

Such is eminently the case of a famous text which can be read in Thomas Aquinas' commentary on the *Metaphysics* of Aristotle, and nothing could be more natural. If there is a moment when the thought of Thomas Aquinas is bound almost to coincide with pure Aristotelianism, it normally should be while he is explaining Aristotle's own thought.

The text at stake is a passage of *Metaphysics*, Book IV, Chapter 2, which we have already met with, while dealing with Aristotle himself. In the short Chapter 1, Aristotle has just said that there is a science which deals with being *qua* being (τὸ ὄν ᾗ ὄν) as well as with what belongs to it inasmuch as it is being. In Chapter 2, he will inquire into the meaning of the word "being." According to him, being is said in several different ways, but always in relation to one and the same fundamental reality, which is οὐσία. Certain things are called "beings" because they themselves are "substances" (or realities = οὐσίαι); others, because they are properties of some substance, and others because they beget some substance or else destroy it. If, therefore, there is a science of all that which deserves the title of "being," it is because all that which receives that name, receives it because of its relation to reality (οὐσία). Reality, then, along with οὐσία, its principles and its causes, is the proper object of the science of being. Moreover, since it deals with being, that science must deal with all its aspects, especially with "oneness," for, "to be" and to be "one" are one and the same thing (ταὐτὸ καὶ μία φύσις); which leads us to the conclusion that οὐσία (reality or substance), *being* and *one* are equivalent terms. Hence the oft-quoted formula which we have already mentioned: "A man," "being man," and "man" are the same thing. For, indeed, the reality signified by those various formulas is the same: "Just as the reality (or substance = οὐσία) of each thing is one, and is not so by accident, so also it is some being (ὅπερ ὄν τι)." The intention of Aristotle in this passage is therefore clear: Metaphysics shall deal with "oneness," as it deals with "being," because oneness and being are simply two other names for reality (οὐσία) which both *is*, and is one in its own right. If there is a doctrine of the identity of being and substance, this is one, and Averroes was well founded in thinking that he was vindicating the authentic thought of Aristotle when he criticized Avicenna for teaching that existence was to the essence of reality, if not exactly an accident, at least a happening.

Confronted with such a text, what is Thomas Aquinas going to do? Under the circumstances a commentator, he will just say what that text means, and he will do it with the less scruple as, within its Aristotelian limits, that text is absolutely right. First of all, what it says about "being" and "oneness" is true from the point of view of Thomas Aquinas himself: "*One* and *being* signify a single nature as known in different ways." It is also true concerning the relation of essence (οὐσία) to existence itself, for, indeed, to beget a man is to beget an existing man, and for an existing man to die is precisely to lose his actual existence. Now, things that are begotten or destroyed together are one. Essence then is one with its own existence. These various words, "man," "thing," "being" (*ens*) and "one" designate various ways of looking at determinations of reality which always appear or disappear together. The same reality, therefore, is a "thing" because of the fact that it has a quiddity or essence; it is a "man" because of the fact that the essence it has is that of man; it is "one" because of its inner undividedness; last but not least, it is a "being" in virtue of the act whereby it exists (*nomen ens imponitur ab actu essendi*). To conclude, these three terms, *thing*, *being* and *one*, signify absolutely the same thing, but they signify it through different notions.[10]

The solid block of Aristotle's substance is here to be found in its perfect integrity, and Thomas Aquinas will never attempt

---

[10] Aristotle, *Metaphysics*, Γ, 2, 1003 a 33-1004 a 9, and Thomas Aquinas, *In Metaph.*, lib. IV, lect. 2.

to break it up. Yet, it would be a serious mistake to infer from such a text that, even while commenting upon Aristotle, he had forgotten his own distinction between essence and existence. At any rate, his own notion of existence is there, and it makes itself felt at the very moment when Thomas reminds us that the noun "being" is derived from the verb "to be," which means the very act of existing. But that was not the occasion for him to apply the distinction of essence and existence, because, if, in a being, its "to be" is other than its "essence," the very thing which arises from the composition of its "to be" with its essence is in no way distinct from its intrinsic oneness or from its being. In other words, the Aristotelian substance remains intact in the doctine of Thomas Aquinas.

Yet, the Aristotelian substance cannot enter the world of St. Thomas Aquinas without at the same time entering a Christian world; and this means that it will have to undergo many inner transformations in order to become a created substance. In the world of Aristotle, the existence of substances is no problem. To be and to be a substance are one and the same thing, so much so that no question can be asked as to the origin of the world, any more than any question can be asked about its end. In short, Aristotelian substances exist in their own right. Not so in the Christian world of Thomas Aquinas, in which substances do not exist in their own right. And this difference between these two worlds should be understood as both radical and total. The world of Aristotle is not a world which its philosopher has neglected to conceive as a created one. Because the acme of reality is substance and, in substance itself, essence, Aristotelian being is one with its own necessity. Such as its philosopher has conceived it, *it cannot possibly not exist.* On the contrary, the created world of Thomistic substances is radically contingent in its very existence, because it might never have existed. And it is not only radically contingent, but it is totally so. Even while it is actually existing in virtue of its first cause, it remains true to say that it might at any time cease to exist. But we are not yet saying enough, for, even though it were demonstratively proven that this created world is destined always to exist, it still would remain a permanently contingent world. Unless one understands this, one will never understand why the problem of the eternity of the world appeared to Thomas Aquinas as philosophically indifferent. I do not think I am betraying him if I say that, had he not learned to the contrary from divine revelation, Thomas Aquinas would have found it quite natural to think of the world as being now as it always was and always will be, world forever, because, were it so, such an absolutely eternal world would still remain an eternally contingent world whose actual existence still would remain an eternal gratuity.

In his *Summa Theologica*, Thomas Aquinas has expressed his view on this fundamental point by means of an example which, though it is itself out of date, says it as forcefully as possible. In the physics of Aristotle, the diaphanous media, such as air or water, for instance, are the receiving subjects of light. Now, while light permeates such subjects completely, it never mixes with them. Light is in them, but it does not belong to them, and this is so true that, as soon as light ceases to shine, diaphanous subjects at once fall back into that nothingness of light which we call darkness. It is not so with all physical energies. For instance, when fire warms a certain quantity of water, that water actually assimilates warmth, so that it keeps warm, at least for some time, after being withdrawn from fire. On the contrary, that same water does not assimilate light as it does warmth, nor, for that matter, does air. Air may become bright, but it never shines as does the sun, which is the source of light, and this is why, as soon as the sun is hidden, everything grows dark. Now, it is in such guise that God is cause of existence. Just as the sun is not cause of light in *fieri*, but in *esse*, so God does not render things able to be, He makes them be. In other words, God does not grant things an existence which they could keep, be it only for one moment, if He suddenly ceased to give it. "Because," Thomas says, "[light] is not rooted in air, it ceases with the action of the sun: *quia non habet radicem in aere, statim cessat lumen, cessante actione solis;*" and "All creatures are to God as air is to the sun which makes it bright: *sic autem se habet omnis creatura ad Deum, sicut aer ad solem illuminantem.*"[11] It would be difficult indeed to find stronger expressions: existence has no root in even actually existing things. In short, whereas the substance of Aristotle exists *qua* substance, existence never is of the essence of any substance in the created world of Thomas Aquinas.

Nothing looks more precarious than a thus-conceived world, in which no essence can ever *be* its own act of existing, yet the world of Thomas Aquinas is made by God to wear as long as that of Aristotle, that is, never to wear away. Why is it so? This is, I think, one of the most difficult points to grasp in the whole metaphysics of Thomas Aquinas, because we are here invited to con-

---

[11] Thomas Aquinas, *Summa Theologica*, I, 104, 1, Resp. Cf. *In II de Anima*, lib. II, lect. 14, ed. by Pirotta, n. 403-421.

ceive creatures as being, at one and the same time, indestructible in themselves, yet wholly contingent in their relation to God.

If we look at the world of creatures from the point of view of its existence, then it is true to say that it has no existence of its own. Existence is *in* it, just as light is in the air at noon, but the existence of the world never is *its* existence; so that, in so far, at least, as the world itself is concerned, it can lose existence at a moment's notice, or, rather, without previous notice. On the other hand, if we look at this existing world from the point of view of its substance, there are aspects in it that tally with such a view, but there are others that do not. We all are but too familiar with the sight of death, and, because we know that there is at least one death that lies in store for each of us, we easily realize the precariousness of existence in existing things. All is vanity and vexation of spirit. Yet, at the very same time, poets, at least, are fully aware of the scandalous indifference of Nature to the precariousness of human existence—a too easily explainable indifference indeed, since men pass away while nature itself does not pass away. And science is here of one mind with poetry, just as science itself is of one mind with Aristotle's metaphysics in so far, at least, as existence is concerned. For this world is, if not *such as* it was, at least *as* it was, and now is and ever will be a world forever. And the created world of Thomas Aquinas is just like that, because it is a world of Aristotelian substances which *are* in their own right. It is both a substantially eternal and an existentially contingent world.

What makes it hard for us to reconcile both points of view is but an illusion. Exactly, it is the common illusion that corruptibility is of the essence of temporal beings. In fact, it is not so. Corruptibility is of the essence of substantially composite beings, because their very composition entails a possibility of decomposition and thus makes them to be corruptible. Such, for instance, is the union of form and matter in plants, in animals, in man. But, even in such composite beings, their constituent elements themselves are simple, and consequently they are indestructible. When a man dies, his "body" at once begins to decay and soon becomes that "I know not what," for which, as Bossuet says, there is no name in any language. Yes, indeed, the "body" passes away, but the very matter of that body does not pass away, because, as a first principle, matter is both simple and incorruptible. And, for the very same reason, the soul of that body does not pass away, because, inasmuch as it is a spiritual substance, it also is both simple and incorruptible. This is the very reason why, in Thomas Aquinas' philosophy, the immortality of the human soul is an immediate evidence. It stands in no need of being proven. If anything had to be proven about it, it would rather be that the human soul is *not* immortal, and one does not see how such a proof could possibly be formulated. Inasmuch as it is pure form, the human soul *is* in its own right. It is as any subsisting form is, since, in order to cease being, it would have to cease being a form.[12] In other words, if God creates a circle, He has to make it round, and the roundness of that circle is inseparable from it. So, also, if God creates a human soul, He creates a "being," and, since it is a simple spiritual form, there is in it no occasion for decomposition to creep in. In so far, at least, as its *substance* is concerned, such a soul cannot lose its existence.[13] True enough, existence could be taken away from it, but of itself it cannot lose it. Man can kill himself, because he can separate his soul from his body, but there are two things he cannot kill, the matter of his body and his soul.

This sharp contrast between the point of view of existence and that of substance is thrown into relief by the very order of demonstration in the *Contra Gentiles*, in which, after proving, in II, 54, that "the composition of substance and existence is not the same as that of matter and form," Thomas Aquinas at once proceeds to prove, in the very next chapter, that "intellectual substances are incorruptible." And both statements are true, for even simple substances could be existentially destroyed, but they cannot become substantially corrupted.

To be sure, readers of Thomas Aquinas sometimes wonder how this can be. How is it that those very substances in which existence never takes root can nevertheless be everlasting in their own right? If, from moment to moment, they may cease to be, why should we say that they never will cease to be? But this is the very illusion we should get rid of if we want to understand the meaning of this doctrine. Even simple forms are engaged in time, if they are forms of a matter which they do not fully actualize. The more fully to actualize it, they operate, they change and they endure in time. Such is their life, made up of so much give and take that they require a lot of endurance to endure, and, when they have no more, they die. Man is not everlasting, precisely because to be is for him to last, but there are two things in him that are everlasting, precisely because, taken in themselves, they do not *last*, they *are*: the matter of his body and his soul. Engaged

[12] Thomas Aquinas, *Qu. disp. de Anima*, art. 14, Resp.
[13] Thomas Aquinas, *Sum. Theol.*, I, 50, 5, Resp. and I, 75, 6, Resp.

163

in time through its operation, the human soul transcends time by the very simplicity of its being. The soul does not enjoy being a moment at a time. Its duration is not a chain of instantaneous acts of existing, each of which has to bridge an infinitesimal gap of nothingness. The being of true substance is whole, and, because it is such out of its own nature, it is not such a gift as stands in need of being renewed from moment to moment. God is not eternally busy retailing existence to beings, nor are substances applying for it from moment to moment. The gift of existence is irrevocable, when it is granted to beings which, as regards themselves, are unable to lose it.

Thus, God is perfectly free not to create substances, and He remains perfectly free to annihilate them after creating them, but that is God's own business; and if we look at substances themselves, or at least at simple substances, there is in them no reason why they should perish. On the contrary, no special act is required on the part of God to keep them in existence; God has not to re-create from moment to moment what has, out of itself, no moments; one and the same continued act of creation, that is, a non-lasting act of creation, is enough to keep them existing. As Thomas Aquinas himself forcefully says, concerning immaterial substances, since they are immaterial: "There is in them no potency towards non-being: *in eis non est potentia ad non esse.*" But, you will say, God still can destroy them, and, since their own existence has no roots in those substances, nothing can be more precarious than their very being. Not so in the mind of Thomas Aquinas, because, if you look at simple substances such as they actually are, it is obvious that they are made to endure. There is no more potency to non-being in a substance than there is potency to non-roundness in a circle, which entails for us the obligation literally to accept Thomas Aquinas' astounding statement about created beings in general: "The natures of creatures point out the fact that none of them shall be reduced into nothingness: *creaturarum naturae hoc demonstravit ut nulla earum in nihilum redigatur.*"[14] And indeed men do die, but they are not reduced to nothingness, for the very matter of their bodies still remains, already entering the composition of some new substance, and, as to their souls, they go on subsisting in themselves, and will go on doing it indefinitely.

We now find ourselves in a position accurately and technically to describe the relation of actual existence to God in the world of Thomas Aquinas. There is, *for* all creatures, a possibility not to be or, as Thomas himself says it, a potency to non-being (*potentia*

[14] *Ibid.*, I, 104, 4, Resp. and ad 1 m.

164

ad non esse), but that possibility is not *in* them. At least there is no such thing in simple substances. In composite substances, yes; in simple substances, no. A composite substance, precisely in as much as it is composite, is indeed corruptible, but it is not so because God could annihilate it; it is so because, out of itself, any composition entails the possibility of its own decomposition.[15] On the contrary, when taken in itself, form as such is fully entitled to its own being, or, should we prefer to say it the other way around, being, of its very nature, belongs to form: *esse secundum se competit formae*.[16] All that we now have to do is to bring both aspects of created being together, that of its efficient cause, which is God, and that of its formal or material causes, which are matter and form. To do so will be nothing else than to bring together the two orders of existence and of substance. Existence is not what makes things to be either corruptible or incorruptible; it is what makes them to be corruptible or incorruptible existents; on the other hand, substance is not what makes things to exist, it is what makes them to exist either incorruptibly (if it is simple) or else corruptibly (if it is composite). Consequently, the efficient cause for actual existence is and always remains outside actually existing substances, either corruptible or incorruptible; but the formal cause whereby this substance exists in an incorruptible way while that substance exists in a corruptible way rests with the substance itself, as being bound up with the definite nature of its substantiality. Thus, since the power which God has to annihilate anything is not what makes corruptible things to be corruptible, it does not, either, deprive incorruptible things of their corruptibility. "Corruptible" and "incorruptible" are *essential* predicates, because they follow essence itself taken as a formal or as a material principle,[17] and this is why the world of Thomas Aquinas can be both incorruptible like the world of Aristotle, yet, absolutely speaking, destructible by the will of God. True enough, the annihilation of the world remains in itself possible, but for it to happen would take just as ineffable a marvel as its creation once was. And an almost scandalous marvel to boot, since it would mean that *incorruptible* substances have been created in order to be, not at all corrupted, for, indeed, corrupted they cannot be, but annihilated. This is exactly what Thomas Aquinas meant when we heard him say that the natures of creatures *demonstrant*, that is, point out, that no one of them shall ever be reduced to nothingness. To conclude: "To be" belongs

---

[15] *Ibid.*, I, 50, 5, ad 3[m].   [16] *Ibid.*, Resp.
[17] *Qu. disp. de Anima*, art. 14, ad 5[m].

by itself to the forms of creatures, supposing, however, the influx
of God. Hence, potency to non-being (that is, the possibility not
to exist), in spiritual creatures as well as in heavenly bodies, lies
more in God, Who can subtract His influx, than it is in the form
or in the matter of such creatures: *"Esse per se consequitur formam
creaturae, supposito tamen influxu Dei, sicut lumen sequitur diaphanum aëris, supposito influxu solis. Unde potentia ad non esse
in spiritualibus creaturis et corporibus caelestibus magis est in
Deo, qui potest subtrahere suum influxum, quam in forma vel materia
talium creaturarum."*[18]

Such is the way the world of Aristotle can enter the Christian
world of Thomas Aquinas, but there remains now for us to see
that, while it enters it whole, it also becomes wholly different.
The world of Aristotle is there whole in so far as reality is substance. It is the world of science, eternal, self-subsistent and such
that no problem concerning existence needs nor can be asked
about it. It is one and the same thing for a man in it to be "man,"
to be "one" and "to be." But, while keeping whole the world
of Aristotle, Thomas Aquinas realizes that such a world cannot
possibly be "metaphysical." Quite the reverse, it is the straight
"physical" world of natural science, in which "natures" necessarily
entail their own existence; and, even though such natures may
happen to be gods, or even the supreme God, they still remain
natures. Physics is that very order of substantial reality in which
existence is taken for granted. As soon as existence no longer
is taken for granted, metaphysics begins. In other words, Thomas
Aquinas is here moving the whole body of metaphysics to an
entirely new ground. In the philosophy of Aristotle, physics was
in charge of dealing with all "natures," that is, with those beings
that have in themselves the principle of their own change and of
their own operations; as to those true beings which are unchangeable, they make up the order of metaphysics, in virtue of their
own unchangeability. In the new philosophy of Thomas Aquinas,
even unchangeable beings still remain natures, so that their
handling falls within the scope of the philosophy of nature. Some
of his readers sometimes wonder at the constant readiness of the
"Angelic Doctor" to thrust angels into the very middle of his
discussions concerning man or any other natural beings. Then
they say that, of course, it helps him, because angels provide
such convenient examples and means of comparison. In point of
fact, if Thomas Aquinas is so familiar with angels, it is because
to him they are just as "natural" beings as men themselves are,

[18] *Sum. Theol.*, I, 104, 1 ad 1ᵐ. Cf. *De Potentia*, q. 5, art. 1.

only they are better natural beings. With Thomas Aquinas, the supernatural does not begin with a certain class of substances. Precisely because composite substances are natures, only that which is beyond such substances can be said to be *supernatural*. But, even within these composite substances, where the physical ends, the metaphysical begins, and, since there is nothing else beyond nature than its own existence, metaphysics begins with the consideration of existence. In short, Thomistic metaphysics is existential in its own right.

Yet, Thomistic philosophy is no existentialism, at least as the word is now understood, unless one prefers to say that it is existentialism as it should be understood. The crucial problem which has always worried the mind of Kirkegaard (how is it that, in man, existence is to be seen side by side with eternity?) is here meeting at last the sole principle which can lead to its solution. The error of Kirkegaard, as well as of all his modern followers, has been to mistake existence in time for existence as such. For, to endure in time is indeed to exist, and temporal existence is for us the more manifest mode of existence, but man does not exist in time only, he also transcends time inasmuch, at least, as he is, right now, communicating with his own eternity. He does so inasmuch as he is an intellectual substance which, as such, transcends both matter and mortality. And this is why there is nothing scandalous, or even paradoxical, in the fact that, although he is engaged in temporal existence, man naturally deals with eternal things, such as objective truth, objective goodness and objective beauty. For, indeed, such objects owe their very eternity to that of forever enduring subjects, of which man himself is one. Not eternity, but time, is the problem, since time is what ceaselessly interrupts man's own eternity. And here, at least, many of the great philosophers we could consult would be of one mind: from Plato to Aristotle, and to Kirkegaard himself, man's main business in life is to see to it that there be no such thing as lost time, and to use passing time itself as a means to achieve one's own eternity. That end is in sight for each of us, not at all when we wish, with Faust, for one exceptionally beautiful moment to stop, but when we can say with Rimbaud, be it for a split second: "Elle est arrivée. Quoi? L'éternité."[19]

But why should we quote modern poets? Thomas Aquinas himself used to resort to another and much older poetry which still remains the most beautiful there ever was, that of Scripture.

[19] "It is come. What? Eternity," in A. Rimbaud, *Eternité*, and quoted later in *Une saison en Enfer*.

For it is written in *Ecclesiastes*, III, 14: "I have learned that all
the works which God hath made, continue forever." If it is true
that all the works of God are there to stay, then each of us is
already in the very midst of his eternity, surrounded on all sides
by beings no less eternal than he himself is. The current view
of the world as of a realm of progressively decaying and wearing
away beings expresses just the reverse of what reality actually is.
It betrays reality at least in so far as actual being entails actual
existence, for, indeed, not to pass away, but to be for ever and
ever, that is what it is to exist.

The technical result of the Thomistic reformation of metaphysics has been a twofold one. First, it has brought about a
clear realization of the specific nature of efficient causality. It is
not easy to find a clear-cut notion of the efficient cause in Aristotle's
philosophy, save only where he deals with problems related to the
making of objects by human artisans. He knows very well what
it is "to make" artificial things, but he does not seem to think
that their very being stands in need of being either produced or
made. Such beings appear to him as so many terms of certain
motions, whose final causes they are. Of course, there is a cause
for each motion, and it is one of the four kinds of natural causes,
but Aristotle does not consider it as the cause of the existence of
that motion. Indeed, how could he, since motion never begins
nor ceases? He merely sees it as the "origin" of this and that
particular motion. Universal motion is, so to speak, constantly
relayed from being to being, so that each particular nature becomes
the starting point of particular motions which, in their turn, result
in particular beings.[20] On the contrary, in Thomas Aquinas'
aetiology, the Aristotelian "moving causes" (τὰ κινοῦντα αἴτια)
become so many "efficient causes," so that, even when that which
a cause produces is motion, it actually makes it to be. In such
cases, to move truly is to display an efficient causality, whose
effect is motion.

The second consequence of the Thomistic reform of metaphysics has been to introduce a clear-cut distinction between the
two orders of formal causality and of efficient causality. Formal
causality is that which makes things to be *what* they are, and,
in a way, it also makes them to be, since, in order to be, each and
every being has to be a *what*. But formal causality dominates the
whole realm of substance, and its proper effect is substantiality,
whereas efficient causality is something quite different. It does

[20] Aristotle, *Metaphysics*, Λ, 3, 1070 a 21. Cf. B, 2, 996 b 22-23, and Z, 7,
1032 b 21-22.

not make beings to be what they are, it makes them "to be." Now the relations of these two distinct types of causality are as follows. First, they cannot be deduced from each other: from the fact that a thing is, no conclusion can be drawn as to what it is, just as, conversely, from our knowledge of what a thing is, no inference as to its actual existence can be correctly deduced. Any such attempts are bound to result in so many failures, even if they are made on the notion of God; whence it appears that they must still more necessarily fail, if they are tried on the notion of any contingent being. On the other hand, Thomas Aquinas maintains the Aristotelian principle that causes which belong in distinct orders of causality can exert reciprocal causality. In this case, efficient causality can give existential being to substance, just as, conversely, formal causality can impart substantial being to actual existence. Where there is no existence, there is no substance, but, where there is no substance, there is no existence. It is then literally true to say that existence is a consequence which follows from the form of essence, but not as an effect follows from the efficient cause.[21] Let us here return to an example which Thomas Aquinas has already used. No one doubts that light is the cause of brightness in air, yet, in its turn, the diaphaneity of air causes the existence of that very light in air (causa essendi), since it enables light to be there by enabling air to receive light. So, also, by constituting substances, the forms give rise to the receiving subjects of existence, and, to that extent, they are causes of existence itself.[22] In short, forms are "formal" causes of existence, to the whole extent to which they contribute to the establishment of substances which are capable of existing.

This is a cardinal point in the doctrine of Thomas Aquinas. To posit substance as the proper receiver of existence (proprium susceptivum ejus quod est esse)[23] is not to posit it as a "container" into which existence has but to flow in order to make it be. So long as there is no existence, there is no receptacle to receive it. Existence is here fulfilling an entirely different function. As we have already described it, the substance is "that which" exists, and it is id quod est in virtue of its form. Form then is ultimate act in the order of subtantiality. In other words, there is no form of the form. Consequently, should we have to ascribe "to be" or "is" to a form, it could not be considered as a form of that

---

[21] Thomas Aquinas, Qu. disp. de Anima, art. 14, ad 4[m]. Cf. ad 5[m]; and In Boethium de Trinitate, q. V, art. 4, ad 4[m], ed. P. Wyser, p. 50, l. 19—p. 51, l. 11.
[22] Thomas Aquinas, Contra Gentiles, II, 54 ("Deinde quia . . .").
[23] Ibid., II, 55.

form. No point could be more clearly stated than is this one in the metaphysics of Thomas Aquinas. The form truly is "cause of being" for that subject in which it is, and it is not such owing to another form (*forma non habet sic esse per aliam formam*). To repeat, forms have not to be posited in their acts of forms by another form; quite the reverse: form reigns supreme within the order of substance, in its own being of form and in its own formal actuality. If form still requires and still has to receive a complement of actuality, that complementary actuality cannot belong in the order of formal actuality, but it belongs in an altogether different order, that of existential actuality. What substance can and must receive over and above what makes it to be "that which it is," is existence, which is imparted to it by some efficient cause: *habet tamen causam influentem ei esse*. Thus, the act through which substance actually exists can and even must be added to that other act in virtue of which its form makes it to be a substance. It can be added to it because, though all forms are acts, not all acts are forms. And it must be added to it, in order that substance *be*. In case we find good reason to posit it, the composition of essence with existence shall have to be that of an act, which is not itself a form, with the form of a subsisting being.[24]

It is therefore somewhat surprising to read such statements as this: "Thomists always presuppose that existence is a form properly so called and that it should be handled as such: which is the very point at stake, and the one which Suarez perseveringly denies, but which his adversaries always take for granted, yet never prove."[25] Leaving aside the philosophical debate between Thomists and Suarezians, this at least can be said, that it will never end, if the doctrine ascribed by Suarezians to Thomists is not that of Thomas Aquinas. To those, at least among the Thomists, who agree with Thomas Aquinas, existence is emphatically *not* a form, and, to the best of my knowledge, he himself has never said that it was. What he has said, and more than once, is that existence is "formal" with respect to all that which is in the existing thing.[26] What he means in such cases is that, analogically speaking, existence is to form as form itself is to matter. In both cases, the relation is that of "the received to the receiver (*receptum ad recipiens*)". It is therefore true that, to the extent to which act stands on the side of actuality and not of potency, existence

[24] Thomas Aquinas, *De Spiritualibus creaturis*, art. 1, ad 5[m].
[25] P. Descoqs, *Le Suarezisme*, in *Archives de Philosophie*, Vol. II, 2 (Paris, Beauchesne, 1924), p. 205.
[26] Thomas Aquinas, *Sum. Theol.*, I, 8, 1, Resp. Cf. I, 4, 1, ad 3[m].

behaves formally, not materially, with respect to essence. And why did not Thomas Aquinas say "actual" instead of "formal?" Simply because, as has just been seen, though existence is the supreme actuality of any existing substance, it is not act with respect to all that there is in that substance. If form is supreme in its own order, existence cannot be the act of essence *qua* essence. In other words, existence does not monopolize the whole actuality of existing substance. Rather, just as essence is in potency to the act of its own existence, so also is the act of existence in potency to the formal act of its own essence. If existential actuality is higher than formal actuality, the reason for it is that the very core of reality is existence. Thus, existence may well be said to be "formal," but it is not a form. Were it a form, it would be an essence, which it is not. For, indeed, there is no essence of existence, although there is essence in each and every existent.

A composition of essence with existence which is so conceived, then, is not inconsistent in itself, but has it been posited by Thomas Aquinas, and, if so, in what terms?

In at least one text, Thomas Aquinas has spoken of a "real composition" (*realis composito*); but most of the time he has simply said that they differ "in reality" (*re*). These and other similar expressions sufficiently account for the fact that his position is today designated by such denominations as the "real distinction" or the "real composition" of essence and existence.

What such formulas mean is, first of all, that each actually existing individual is, *qua* existing, a thing distinct from its own essence. This thesis should be understood as the properly Thomistic answer to the classic problem of universals. The question was: "How can the essence of the species be both one in itself and many in the plurality of individuals?" And philosophers had vainly looked at the essence of the species for an answer. What is new in Thomas Aquinas' answer is that he finds the answer in the order of existence. Actually existing individual beings are "beings" because of their own existing (*esse*). In other words, they are "beings" because of their own "to be," and this is why, within one species, whose quiddity is the same for all, each "being" is a distinct individuality. It is distinct, first, from any other being that belongs in the same species, and next it is distinct from its own quiddity, since its own being belongs to itself alone, while its quiddity is the same for all the members of the same species. Thus, the composition is "real," because its result is a *res* (a thing), and the distinction also is "real" because its act of existing is what makes that thing to be, not a mere quiddity, but an actually

171

real "being."[27] In short, what "real" composition or distinction seems to mean in the texts in which Thomas Aquinas himself uses such expressions, is that the existential actuality which a subsisting being owes to its own "to be" is radically other than what, in the substance itself, makes it to be "such a thing."

Justifiable as they are, we should not allow such formulas to mislead us into thinking that "to be" (esse) is itself a thing. "To be" (esse) is what makes an essence to be "a being," and, since the essence itself needs to receive it in order that it be, even while it has its own act of existence, it remains distinct from it. True enough, and the opponents of Thomas Aquinas are not yet weary of repeating it, unless it had already received actual existence, the essence of the substance could not be distinct from its own existence, since, were it otherwise, the essence would be nothing. Yet it is true that essence is really other than its own existence in virtue of its very act of existing, for, indeed, its act of existing is what enables essence to act as a formal cause, and to make actual being to be such a being. The very common mistake about this fundamental thesis of Thomism is due always to the same overlooking of the reciprocal character of efficient causality and of formal causality.[28] "To be" is not a thing distinct in itself from "essence" as from another thing. It is not, for the simple reason that, taken in themselves, "to be" and essence are not "things." Their composition alone is what makes up a thing, but they both become, so to speak, "real" because "to be" then is to be a "being," just as "to be such" is to be "such a being." Actual existence, then, is the efficient cause by which essence in its turn is the formal cause which makes an actual existence to be "such an existence." Since they represent irreducibly distinct modes of causality, essence and existence are irreducibly distinct, but the reality of their distinction presupposes their composition, that is, it presupposes the actual reality of the thing. Existence is not distinct from essence as one being from another being; yet, in any given being, that whereby a being both is and actually subsists is really "other than" that whereby it is definable as such a being in the order of substantiality.

This fundamental thesis entails far-reaching consequences. For, although it was not posited by Thomas Aquinas as a means of distinguishing finite beings from God, once it was posited, it

---

[27] Thomas Aquinas, *Qu. disp. de Veritate*, q. 27, a. 1, ad 8ᵐ (*realis compositio*). Cf. *In I Sent.*, d. 19, q. 2, a. 2, Solutio (*differt . . . re quidem*).

[28] "*Causae ad invicem sunt causae, sed in diverso genere,*" Thomas Aquinas, *In Metaph.*, Bk. V, ch. 2, lect. 2.

at once settled the whole question. *If* there is a distinction between essence and existence in each and every being, then any being is distinct from God in virtue of the composition which makes it to be "a being." In purely spiritual substances, such as angels, for instance, there is at least one composition, namely, that of its essence with its act of existing. In corporeal substances, such, for instance, as men, there are compositions: that of form with matter, which makes up substance, and that of the thus-constituted substance with its own act of existing. Thus, in a purely spiritual substance, in which substance is pure form, the composition of form with existence is enough to make up an actual being, but in a corporeal substance the composition of matter and form enjoys a metaphysical (not temporal) priority over the composition of the thus-constituted substance with its own act of existing. It should not be forgotten, however, that we are not here describing two different moments of the same composition, but two different *orders* of composition. For, indeed, in a corporeal being the substance *is* not in virtue of either its matter or its form; in other words, the act whereby the substance exists is neither its matter nor its form, but it is received by that substance through its form.[29]

Let us investigate more closely the respective natures of these two orders of composition. Both of them are compositions of potency and act. On the one hand, form is to matter as act is to potency; on the other hand, "to be" is to substance as act is to potency. But, since we already know that these two compositions do not belong in the same order, the act whereby a substance *is* must belong in another order than does the act whereby a substance "is a substance." Thomas Aquinas himself says: "The composition of matter and form is not of the same nature as that of substance and existence [*esse*, to be], although both of them are compositions of potency and act."[30] What makes it hard for us to realize the difference is precisely that they both result in one and the same effect, namely, a "being." This is why, as has already been said, the form of a substance is, *in its own order*, a cause of existence; it is, as Boethius used to say, a *quo est*,[31] a "thing whereby a being is." Form is formal cause of existence, inasmuch as it is the supreme constituent of the substance which exists in virtue of its *esse*, or act of existing. To go back to Thomas

[29] Thomas Aquinas, *De Substantiis separatis*, cap. VI.
[30] "*Nec est autem ejusdem rationis compositio ex materia et forma et ex substantia et esse, quamvis utraque sit ex potentia et actu*," Thomas Aquinas, *Contra Gentiles*, II, 54.
[31] "*Forma . . . potest dici* quo est, *secundum quod es! essendi principium*," loc. cit.

Aquinas' pet example, form is cause of existence, just as its diaphaneity is the cause why air shines and why there is light. To
get light, it takes both the sun and the air's diaphaneity, just as,
in order to get actual being, it takes both to be and substantiality.
In short, form is the cause of actual existence, inasmuch as it is
the formal cause of the substance which receives its own act of
existing.[32] This is why, as Thomas Aquinas so often says, *esse
consequitur formam:* to be follows upon form. It does, indeed,
because, where there is no form, there is nothing that can be. And
the same reason accounts for the formula so sharply criticized
by Siger of Brabant, namely, that "to be" is *quasi* constituted by
the principles of an actual essence.[33] In point of fact, Thomas
Aquinas has sometimes been even more positive about it, since,
as he has said at least once: "To be is always to be found in a thing,
and it is the act of a being, which results from the principles of that
thing, just as to light is the act of a lighting thing: *esse in re est,
et est actus entis, resultans ex principiis rei, sicut lucere est actus lu-
centis."*[34] If "to be" always belongs to a being, it certainly results
from the constituent principles of that being.

Yet, it is also true that any being results primarily from its
act of existing as from one of its primary constituents, for, if
the form is what makes it to be such a being, "to be" is what makes
it to be a "being." Precisely because existence reaches substance
in and *through* its form, forms have to receive existence in order
that they become "beings." But Thomas Aquinas could not
posit existence (*esse*) as the act of a substance itself actualized
by its form, without making a decision which, with respect to the
metaphysics of Aristotle, was nothing less than a revolution.
He had precisely to achieve the dissociation of the two notions of
form and act. This is precisely what he has done and what probably remains, even today, the greatest contribution ever made
by any single man to the science of being. Supreme in their own
order, substantial forms remain the prime acts of their substances,
but, though there be no form of the form, there is an act of the
form. In other words, the form is such an act as still remains in
potency to another act, namely, existence. This notion of an
act which is itself in potency was very difficult to express in the
language of Aristotle. Yet, it had to be expressed, since even

[32] "*Per hoc enim in compositis ex materia et forma, dicitur forma esse principium
essendi, quia est complementum (i.e.,* the perfecting act) *substantiae, cujus actus
est ipsum esse; sicut diaphanum est aeri principium lucendi, quia facit eum proprium
subjectum lucis,*" Thomas Aquinas, *Contra Gentiles,* II, 54.
[33] Cf. Thomas Aquinas, *In IV Metaph.,* lect. 2, ed Cathala, n. 558.
[34] Thomas Aquinas, *In III Sent.,* d. 6, q. 2, a. 2, Resp.

174

"those subsisting forms which, because they themselves are forms, do not require a formal cause for both being one and being, do nevertheless require an external acting cause, which gives them to be."[35] In order to receive its to be, a form must needs be in potency to it. "To be," then, is the act of the form, not *qua* form, but *qua* being.

This is to say that "to be," or to exist, is the supreme act of all that is. And the reason for it is clear, since, before being anything else, that is, this or that substance, any substance *is*, or is a "being." The form of a horse makes it "to be a horse;" it does not make it to be, nor, consequently, does it make it to be a being. And so, if being comes first in reality, then the existential act which causes it should come first among the constituent acts of concrete reality. But this is not an easy thing to say. Using the terminology of Boethius, to which he gives an entirely new meaning, Thomas Aquinas will say, for instance, that "to be is the ultimate act, which is participable by all, yet itself participates in nothing; hence, if there is such a thing as a self-subsisting *to be*, which we say that God is, we also say that it participates in nothing. But the case of other subsisting forms is not the same, because they must participate in existence itself (*esse*, to be) and, consequently, be related to it as potency to act. Thus, because in a way (*quodammodo*) they are in potency, they can participate in something else."[36] Forms are in potency, at least in a way, precisely because, although fully actual in their own formal order, they are not so with respect to existence. Hence the manifold formulas used by Thomas Aquinas in order to express the primacy of "to be" in the order of being: "*To be* is the act of the subsisting forms: *Ipsum esse est actus formae subsistentis.*"[37] Again: "*To be* is the actuality of all acts, and that is why it is the perfection of all perfections: *esse est actualitas omnium actuum, et propter hoc est perfectio omnium perfectionum.*"[38] And again: "*To be* is the actuality of all things, and even of forms themselves: *ipsum esse est actualitas omnium rerum et etiam formarum.*"[39] Where he is merely following his pen, Thomas Aquinas is liable to go still farther and to say, as he once did: "Each and every created being shares, so to speak, in the nature of existence: *quodcumque ens creatum participat, ut ita dixerim, naturam essendi,*"[40] which of course does not mean that "to be"

[35] Thomas Aquinas, *Qu. disp. de Anima*, art. 6, ad 9[m].
[36] *Ibid.*, art. 6, ad 2[m]   [37] *Ibid.*, art. 6. Resp.   [38] *Ibid.*, q. 7, art. 2, ad 9[m].
[39] Thomas Aquinas, *Sum. Theol.*, I, 8, 1, ad 4[m].
[40] *Ibid.*, I. 45, 5 ad 1[m]. Cf Anselm, *Monologium*, III; *PL*, Vol. 158 col. 147 Cf. also *Qu. disp de Potentia*, q. 7, a. 2, ad 9[m].

is itself a nature, and still less that it *has* a nature, but that, as Saint Anselm had already said, God is the very *natura essendi* in which each and every being, so to speak, participates.

When correctly understood, the Thomistic metaphysics of being appears as established on a ground whose very nature its opponents do not even seem to suspect. How, they ask with persistence, can essence enter into composition with existence, if, apart from existence, essence in itself is nothing?[41] As so formulated, the objection is irrefutable, and this is probably why its authors obstinately refuse to move to another ground; but the reason why they triumph so easily is that their adversary is not there. Thomas Aquinas himself stands on an entirely different ground. He is not composing an essence which is not with an existence which is not a thing, and he does not do it because he does not make the mistake which his opponents reproach him with making, namely, to consider existence as an essence. They themselves are making that radical and decisive mistake, because their own essentialism makes it impossible for them to think of anything otherwise than as of an essence. Hence their faultless argumentation: all that which is real is essence; existence is not an essence; hence existence is nothing. And, since each and every essence is an object of both concept and definition, the very fact that there is no concept of existence as such is to them a sure sign that existence itself is nothing. "Existence," they say, "*existentia, id quo formaliter ens constituitur actu*, that is, that whereby being is constituted in act, is not a concept, but a pseudo-concept." In short, as opposed to essence, it remains a "perfectly empty logical form," the only actual existence there is being that of individual, perceivable or conceivable reality.[42]

In a way, this is to raise as an objection to Thomas Aquinas what has always been his own doctrine, namely, that there is indeed no existence outside perceivable or conceivable things, that is, outside actually existing beings. In another way, this is to show complete blindness with respect to the very problem at stake. For the whole argumentation rests upon the fundamental assumption that there can be no real distinction where there is no distinct conceptual representation. God Himself, essentialism boldly says, cannot think of finite existence except in so far as it really identifies itself with that which it actualizes, and wherein it is but the "rela-

---

[41] P. Descoqs, *Thomisme et scolastique*, in *Archives de Philosophie*, Vol. V, 1 (Paris, G. Beauchesne, 1926), p. 103. Cf. *Archives de Philosophie*, Vol. X, 4 (1929), p. 589.
[42] *Ibid.*, Vol. I, p. 112.

tion to the cause whence it proceeds."[43] But the whole problem is precisely to know if existence can be nothing else than either an empty logical concept in the mind or a relation in the thing. It cannot be, if to be an act is to be a form, but it can be, if there can be such an act of the form as is not itself a form; and, since it is not a form, such an act has no essence distinct from itself, and hence can be neither perceived nor even conceived apart through any kind of conceptual representation. God *knows* essences, but he *says* existences, and He does not say all that He knows.

What is here at stake is not mere formal correctness in logical reasoning; it is an option between two radically different metaphysics of being. In fact, what is at stake is the metaphysical realization of the autonomous character of the order of existence, and this is a realization which is impossible to anyone who approaches being only by way of conceptual representation. As a concept, "to be" is indeed a pseudo-concept, but "to be" might well escape representation in virtue of its very transcendence. When we say that God is only *to be* (*Deus est esse tantum*), we are not falling into the error of those who said that God was that universal being (that is, *being* taken as a mere universal) owing to which each and every thing should be said to be as through its form. Quite the reverse: the only instance in which "to be" is absolutely pure of any addition or determination is also the only instance in which being is absolutely distinct from all the rest. God does not owe His *esse* to His own individuality; rather, supreme and unique individuality necessarily belongs to Him, and He *is* He, precisely because He alone is "to be" in its absolute purity: *"Unde per ipsam suam puritatem est esse distinctum ab omni esse."*[44] It should not be said then that "to be" cannot truly be act because, out of itself, it is not an act but the emptiest of universals; rather, it should be said that, because pure "to be" is in itself the supreme and absolute act, it cannot be a universal. And, if this be true of God, it should also hold true in the case of finite beings. For "to be" is, in things, the very act by which they are actual beings whose essences can be conceived as universals by way of conceptual abstraction. Matter is non-being apart from its form; form itself is non-being apart from its own to be; but substances are not nothing; they are acts, namely, they are forms which themselves participate in their ultimate act of existing.[45]

[43] *Ibid.*, pp. 121-122. Cf. pp. 111-112.
[44] Thomas Aquinas, *De ente et essentia*, cap. VI (IV).
[45] *"Si igitur per hoc quod dico* non ens, *removeatur solum esse in actu, ipsa forma*

As understood by Thomas Aquinas, being appears therefore as both radically contingent and literally indestructible in virtue of its composition of essence and existence. It is radically contingent because, with the exception of God Himself, Who is the pure act of existing, everything else hangs on some act which it cannot have unless it first receive it. At the lowest level of reality is matter, which cannot itself directly receive existence, or, in other words, cannot even be created alone. Matter is always the matter of a form; it can be but "concreated" with a form, so that existence reaches it only through the form with which it is concreated. But the very nature which is thus constituted of form and matter still needs to receive existence in order to be a "being." Just as matter is in potency to form, the nature to which that matter belongs is itself in potency with respect to the act of existing which makes it to be a "being."[46]

On the other hand, this radically contingent being is also indestructible, and what makes the combination of these two characters look paradoxical is a mere illusion. It is the same ever-recurring illusion, namely, the pseudo-primacy of essence over existence. We naturally begin by imagining some essence, which we conceive as the very core of some future being. It seems to us that, when such a being will finally be, it will be, before anything else, the very essence which, now a mere possible, will then have become real. If a metaphysician tells us that such a being receives its existence from an external cause and never ceases to receive it, its essential caducity is but too manifest, and we can then only wonder in what sense it could enjoy any degree of ontological stability.

Things will, however, appear quite different if we remember that reality is not essence, but being. Essence itself is primarily form, and form is what existence makes to be a being which, if it has a matter, makes its matter to be. What the contingency of existence means is, that all actual beings are contingent with respect to their cause, and this is but another way of saying that they might not exist; but, if they are actually produced by their cause, they do exist, and what they are in themselves is being. The primacy of existence means precisely that the radical con-

---

secundum se considerata est non ens, *sed esse participans. Si autem* non ens *removeat non solum ipsum esse in actu, sed etiam actum seu formam per quam aliquid participat esse, sic materia est non ens; forma vero subsistens non est non ens, sed est actus, qui est forma participativa ultimi actus, qui est esse,"* Thomas Aquinas, *De Substantiis separatis,* cap. VI; in *Opuscula.* ed. by P. Mandonnet, Vol. I, p. 97.

[46] Thomas Aquinas, *De Spiritualibus creaturis,* art. 1, Resp. Cf. *Qu. disp. de Potentia,* q. III, a. 4, Resp.

tingency of finite beings has been overcome, and, once it has been overcome, we should no longer worry about it. Such is the true Thomistic meaning of the neoplatonic formula borrowed from Plotinus himself through the *Liber de Causis*, that the first created thing is actual being: *"Prima rerum creatarum est esse."* In Thomas Aquinas, the formula no longer means that actual being is the first effect of some higher principle which itself *is* not; on the contrary, it means that the very first effect of the Pure Act of existing is the very existence of what it causes. In other words, the very first thing that can be said of its effects is that they *are*. Of course, if they are, they are something, perhaps a pure form, or maybe a nature composited of both matter and form, but, before being anything else, each of them is a "being," because it *is*. "The first effect of their cause, then, is to make them to be, an effect which is presupposed by all the others and which itself presupposes no other: *Primus autem effectus est ipsum esse, quod omnibus aliis effectibus praesupponitur et ipsum non praesupponit aliquem alium effectum."*[47] And to be is not only what comes first in everything; for, since it is what makes it to be a "being," it is, so to speak, involved in all that any being actually is. But we should perhaps rather say that the whole being is involved in its own to be, since it is owing to it that it is a being. "To be" thus permeates the innermost recesses of each and every being. In Thomas Aquinas' own words, "Being is the most common of all effects [since it is presupposed by all others], the first effect, and the innermost of all effects: *Ipsum enim esse est communissimus effectus, primus, et interior omnibus aliis effectibus."*[48] Thus, contingent as it may be with respect to its cause, reality is "being," and it is so to the core, as appears from its very name. In the very formula, "that which is," there is the "that which," that is, the substance which is the proper receiver of existence, and there is the "is," which that substance receives.[49] In other words, being is that which is *"be-ing "* in virtue of the very "to be" which it exercises. The noun *ens* (being) means *esse habens* (having *esse*, to be), so that it is derived from the very verb *esse* (*to be*): *"Hoc nomen ens . . . imponitur ab ipso esse."*[50] In such a doctrine, the word "being" can never be used without meaning both the thing which a certain being is and the existential act which makes it

---

[47] Thomas Aquinas, *Qu. disp. de Potentia*, q. III, a. 4, Resp.
[48] *Ibid.*, q. III, art. 7, Resp. Cf. *Compendium theologiae*, Pars. I, ch. 68.
[49] Thomas Aquinas, *Cont. Gentiles*, II, 55.
[50] Thomas Aquinas, *In IV Metaph.* lect. 2, ed. Cathala, n. 558. Cf. *In XII Metaph.*, lect. 1, n. 2419.

to be a "being."[51] Taken in itself, existential being is solidly full, totally blended together, as it were, by the very act in virtue of which it actually is.

A second character of existential being immediately follows from the first one. It is that the relation of its essence to its existence, instead of being the irreducible paradox which it is in the doctrine of Kirkegaard, appears as perfectly normal. More generally speaking, the classical antinomy between being and existence here simply disappears.

Being, philosophers are accustomed to say, is just what it is: it is its own essence, and it must therefore exhibit the characters of essence, which are essential selfhood and essential immutability. On the other hand, actual existence is perpetual otherness, because it is perpetual becoming. Whether it be asked in the terms once used by Plato: "What is it which always is and never becomes, and what is it which is always becoming but never is?" or whether it be raised in the terms used by Kirkegaard and modern existentialism: "If x is, x does not exist," the problem remains the same. It always rests upon the assumption that essence and becoming are incompatible, whereas, the very reverse is true. Far from being incompatible with becoming, essence is both the final cause of becoming and the formal condition of its possibility.

Where existence is alone, as is the case in God, Whose essence is one with His existence, there is no becoming. God is, and, because He is no particular essence, but the pure act of existence, there is nothing which He can become, and all that can be said about Him is, *He Is.* On the contrary, as soon as essence appears, there also appears some otherness, namely, the very otherness which distinguishes it from its own possible existence and, with it, the possibility of becoming. This is particularly clear in the case of man, with which modern existentialism is almost exclusively, or, at any rate, chiefly concerned. It is of the essence of man to belong in the order of corporeal beings. This does not mean that intellectual souls, which are the forms of human beings, are fallen into their bodies and struggling to get out of them; rather, it means that they stand in need of such bodies in order both to subsist and to act. The cause of such a need on the part of souls is a certain incompleteness in actuality. Were they able to stand alone and to perform by themselves their own operations, they would be fully actual in themselves, that is, they would be pure subsisting forms, and no material element would enter their definition. On the contrary, since the essence of a human soul entails its relation to

[51] Thomas Aquinas, *In I Perihermeneias*, lect. 5, n. 20.

body (or else it would be a pure spirit, not a soul), it seems clear that, out of itself, such a form as a human soul is an act that stands in need of some further actualization. It does not need to be confirmed in its own nature: as has been said several times, there is no form of the form nor any act of the form *qua* form, but it still does need to become more fully that which it is. "Become what thou art" is for such a form an imperative order, because it is inscribed as a law in its very nature. And this is a purely existential problem, since the question never is for a soul to become *what* it is (it is such *qua* form) but *to become that which it is.* In other words, a human soul has more and more to actualize its very definition.

It thus appears that no form engaged in matter can simply and solely *be.* For it, "to be" is to become, and its "being" *is* "becoming." Always in existential potency to the absolute fullness of its own being, such a form is bound to exert manifold operations in order to fill the privation of actuality which it suffers: not a privation of essence, but that of a substance which still fails completely *to be* its own essence, and which, in order more fully to be, must achieve its own being by exerting a series of operations, each of which shall ultimately bring it a step nearer its own completion. To do so is to move, to change, to "be-come," that is, progressively to arrive at its own being. Such is the law wherever there is matter. For, since to need matter points out a certain privation of being in the form, wherever there is matter, there also is in the form a potency to a more complete existential actualization. Hence the very motion or change which is required to achieve it. In short, since matter is there in view of its form, it is one and the same thing for a form to actualize its matter more completely and for itself more completely to be.[52]

To get rid of the current notion of essence is here an absolute necessity. Unless we do so, such a metaphysics of being as that of Thomas Aquinas cannot be understood at all. Essences are commonly conceived as abstract entities, which cannot suffer any change because their very nature is to be just what they are. First conceived by Plato as comparatively simple, they have become infinitely complex since the time of Leibniz, when the new resources provided by the infinitesimal calculus made it possible to include within their unity an infinite number of determinations. Yet, even after Leibniz, essences have always remained the fully achieved and purely static unities of possible subjects taken with the totality of all their determinations. In Julius Caesar's

[52] Thomas Aquinas, *Cont. Gentiles,* III, 20.

essence, Leibniz says, the crossing of the Rubicon is eternally included, just as, according to Kant, were there such an essence as that of the Wandering Jew, it should include each and every time and place of his endless peregrinations.

Now, it may be true that, in God's eternal cognition, essences are just like that, but the common mistake of both essentialists and existentialists is to think that the eternal essence of a being subject to becoming does not include the knowledge of its actual existence as cause of its becoming. The ideas of all possible essences are to be found in God, and they include determinately all the determinations which would belong to the corresponding beings, if only they were created. But only some among those possibles are actually created, and their choice rests with the divine will. This further determination to actual existence is what turns the corresponding essences into so many divine ideas, in the full sense of the term. When thus conceived, ideas represent possible beings, including both their actual existence and their becoming. In other words, if *esse* (to be) is the supreme act of creatures, their idea must needs include it as the active energy through which the corresponding essence shall progressively receive all its determinations.

Essences are often conceived as *possible* beings, whose reality coincides with their very possibility. But we should be careful to distinguish between essential possibility and existential possibility. For, indeed, they belong in two distinct metaphysical orders, so much so that there is no way for us to reach the second one through the first one. An essence is possible, *qua* essence, when all its determining predicates are compossible. If they are, the existence of the corresponding being is possible; if they are not, it is not. And this is true, but it is true only in the order of essential possibility, not at all in the order of existential possibility. Many metaphysicians seem to imagine that an essence cannot exist, so long as it has not received all its determinations, that, as soon as it has received them, it is bound either to burst into existence or, at least, to receive it. Now, a twofold error is responsible for such an illusion. The first one is not to see that to be fully completed in the order of essentiality does not bring an essence one inch nearer actual existence. A completely perfected possibility still remains a pure possibility. The second error is to forget that the essence of a possible being necessarily includes the possible existence through which alone it can achieve its essential determination. To repeat, essential possibility is no sufficient reason for existential possibility, and, since its essence is what a being is going to become, if it exists, existence itself necessarily enters the calculation of its essential possibility. Thus, Julius Caesar does not cross the Rubicon because that is eternally included in his essence; it is eternally included in his essence because his essence is that of a Rubicon-crossing man. Such determinations have eternally to be known as existential, if they are to be known at all. Essences may well represent the balance sheets of so many already fulfilled essential possibilities, but actual existences are their very fulfilling, and this is why essences are actually becoming in time, despite the fact that a time-transcending knowledge eternally sees them as already fulfilled.

Actual and individual essences then are not static, because their own becoming is presupposed by their very definitions. Their progressive self-determination through acting and operating, that is, through the change of which time is but the numbering, is not extraneous to their eternal ideas; rather, it is eternally included in them. God is an immobile knowledge of becoming *qua* becoming. But, if it is so, there is no antinomy between eternity and existence in time. For Him Who Is there is no time, because He is to Himself His own essence, so that His own "now" is identically His own *is*. In short, because He Is, there is nothing that He can become, so that He is eternity.

To posit essence or supreme essentiality as the supreme degree of reality is therefore the most disastrous of all metaphysical mistakes, because it is to substitute *essentia* for *esse* as the ultimate root of all being. The whole of metaphysics is here at stake. If God is *esse*, He is He Whose own "to be" constitutes His own essence. Hence both His unicity and His singularity. Fully posited by its "to be," essence here entails neither limitation nor determination. On the contrary, finite essences always entail both limitation and determination, because each of them is the formal delimitation of a possible being. Yet, if such a possible essence actually receives existence, it is a being, owing to its own act of existing, so that, even in the order of finite being, the primacy of existence still obtains. Its act of existing is what insures the unity of the thing. Matter, form, substance, accidents, operations, everything in it directly or indirectly shares in one and the same act of existing. And this is why the thing is both being and one. Existence is not what keeps elements apart, it is what blends them together as constituent elements of the same being. For the same reason, temporal existence is neither the ceaseless breaking up of eternity nor the perpetual parceling out of being; it is rather their progressive achievement through becoming. Thus, becoming through *esse* is the road to fully determined being, just as time is the road to eternity. Man is not struggling in time not to lose eternity, since, like all true spiritual substances, he is eternal in his own right; but, if he must become in order the more fully to be, it is of the essence of man to be, in time, a self-achieving and self-eternalizing being.

The full import of this conclusion will perhaps appear more clearly if we consider a third characteristic of existential being, namely, its intrinsic dynamism. Because abstract essence is static, while existence is dynamic, such a metaphysics of being must needs be a dynamic one. The very existence of finite essence is the first and immediate effect of the first and absolute existential Act. To repeat, *prima rerum creatarum est esse.*[53] Born of an existential act, "to be" is itself an existential act, and, just as it is effect, so also it is cause. Even finite being is, in its own way, cause of being. This is why, in a chapter of his *Summa Contra Gentiles* (III, 69), Thomas Aquinas puts so much speculative passion into refuting the error of "those who deprive natural things of their own actions." He goes at it tooth and nail, because the very nature of being is here at stake. Not: to be, then to act, but: to be is to act.

And the very first thing which "to be" does, is to make its own essence to be, that is, "to be a being." This is done at once, completely and definitively, for, between to be or not to be, there is no intermediate position. But the next thing which "to be" does, is to begin bringing its own individual essence somewhat nearer its completion. It begins doing it at once, but the work will take time and, in the case of such corporeal beings as men, for instance, it is bound to be a slow process. It takes each of us a lifetime to achieve his own temporal individuality. True enough, essence itself is there from the very beginning, and, in a way, it is whole, but its wholeness is not that of a thing. The essence of the symphony is in the mind of the composer, and, since it is its essence to be a symphony, it will have to be it, but it will not exist until the last bar of its score has been orchestrated, and even that will not be the end of its becoming. So also with natural essences. Each of them is the progressive becoming of its own end. In short, the actual perfecting of essences is the final cause of their existences, and it takes many operations to achieve it.

Existence can perform those operations. Because *to be* is to *be act*, it also is to be able to act. Now, as an act is, so will be its operation. If a being acts *qua* being, it will be cause of being.

[53] Cf. above, p. 179

Because God is pure act of existence, His first effect is existence, and He is the first cause why everything else exists.[54] But those existing things which God creates, are His images precisely inasmuch as they exist. If, therefore, God has made them like unto Himself by giving them existence, He has consequently made them like unto Himself by giving them causal efficacy, that is to say, by granting them the power to exert causal actions of their own.[55] Such is the reason why, although no finite being can create existence, each of them can at least impart it. In any relation of efficient causality, something of the *esse* (to be) of the cause is somehow imparted to its effect. Such a relation then is an existential one, and it is no wonder that all attempts to reduce it to some analytical relation have been unsuccessful. Hume was perfectly right in refusing to consider causal relations as deducible from the essences of the causes, and Kant was simply dodging the difficulty by transferring to a category of the understanding the synthetic nature of a relation which is grounded in things. From no essence will there ever spring any causal efficacy; as to the *a priori* synthetic judgment of Kant, it is nothing more than the mental dummy of being's existential causality. *Esse* (to be) is the ceaselessly overflowing source of its effects, and, if the relation of such effects to their causes is unintelligible in a world of abstract essences, it is quite intelligible in a world in which to be is to act, because beings themselves are acts.

This intrinsic dynamism of being necessarily entails a radical transformation of the Aristotelian conception of essences. True enough, Aristotle's metaphysics was already a thorough dynamism, but it was a dynamism of the form. The form of the being-still-to-be was there, acting as both the formal law of its development and as the end to be reached by that development. Aristotelian beings were self-realizing formal types, and the only cause for their individual variations rested with the accidental failures of various matters completely to imbibe the forms. Individuals then were little more than abortive attempts to be their own forms; none of them could add anything to its species; rather, there was infinitely more in the species than there was in the whole collection of its individuals. Because Aristotelianism had been a dynamism, Thomas Aquinas has seen his way to including it within his own metaphysics of being, but, because it had been a dynamism of the form, he has had to deepen it into a dynamism of *esse* (to be). When he did it, the whole philosophical outlook on reality at once became different. Each and every individual, even among

[54]Thomas Aquinas, *Cont. Gentiles*, I, 10; I, 13; II, 15.   [55] *Ibid.*, III, 69.

BEING AND SOME PHILOSOPHERS

corporeal beings, was henceforward to enjoy its own *to be*, that is, a to be of its own; and this is why, in such a doctrine, to be is not univocal, but analogical in its own right. True enough, corporeal individuals still remain individuated by matter, but. if they owe matter their individuation, they are indebted to their to be for their individuality. For, indeed, "all that which is has its to be: *Omne quod est, esse habet,*"[56] and "that to be is its own: *Unumquodque est per suum esse.*"[57] It is also true that such individuals still are determined by their forms, but they no longer are the automatic self-realizations of forms merely hampered by the natural indocility of matter; they are individualities in the making, each of which is being actively built up by its own *esse*. And this, of course, is eminently true in the case of man, whose soul is itself an intellectual substance. There still is formal causality in such a doctrine, and it remains whole, but it has been metamorphosed by its subordination to efficient existential causality. Instead of a self-achieving end, form becomes an end to be achieved by its own *esse*, which progressively makes it an actual being. To be (*esse*) is to act (*agere*), and to act is to tend (*tendere*) to an end wherein achieved being may ultimately rest.[58] But there is no rest for being in this life, where to be is to become. And this is why aetiology is here part and parcel of the metaphysics of being. "To be" is to be cause, that is, both immanent cause of its own being and transitive cause of other beings through efficient causality. Matter itself is no longer here as a mere obstacle, blindly aspiring to form; it is also a help. Actively engaged in it, the soul is giving itself the body which it needs; it progressively builds it up through physiological operations which pave the way for intellectual operations. Hence, in the end, the infinite variety of human minds, all human in the same measure and in the same way, yet all different, as though each of them were less the stereotyped copy of their common species than a monotype endowed with singular originality.

"To be" does it, and it can be done by nothing else. Saints, philosophers, scientists, artists, craftsmen—no two men are the same, because even the humblest among them ultimately is his own "to be;" yet none of them is really alone. To be is not to be a solitude. Each and every man can share in the common good of his species, and nothing that is human remains foreign to him.

[56] Thomas Aquinas, *Qu. disp. de Potentia*, q. VII, art. 2, ad 9m.
[57] Thomas Aquinas, *Contra Gentiles*, I, 22. See E. Gilson, *Le Thomisme*, p. 134, note.
[58] Thomas Aquinas, *Qu. disp. de Veritate*, q. 21, art. 2, Resp.

Nay, nothing that *is*, is foreign to him. A member of the universal brotherhood of being, he can experience in himself that being is "tending to," and he can see that everything else is acting to some purpose, a purpose which is indeed everywhere the same, namely, to be. His end, then, is in his beginning, and what is true of him holds true of everything else. All beings, from the most exalted to the humblest ones, are just as really distinct and as ultimately alike as the children of the same father; for, indeed, they all have the same Father, and He has made them all in His image or resemblance. They act because they are, and they are because His name is *He Who Is*.

Just as aetiology hangs on ontology, so also does epistemology. If to know is to know things as they are—for otherwise they are not known at all—to know them is to reach, not only their forms, but their very "to be." Unless it penetrates reality up to its innermost core, knowledge is bound to miss what is the very core of its object. There was a deep truth in Kirkegaard's statement, that any general knowledge about existing beings entails reducing them to the abstract condition of mere possibles. It was true, because, since being minus actual existence is, at best, possibility, the abstract knowledge of existence itself still remains knowledge of its possibility. But this is true only of abstract essences; it is not true of the essence of actual existence. To know existential being is not to know its essence only; it is not to know that it enjoys existence in a general way; it is not even to know existences; precisely, it is to know existents, which is but another word to designate in its fullness this ever-new notion of "being."

If this be true, real knowledge necessarily includes essence, since to know a thing is to know what it is, and this is why the first operation of the mind is to form such concepts as express what things are. Such is the situation with the very notion of being, the most common of all, which expresses all that "which has existence" (*ens: esse habens*). The truthfulness of such a concept fully appears when it is related to its object by a judgment; for then we see that it correctly expresses what the essence of a being truly is. In such cases, truth is correctly grounded in the very essence or quiddity of its object. Yet, such an object still remains an abstract and general one, so that its truth also remains an abstract and general one, applying to possible being as well as to actual beings. In short, it is not yet the knowledge of a "thing."

In order to go further, another class of judgments is required, namely, those by which we state that what the thing is, actually

187

is, or exists. Such is the composite operation which we call a judgment of existence. By saying that *x is*, we mean to say that *x* is a certain *esse* (to be), and our judgment must needs be a composite operation precisely because, in such cases, reality itself is composite. Existence is synthetically united with essence in reality, owing to the efficient causality of its cause, and the synthetic nature of their actual relation entails the synthetic nature of the mental act whereby we express it. If our existential judgment is true, however, it is so because that to which we ascribe existence actually is, or exists. In short, it is true when the data of abstract, intellectual knowledge and those of sensible intuition fully agree. When they do, there still is no *objective* knowledge of a *subjective* existence, which Kirkegaard has quite rightly described as an intrinsic impossibility, but I have objective knowledge of a subjectively existing being. And this is what true knowledge should be, if for it to be true means to reach its object such as it is. For, indeed, to identify subjectivity with existence, as Kirkegaard always did, was but to turn existence into one more essence, namely, that whose very essence it is to preclude objectivity. If, on the contrary, actual being is the existential actualization of an objective essence, knowledge not only can, but must, be at one and the same time both objective and existential. It is directly objective through abstract concepts; it is directly existential through a certain class of judgments. If such judgments ultimately aim to reach actual beings, including their very "to be," then their truth must ultimately rest upon the actual "to be" of the thing. "Since," Thomas Aquinas says, "a thing includes both its quiddity and its existence (*esse:* to be), truth is more grounded on the existence (*esse*) of the thing than on its quiddity itself. For, indeed, the noun *ens* (being) is derived from *esse* (to be) so that the adequation in which truth consists is achieved by a kind of assimilation of the intellect to the existence (*esse*) of the thing, through the very operation whereby it accepts it such as it is."[69] Existential judgment expresses that assimilation.

These words are exceptionally meaningful, even in a philosophy which seldom indulges in wasting words. Because things are, true judgments are true inasmuch as they accept them as actual beings, and, because to be a "being" is primarily to be, *veritas fundatur in esse rei magis quam in ipsa quidditate:* truth is more principally

[69] Thomas Aquinas, *In I Sent.*, d. 19, q. 5, a. 1, Solutio, ed. by P. Mandonnet, Vol. I, p. 486. Cf. *In Boethium de Trinitate*, V, 3, Resp., from "*Ad evidentiam* . . . to "*ut in substantiis simplicibus*" ed P. Wyser, p. 38, ll. 1-13.

grounded in the existence (*esse*) of the thing than it is in its essence. And this, I think, is undoubtedly true, because no other description of knowledge can do complete justice to the twofold nature of both actual reality and true knowledge. Both reality and our knowledge of it entail the subjective actualization by existence of an essential objectivity. Being *qua* being is their very unity. Unless such knowledge of reality be possible, no knowledge will ever grasp reality such as it is. The last word of Thomistic epistemology, then, is that our knowledge of being is more than an abstract concept; it is, or it should be, the living and organic unity of a concept and of a judgment. But is such knowledge of reality possible? The question is in itself so important that it requires to be submitted to detailed consideration.

Chapter VI

Knowledge and Existence

To know is to *conceive* knowledge. Every act of intellectual knowledge terminates in an intellection, that is, in what is intellectually known (*ispum intellectum*), and what has thus been conceived is a "conception" (*conceptio*) which expresses itself in words. Now, the intellectually conceived is twofold in kind, as can be seen from the very words which express it. It may be simple, as happens when our intellect forms the quiddity of a thing, in which case its verbal expression is incomplex. It may also be complex, as happens when our intellect compounds or divides (*componit et dividit*) such quiddities. In both cases there is an intellectual act of conceiving and, therefore, a conceived intellection, but what has been conceived in the first case is called a concept (*conceptus*), whereas what has been conceived in the second case is a judgment (*judicium*). To judge is to compose or to separate by an intellectual act two elements of reality grasped by means of concepts.[1]

The verbal expression of a judgment is the *enunciation*, which logicians call a *proposition*. Propositions are usually defined as enunciations which affirm or deny one concept of another concept. All complete logical propositions are made up of two terms, the "subject" of the affirmation or negation, and the "predicate," which is affirmed or denied of the subject. As to the "copula," it is not really a term, because it designates, not a concept, but the determinate relation which obtains between two terms. For this reason the copula cannot be a noun; it is a verb. In point of fact, it is the verb *is*. But there are difficulties concerning the exact meaning of this verb.

Logicians find it a particularly difficult problem, because the verb *is* can perform two different functions and thus give

---

[1] Thomas Aquinas, *Qu. disp. de Veritate*, qu. IV, art. 2, Resp. Cf. *Qu. disp. de Potentia*, qu. VIII, art. 1, Resp. In these texts and in many similar ones, *conceptus—us* should be carefully distinguished from *conceptus—a—um*. The second one may apply to the judgment (which is a *conceptio*, hence a *conceptum*), but it is at least doubtful that Thomas Aquinas ever called a judgment a *conceptus*.

rise to two distinct classes of propositions. It may play the part of a copula which links together subject and predicate: the earth *is* round. Such propositions used to be called *de tertio adjacente*[2] because, in them, the predicate is the third word. But there are propositions in which the verb *is* does not seem to introduce any predicate: Toronto *is*, Troy *is* no longer. Logicians used to call them *de secundo adjacente*, because, in them, the verb comes second, and last, after the subject. Let us call those two classes of propositions "two-term propositions" and "one-term propositions." If there are one-term propositions, how can the classical definition of propositions be valid? And, if the classical definition of propositions is valid, how can there be one-term propositions? In short, if all propositions entail either a composition or a division of concepts, how can there be a proposition in which there is only one concept?[3]

To remove this difficulty, logicians have undertaken to reduce all one-term propositions to two-term propositions. Now, there is a class of propositions which seem to lend themselves to such a reduction. It is the class of those in which the verb is other than *is*. Psychologists call them "judgments of action,"[4] and it can be maintained that, when I say that *Peter runs*, what I mean is that *Peter is running*, just as, when I say that *fire burns*, what I mean is that *fire is burning*. All such one-term propositions could easily be developed into so many two-term propositions. But, if this is so, why should we not deal in the same way with such propositions as *I am*, or *God is?* To say that *I am* merely means that *I am being*, just as to say *God is* means that *God is being*. The meaning remains the same, yet the thus-developed propositions

---

[2] This formula seems to have been suggested by a few words of Aristotle in his *De Interpretatione (Perihermeneias)*, X, 4. For an objective modern presentation of the Scholastic theory of judgment, see, for instance, Joseph Fröbes, *Tractatus logicae formalis* (Romae, Pont. Univ. Gregoriana, 1940), Vol. I, lib. 2, cap. 1, pp. 98-115. Cf. by the same author, *Psychologia speculativa* (Freib. i. Br., Herder, 1927), Vol. II, p. 58: *De natura actus judicii*, thesis V, and lib. I, cap. 2, n. 2, Vol. II, pp. 52 ff.

[3] This difficulty has prompted John of St. Thomas to distinguish between the verb as part of an enunciation, in which case it is a term (*terminus enuntiativus*), and the same verb as part of a syllogism, in which case it is not a term (*i.e.*, not a *terminus syllogisticus*). From this point of view, the enunciation *Petrus currit* (Peter runs) is made up of two terms (*currit* being here a predicate); so also in the case of *Petrus est*. On the contrary, *est* is not a term in the syllogistic proposition *Petrus est albus*. See John of St. Thomas, *Logica*, I P. Quaest. disp. q. I, arts. 2 and 3 (Taurini-Romae, Marietti), Vol. I, p. 97. Cf. p. 91. The whole difficulty rests with the assumption that in *Petrus currit* the verb is a predicate.

[4] J. Fröbes, *Psychologia speculativa*, lib. I, cap. 2, Vol. II, p. 54: *"judicia proprietatis vel activitatis* equus *currit: ibi perceptio resolvitur in subjectum et activitatem, quae denominatur et ut proprietas de subjecto asseritur."*

191

are regular two-term propositions, in which *is* performs its regular function as copula between a predicate and its subject.

Let us suppose, which is far from evident, that *I am running* means exactly the same thing as I *run*. If *running* is not truly a predicate, but a mere part of the verbal form *is running*, *is* does not play the part of a copula, and what is left is a one-term proposition made up of the subject *Peter* and of the verb *is running*. If, on the contrary, *running* can be held to be a predicate, *is* becomes a mere copula. The proposition then truly is a two-term one, but it is so precisely because the verb no longer means the predicate; it means only our affirmation that the predicate belongs to the subject. In other words, for a proposition to be a two-term one, its verb must be a mere copula which does not include the predicate in its own meaning. This is so true that some languages, Russian for instance, completely do away with the copula and yet are immediately intelligible even to readers whose own mother tongue makes constant use of it. "He old," "she lovely," "they students" do not raise the slightest difficulty in any mind,[5] and nothing can be more clear than the following translation of a correct Russian syllogism: "All men mortal; Socrates man; Socrates mortal." The propositions which enter the composition of such a syllogism are true two-term propositions, and even without a copula their meaning is complete; which proves that even in classical logic the copula does not signify by itself: it always bears upon the predicate, not in order to signify the predicate, but to signify its union with a subject.

But even though, *dato non concesso*, judgments of action could be correctly developed into so many two-term ones, the same operation could not be validly performed on judgments of existence, that is, on those one-term propositions in which the verb is the verb *is*. In all such cases the verb signifies by itself, and this is why it cannot become a copula. It cannot, because, if we develop such one-term propositions into two-term propositions, the predicate would mean the verb. Verbally speaking, I can replace *God is* by *God is being* or *I am* by *I am being*; but, in the first place, it then becomes apparent that the two propositions are not the same, for it could well be maintained that God never *is being*, precisely because *He is*, and, secondly inasmuch as the two formulas can convey the same meaning, the second one is tautological,

---

[5] A. Mazon, *Grammaire de la langue russe* (Paris, Droz, 1943), arts. 143, 162. Let us note that John of St. Thomas would find no difficulty in this, since, according to him, terms can be united either by a verb, or *"significatione, quarum una determinat aliam."*

whereas the first one is not. In *Peter is running*, the predicate does not signify Peter's existence, but his condition as a running man, and, likewise, *is* does not signify Peter's existence, but remains a bare copula which ascribes to Peter his running determination. True enough, to run is itself an existential act, and this is why the only correct way to signify it as such is, precisely, to say that *Peter runs*, in which case there is neither copula nor predicate. Now, in such cases as *I am* or *God is*, the transformation is not even possible, because in *I am being* or *God is being*, the predicate is but a blind window which is put there for mere verbal symmetry. There is no predicate even in the thus-developed proposition, because, while *running* did not mean the same thing as *is*, *being* does. In other words, *is-running* does not mean *is*, but *runs;* whereas, *being* obviously means *is;* and this is why, in the first case, the verb is a copula, which it is not in the second case. The metaphysical truth that existence is not a predicate is here finding its logical verification.

The same conclusion can be formulated in two different ways, according as our approach to the problem is a metaphysical or purely logical one. Metaphysically speaking, there is no abstract essence of existence. Existence is not a "thing," it is an act, namely, the primary act of being. And this is why I cannot abstract existence from any being. If what I am conceiving does not exist, I can mentally separate the concept of the thing from existence by denying that the thing is, that is, by asserting that it is not. *Troy is not* signifies that there now is no such thing in the world as King Priam's city. Existence then cannot play the part of a predicate, because it cannot be a term in a proposition. Logically speaking, any attempt to make it a predicate is doomed to failure, because, in existential judgments, *is* never loses its existential connotation, so that it cannot become a copula. In *I am being*, instead of the three known parts of predication, we really have four: (1) the subject, *I*; (2) the predicate, *being;* (3) the copula, *is*, which itself means, (4) once more, *being*[6]. Here, James Stuart Mill was right. All we have to add is that, if such propositions are made up of four parts, they nevertheless include only one term and a verb. All the rest is mere verbiage calculated to make us believe that existence falls under the scope of conceptual predication.

Let us call "existential" such one-term propositions.[7] We

[6] J. S. Mill, *Analysis of the Phenomena of the Human Mind* (London, 1869), Vol. I, pp. 174-175.
[7] There can even be one-word propositions, for instance, the Latin *pluit* (it

then shall have to say that no existential proposition can be transformed into a predicative proposition. But the reverse could be attempted, namely, to transform all predicative propositions into so many existential propositions. In point of fact, it has been attempted by Franz Brentano, and it was a very tempting attempt to make. For, indeed, Brentano says, in existential propositions, the verb *is* should make sense, and, since it is agreed that existence is no predicate, there is but one term which *is* can predicate, namely, the subject. But this first moment of the demonstration is already beset with difficulties. Like the opposite thesis which it aims to disprove, it takes it for granted that, in all propositions, the verb is bound to signify a term. If it cannot be the predicate, then let it be the subject! Yet, should this be granted, the problem would remain the same under a different form, namely, what is the meaning of *is?* Is it a copula? If it is, we thereby obtain the classical formula of the principle of identity, *A is A;* an undoubtedly correct formula, but one which is the very reverse of the result intended by such an operation. What we were trying to do was to turn all predicative propositions into existential propositions, and what we are actually doing is turning all existential propositions into predicative propositions. Brentano is right in saying that what is then asserted is not "the union of the character *existence* with A," but he seems to be wrong in saying that what is then asserted is A itself.[8] The proposition *Socrates is* does not at all mean that *Socrates is Socrates.* Neither does it point out *Socrates;* what it points out is the fact that Socrates *is.*

But what Brentano means may well become more clear if we consider the second moment of his proof. If *Socrates is* does not mean either that he has the predicate existence, or that he is Socrates, then to posit Socrates and to posit him as existing are one and the same thing. This time, the thesis of Brentano implies that to assert A is to assert its existence, which is precisely the point at stake. If what Brentano says is true, the assertion of A should be one with the assertion of the existence of A; but such is not the case, for the proposition *A is* does not signify A, it signifies A's existence. In other words, either it is developed into the predicative proposition *A is A*, in which case it does not

---

rains). Existential judgments could also be called "real" (cf. J. Fröbes, *op. cit.*, pp. 101-102), but there might be a slight touch of Suarezian essentialism in such an appellation.

[8] Fr. Brentano, *Psychologie du point de vue empirique* (Paris, Aubier, 1944), p. 213.

signify A's existence, or else it remains a one-term proposition, in which case it does not signify the subject.

The difficulty becomes still more apparent if we follow Brentano in his ultimate reduction of all predicative propositions to existential ones, a reduction which he is bound to attempt if the verb *is* always signifies a term. But the very principle of his reduction works both ways, since it can as easily reduce all existential propositions to merely predicative ones. *"Some man is sick,"* Brentano says, "means the same as the existential proposition, *a sick man is*, or *there is a sick man."* [9] Nothing is less evident. The natural amphibology of the verb "to be" is here once more at work. When I say of some man that he is sick, I am taking his existence for granted, for, unless he *were*, he could not possibly be sick. Yet, I am not signifying his existence; what I do indeed signify is his sick condition, which cannot be taken for granted from the fact alone that he *is*. If, on the contrary, I say that there is a sick man in a room, the very existence of some patient is signified. I remember reading on the walls of London in November, 1945: "There still are Liberals," and, indeed, reading this after the Labor Victory of the preceding elections, I could feel no hesitation as to the meaning of the sentence. It did not mean that some liberals still were Liberals, but that there still existed in Great Britain such men as call themselves Liberals. In similar cases, existence is so clearly at stake, that it stands in need of being forcefully asserted. Some man *is sick* and *there is* a sick man do not mean one and the same thing. And here again Russian may help, for it would render the first proposition by "some man sick," whereas, it would render the second one by "a sick man *is*." Russian is a language in which, in its normal use, the verb *is* never plays the part of a copula, because it has kept whole its existential meaning.

It may not be necessary to follow Brentano throughout his systematic reduction of all classes of attribution to existential assertion, for the mainspring of such operations is one and the same, and they all stumble upon the same difficulty. They all suppose that, as a copula, *is* already means existence. If it does, *all men are mortal* can easily become *an immortal man is not* and *there is no immortal man*. But how can the *are* of the universal affirmative beget the *is not* of the universal negative? Are we to say that to assert existence is the same act as to deny it? For generations, logicians have used as a classical example the proposition *all swans are white*. Has it ever meant to them either the actual

[9] *Ibid.*, p. 218.

195

existence of white swans or the non-existence of black ones? When, after the discovery of Australia, it became known that some swans were black, the *truth* of the universal affirmative went to pieces, but its nature *qua* judgment remained identically what it had always been, namely, a predication. Existential judgments are not predications, nor is there any predication of actual existence. Assuredly, the actual existence of what the terms of a judgment signify is directly or indirectly required for the truth of any predication, but the formal correctness of such a judgment as *all swans are white* is independent of its truth. At any rate, the truth of the actual inherence of a predicate in a subject never entails the truth of the actual existence of the subject. *A Centaur is a fiction* does not mean that Centaurs actually *are* in poetic minds; nor does it mean that some fictions existing in poetic minds *are* Centaurs; it means that what is called Centaur "is a fiction." In short, existence is a prerequisite for the truth of any predication, but it does not directly fall under the scope of predication.

We thus find ourselves confronted with the fact that, since *is* does not mean either a predicate or a subject, its meaning must needs be *wholly contained in itself*. There is no doubt that *is* does not signify apart from a subject, yet it does not signify its subject, and, since logicians as such seem unable to cope with the problem, our only hope is to apply to those whose proper job it is to determine the nature and functions of verbs, that is, the grammarians.

If we do so, we find ourselves confronted with the no less disturbing fact that a large number of grammarians are little more than logicians. Just as it has invaded logic, the metaphysical substantialism of Aristotle has wholly subdued grammar, thus turning it into a mere department of logic and reducing the proposition to abstract predication. It is a meaningful fact that, in seventeenth-century France, for instance, the *General Grammar* of Lancelot had been included, just as it was, in the *Port-Royal Logic*. And it could well be, since it was nothing else than logic. The doctrine of Lancelot concerning verbs is simple. To him, the verb is "a word whose principal function is to signify affirmation." We say "principal" because, over and above that function, the verb can fulfill several other ones. When I say, in Latin, *"sum,"* I am actually saying, "I now am," so that such a verb signifies both the subject and the time of the being in question. But these are mere consignifications of the verb, for it can be found without them, whereas it can never be found without either affirmation or negation. And such is indeed its nature: not to consignify time nor even to signify terms, but to be their affirmation. In Lancelot's own words: "According to this notion, it can be said that the verb itself should have no other use than to mark the binding together in our mind of the two terms of a proposition."

This "should" is a pearl. As if the proper job of grammar were to tell us what spoken usage should be, instead of telling us what it is! Naturally, what language should be in order to please Lancelot is what it should be in order to comply with the rules of formal Aristotelian logic. Whence it follows at once that, to Lancelot, language is unduly complicated. Since the principal function of the verb is to affirm, and since affirmation remains the same whatever may happen to be affirmed, a single verb should suffice for all affirmations. In point of fact, there is such a verb, and it is "to be." If only spoken usage allowed it, we would never use any other one. Just one verb; what a simplification! Not *I live*, or *I sit*, but *I am living, I am sitting* and likewise in all other cases.[10]   In such a doctrine, judgments of existence can obviously be nothing else than judgments of attribution. In the case of all other verbs, men have abridged their speech by creating verbs which signify, at one and the same time, both affirmation itself and what it affirms. In the sole case of the substantive verb "to be," they have not done so, because, in that case, the predicate is understood. *God exists* then, becomes the meaningless *God exists existing*, just as *I am* signifies: *I am a being*, or *I am something*.[11]

Lancelot has not been alone in this conviction, but one of the more interesting among similar cases is that of Bossuet. To say that Bossuet had a fine feeling for the meaning of words would be a clear case of understatement, yet he also became entangled in the same difficulty. On the one hand, Bossuet knew that the object of a concept never is existence, since, as he himself says, "whether an object be or not, we nevertheless understand it." On the other hand, he clearly realized that the verb *is* did not mean existence in general, for I am not thinking of such an indeterminate existence when I say *I am*, or *God is*. Yet, Bossuet was also convinced that all knowledge is related to some concept, so that there should always be a concept where there is meaning. In the particular case of existence, there is no doubt that we have such a concept: since we do know existence, we must needs have some idea of it. Thus, "existence" is the only concept we have which designates

---

[10] Lancelot, *Grammaire générale*, Ch. XIII, in *Logique de Port-Royal*, Part II, Ch. 2.
[11] *Logique de Port-Royal*, Part II, Ch. 3.

existence, yet it designates it in a too indeterminate way to designate actual existence. The only thing to do then is to add something to it. This is what Bossuet achieves by adding "now" to it. Our idea of actual existence is therefore the same as that of "present existence." To be is to be now. If I say *"These roses are," "There are roses"* or *"These roses exist,"* I am saying nothing else than that such roses are at the present time.[12] Such an answer presupposes that the three abstract notions of existence, of time and of the present can make up for the disappearance of a verb. True enough, Bossuet was not very far off the mark, for, if there is a notion which is inseparable from actual existence, it is that of "now." Yet, with all due respect for that great master of words, he was then putting the cart before the horse. "To be" is not "to be now;" rather, "to be now" is "to be." There is no concept whose addition to that of existence can make it signify actual existence, because no concept can signify it. The verb *is* signifies existence, and it signifies it in its own right.

We might have better luck with contemporary grammarians, for whom the logic of Aristotle is but a thing of the past. True enough, such scholars feel in no way concerned with philosophical problems. Language is for them a fact to be objectively studied, such as it is. But this is precisely what we need, and it may well appear, on closer investigation, that grammar is nearer metaphysics than formal logic itself is. The more we rid it of logic, the closer we are to metaphysics.

Now, it is a curious fact that even modern grammarians feel rather puzzled when they meet, not our question, but the grammatical occasion for our question. One of the most recent among them has stated it quite clearly: "The theory of the verb is what has most perplexed all grammarians, ancient and modern, and it is, let it be frankly admitted, the one most bristling with irregularities, exceptions, anomalies, and, in short, difficulties of all sorts."[13] As to himself, he begins his book with a farewell to Priscian,[14] a typical case indeed of scholarly ingratitude, since, when he comes to the dangerous problem of the verb, he finally treads in the footsteps of the patriarch of grammarians.

"The verb," Priscian had said, "is a part of speech, with tenses and modes, but without declension, which signifies actions

---

[12] Bossuet, *Logique*, Bk. I, Ch. 39.

[13] F. Brunot, *La Pensée et le langage. Méthode, principes et plans d'une théorie nouvelle du langage appliquée au Français* (Paris, Masson, 1922), pp. xviii-xix. Cf. p. 898, the last paragraph of the book.

[14] *Ibid.*, p. xix, note 1.

and passions."[15] The verb, our modern grammarian says, "signifies action in time and mode."[16] Obviously, this is quite a different account, and, while what we are here witnessing is not a farewell to Priscian, it is certainly a farewell to Aristotle, according to whom verbs were so many nouns, each of which signified, not an action, but the abstract concept which expressed the nature of an action. Thus, according to Aristotle, what the verb "to depart" actually means is, "departure." Not what I do, but the essence of what I do, is signified by the verb. There is nothing to surprise us in such a doctrine. The theory of the verb appears to grammarians as bristling with irregularities, because you cannot enter the realm of action without entering that of existence, and, if a grammarian is a logician of the sort that Aristotle was, he has no use for action. Hence the striking statement of Aristotle: "In themselves and by themselves, the words we call verbs are really nouns."[17] But, if such is the grammar of logicians, the grammar of grammarians is entirely different, since what the verb there means is action. And this, the same grammarian says in all simplicity of heart, is eminently true of the verb "to be," since "the first of all subjective actions is to exist."[18] I happen to have known that great grammarian and historian of the French language personally. Brunot had written his master book on *Thought and Language* with a view to ridding grammar, once and for all, of all traces of Scholasticism; and this he so successfully did that, at the very moment when the last trace of Aristotelianism disappeared from his own grammar, he found himself in complete agreement with Thomas Aquinas.

What happened to Scholastic grammar is clear enough. In so far as the problem of the verb is concerned, it has been the grammar of a logic in which all judgments are judgments of attribution. No grammarian, no linguist will feel the slightest hesitation in deciding which is the primary function of the verb *is*, namely, whether it is to be a copula or to signify actual existence. To say that *x is*, is to say that *x* exercises the very first of all subjective acts, which is *to be*. The problem is not to know how *is* has come to signify existence, it is rather to know why it has been singled out to play the part of copula.

---

[15] Priscian, *Institutiones grammaticae*, lib. VIII, 1, 1, ed. by M. Herz (Leipzig, Teubner, 1855), Vol. I, p. 369.   [16] Brunot, *op. cit.*, p. 203.
    [17] Aristotle, *Perihermeneias*, cap. III. In *In Perihermeneias*, lib. I, cap. 3, lect. 5, Thomas Aquinas says about this text, that, if verbs are nouns, it is because "even acting and being acted upon are, in a way, things." This *quoddam res* is, of course, Thomism in Aristotelian garb.
    [18] Brunot, *op. cit.*, p. 293.

We do not need to look very far for an answer to that question, but it cannot be a logical one; it must be a metaphysical one. Logic in itself is the science and the art which concerns the formal conditions for the validity of judgments in general. As such, it is directly concerned with the formal validity of judgments, not with their actual truth. Unless a judgment be correct, it cannot be true, but it can be correct without being true. If a judgment aims to be true, it aims, beyond formal and purely logical correction, to achieve an adequate expression of actually existing reality. This is why, as a modern logician has aptly said, every logical assertion presupposes a hypothetical judgment of existence.[19] With this last judgment, logic as such is in no way concerned, yet the judgment is there. Such implicit existential judgments have prompted Brentano to turn all judgments of attribution into so many existential ones. And this, I am afraid, was a mistake, but the fact remains that it is practically one and the same thing for us to formulate a judgment and to conceive it as true. The very choice of classical examples made by logicians of all times would suffice in itself to prove it. If the proposition, *"All men are mortal,"* has become the very type of affirmative proposition, it is because of the settled conviction that, in reality, each and every man ultimately dies. But this is not a logical rule; it is an existential fact. A logically correct judgment is true when what it affirms actually is, and when what it denies actually is not.[20]

The reason why *is* has become a copula is here apparent. Logic has had to deal with judgments such as it found them, and those judgments had not been invented by man in order to provide logic with a fitting matter, but in order to express reality. Now, the first character of reality is to be. When I say that *Peter is sick,* I directly conceive Peter as being in a sick way, that is, I conceive his being as that of a sick man. This is so at least as soon as, stepping out of logic, I become interested in actual truth. The verb "to be" is used as a copula because all judgments of attribution which are true or intend to be true aim to affirm or to deny a certain way of being. In short, *is* has correctly been chosen as a copula because all judgments of attribution are meant to say *how* a certain thing actually *is.*[21]

[19] E. Goblot, *Traité de logique,* 7th ed. (Paris, A. Colin, 1941), p. 43.

[20] "Sed quando adaequatur ei quod est extra in re, dicitur judicium verum esse," Thomas Aquinas, *Qu. disp. de Veritate,* q. I, art. 3, Resp. Cf. John of St. Thomas, *Logica,* P. I, Illustr. q. 1, art. 2: "At vero syllogistica illatio quia non consideratur ut vera, sed ut inferens . . ."

[21] See Thomas Aquinas, *In Perihermeneias,* lib. I, cap. 3, lect. 5, n. 22 (Leonine

If we simply say *that* a certain thing *is*, the judgment in question is a judgment of existence, and it is a perfectly correct one: it is complete without any other term requiring to be understood, with only one term and a verb, that is, the subject and the verb *is*. Why logic as such does not know what to do with such propositions is not difficult to see. Attributive propositions are everywhere related to existence, except, precisely, in logic: "*Logicus enim considerat modum praedicandi et non existentiam rei*," Thomas Aquinas says.[22] Existential propositions, which deal with nothing else than actual existence, are no fitting objects of consideration for the logician. They raise no formal problems, because they do not deal with forms, but with existence, which itself is the act of all forms. If it is a question of saying *how* things are, many problems are liable to arise precisely because things *are* in many different ways. There are as many ways of being as there are ways of being related to actual existence. There is that of matter and that of form, that of substance and that of its accidents, such as quantity, quality, action, passion and all the rest. But, when it comes to existence, everything is simple, for *x* either *is* or it *is not*, and that is all that can be said about it. Existential judgments are meaningless unless they are meant to be true. If the proposition, "*Peter is*," means anything, it means that a certain man, Peter by name, actually is, or exists. *Is* does not predicate anything, not even existence; it posits it, and such a proposition has no business to be quoted in formal logic, except as an example of a whole class of propositions which are not the business of the logician.

Grammar thus confronts us with certain judgments which do not fall within the scope of logic, so much so that, as soon as he handles them in a logical way, the grammarian feels bound to do away with them. There is no reason why such a fact should leave us at a loss. No metaphysician should feel ashamed to take everyday language seriously. The deepest metaphysical problems are involved in the most common formulas we use in everyday life. There is no *a priori* reason to doubt that human thought goes straight to what is perhaps the very core of reality. To scrutinize some words, and particularly the verb "to be," may well prove the safest way to seize knowledge, so to speak, at its source, where it is first cast into the mould of words. Thus grammar is closely related to metaphysics, because it deals with

---

edition, Vol. I, p. 28). Cf. John of St. Thomas, *Logica*, Summularum lib. I, cap. VI (Taurini-Romae, Marietti), Vol. I, pp. 15-16.

[22] Thomas Aquinas, *In VII Metaph.*, lect. 17, ed. Cathala, n. 1658.

that unsophisticated expression of common sense, which common language certainly is. There are not two different truths for common sense and for metaphysics; there is but one and the same truth, more or less deeply grasped and more or less distinctly formulated. Men have not waited for metaphysicians to invent judgments of existence. There actually are such judgments, and, despite the age-old hostility displayed against them by logicians, men cannot pronounce a single sentence in which at least one of them is not directly involved. Their existence then is beyond doubt, but what remains for the metaphysician to do is to define the conditions for their very possibility.

The two prerequisites to the possibility of existential judgments are that reality should include an existential act over and above its essence, and that the human mind be naturally able to grasp it. That there is such an existential act in reality has been established, by showing that all philosophical attempts to do without it have resulted in philosophical failures. That the human mind is naturally able to grasp it is a fact, and, if so many philosophers seem to doubt it, it is because they fail to grasp the cognitive power of judgment. Because it lies beyond essence, existence lies beyond abstract representation, but not beyond the scope of intellectual knowledge; for judgment itself is the most perfect form of intellectual knowledge, and existence is its proper object.

The most serious mistake made by the various metaphysics of essence is their failure to realize the nature of essence. They simply forget that essence always is the essence of some being. The concept which expresses an essence cannot be used as a complete expression of the corresponding being, because there is, in the object of every concept, something that escapes and transcends its essence. In other words, the actual object of a concept always contains more than its abstract definition. What it contains over and above its formal definition is its act of existing, and, because such acts transcend both essence and representation, they can be reached only by means of judgment. The proper function of judgment is to say existence, and this is why judgment is a type of cognition distinct from, and superior to, pure and simple abstract conceptualization.

· Yet, it should not be forgotten that, in concrete experience, essence itself is the setting apart of a portion of concrete reality. The primary error of the metaphysics of essence is to mistake that part for its whole and to speculate about essences as though they were the whole of both reality and its intelligibility. In point of fact, essences should never be conceived as final objects of intellectual knowledge, because their very nature is engaged in the concreteness of actual being. Abstracted from being, they claim to be reintegrated being. In other words, the proper end of intellectual abstraction is not to posit essences in the mind as pure and self-sufficient presentations. Even when we abstract essences, we do not do so with a view to knowing essences, but with a view to knowing the very beings to which they belong, and this is why, if philosophical knowledge is not to remain abstract speculation, but to be real knowledge, it must use judgment to restore essences to actual being.

To judge is precisely to say that what a concept expresses actually is either a being or the determination of a certain being. Judgments always affirm that certain conceived essences are in a state of union with, or of separation from, existence. Judgments unite in the mind what is united in reality, or they separate in the mind what is separated in reality. And what is thus united or separated is always existence, either *how* it is, or *that* it is. In this last case, which is that of the judgment of existence, my mental act exactly answers the existential act of the known thing. Let us, rather, say that such a judgment intellectually reiterates an actual act of existing. If I say that *x is*, the essence of *x* exercises through my judgment the same act of existing which it exercises in *x*. If I say that *x is not*, I mentally separate the essence of *x* from actual existence, because existence does not actually belong to *x*. This is why, while abstraction can correctly conceive apart what is really one, judgment cannot separate what is one in reality. It cannot do it, at least in this sense that, when it does, it betrays its own function and defeats its own purpose. In other words, whereas abstraction is there provisorily to take parts out of their wholes, judgment is there to integrate or to reintegrate those same parts into their wholes. True judgments are normal judgments, and judgments are normal when they unite what is actually united or when they separate what is actually separated. Thus, abstract knowledge bears upon essence, but judgment bears upon existence: *"Prima quidem operatio respicit ipsam naturam rei . . . secunda operatio respicit ipsum esse rei."*[23]

But both operations are equally required for knowledge, which always is a cognition of actual being. Fundamental as it is, the distinction between abstract knowledge and judgment should therefore never be conceived as a separation. Abstraction and judgment are never separated in the mind, because essence and

[23] Thomas Aquinas, *In Boethium de Trinitate*, qu. V., art. 3, ed. P. Wyser, p. 38, ll. 8-11.

existence are never separated in reality. I may well abstract the essence of a certain being and deal with it for a while as though it were unrelated to the being from which I abstracted it, but it is not, for *essentia* always belongs to an *esse*, and, even while I conceive it apart, essence never cuts loose from actual being; it is, rather, bound to it by a life line, and, if that line is cut off, essence is dead. No knowledge will ever come out of it. Such is eminently the case for the notion of being. Thomas Aquinas was fond of repeating, with Avicenna, that being is what falls first into the mind, and this is true; but it does not mean that our cognition is an abstract cognition. What comes first is a sensible perception whose object is immediately known by our intellect as "being," and this direct apprehension by a knowing subject immediately releases a twofold and complementary intellectual operation. First, the knowing subject apprehends *what* the given object is, next it judges *that* the object is, and this instantaneous recomposition of the existence of given objects with their essences merely acknowledges the actual structure of these objects. The only difference is that, instead of being simply experienced, such objects now are intellectually known.

If this be true, being is not and cannot become an object of purely abstract cognition. As has been said, there is something insidiously artificial in dealing with even abstract essences, as though the bond which ties them to actual existence could actually be cut; but what is still more artificial and more perilous is to deal in a purely abstract way with such a metaphysical monster as the abstract essence of being. For, indeed, there is no such essence. What is conceivable is the essence of *a being*, not that of *being*. If the correct definition of being is "that which is," it necessarily includes an *is*, that is, existence. To repeat, every *ens* is an *esse habens*, and unless its *esse* be included in our cognition of it, it is not known as an *ens*, that is, as a *be-ing*. If what we have in mind is not this and that being, but being in general, then its cognition necessarily involves that of existence in general, and such a general cognition still entails the most fundamental of all judgments, namely that being is. In short, the very notion of a purely essential cognition of being is self-contradictory, and, because being imperiously demands the immediate recognition, through judgment, of the *esse* which it includes, its knowledge is both essential and existential in its own right.

If thoroughly understood, this conclusion involves another one, which is of decisive importance for metaphysical speculation as a whole, namely, that all real knowledge is by nature both essential and existential. Being does not come first in the sense that what comes next no longer is being. Being comes first and it stays there. Being accompanies all my representations. But even that is not saying enough, for each and every cognition is a cognition of being. I never get out of being, because, outside it there is nothing. What I begin by espying from afar is first to me just a "being;" if it comes nearer, I know that it is an animal, but it still is "a being;" let it come near enough, and I will know that it is a man, then, finally, Peter, but all these successive determinations of the known object remain as so many more and more determined cognitions of a being. In other words, where no actual being, taken with its act of existing, answers my knowledge, there is no knowledge at all. Being, then, is not only the first and primary object of intellectual cognition, it is the cognition into which every other one ultimately resolves: *"Illud autem quod primo intellectus concipit quasi notissimum et in quo omnes conceptiones resolvit est ens."*[24] And, since *ens* (being) includes its own *esse* (to be), each and every real knowledge ultimately is resolved into the composition of an essence with its own existence, which are posited as one by an act of judging. This is why judgment ultimately bears upon *esse* (to be), and also why the truth of cognition ultimately rests upon the fact that its object is, rather than on our abstract knowledge of what the thing is; for all true knowledge is resolved into being, and, unless we reach "to be," we fail to reach "being."

Considered from the point of view of this realism of being, both essentialism and existentialism appear as little more than two opposite yet equally unsatisfactory abstractions. Cognition requires considerable speculation about essences, but even our abstract knowledge of essences is not merely "specular" in the Kirkegaardian sense of the word. Intellects are not mirrors which passively reflect reality, and concepts are not the merely passive reflexions of their objects. Still more than do sensations, concepts express the common act of the knower and of the known thing. To know a thing is *to be it* in an intellectual way. The classical refutation of *adequatio rei et intellectus* which derides it as a copy theory, according to which the concept is supposed to be a passive reflexion of reality, entirely misses its point. It may well apply to naive essentialism, but it by no means applies to a noetic in which the knowledge of essence rests upon the vital conjunction of two acts of existing. Even abstract knowledge is not the mere

---

[24] Thomas Aquinas, *Qu. disp. de Veritate*, qu. I, art. 1, Resp.

copying of an essence by an intellect; it is the intellectual becoming of an actual essence in an intellectual being.

The noetic of abstract essences lies open to irrefutable criticism, because it overlooks the fact that what is most essential to essences is their very relation to existential reality. For the same reason, the realism of the *res* (things) lays itself open to the same objections. It puts reality before existence instead of putting existence into reality, and, because it misses existence, it misses reality. Knowing is an act as deeply rooted in existence as being itself is. Just as the first act of a knowing being is to be, so its first operation is to know, that is, to operate as it must in its capacity of knowing being. "To be" then is first in the order of cognition, and it remains so even in the order of self-cognition. It is quite true to say that, if I know that I think, I know that I am, but this does not mean that I am because I think; rather, I think because I am. Whence it follows, first, that there is no incompatibility between thought and existence. For an intellectual being such as man, thought is not the abstract objectification of existence, nor is existence the ceaseless breaking up of thought. To think is to act, just as to be is to act. In an intellectual substance, thought is the operational manifestation of its very act of existing. But, along with this alleged opposition between thought and existence, the opposition between actual existence and the knowledge of another existence immediately disappears. If I think because I am, and, if what I am thinking about actually is, I do not *think*, I *know*. Normally, man is not a thinker; he is a knower. Man thinks when what he knows is his own thought, man knows when what he is thinking about is an actually existing thing. To know another being, then, always is to grasp its essence within its given existence, and, far from excluding it, all real knowledge includes a judgment of existence which is the last moment of a vital exchange between two actually existing beings.

In short, true realism is neither a realism of *essence* nor a realism of *thing;* it is the realism of being, and this is why it is both an immediate and natural realism. Being is neither intuited by a sensibility nor understood by an intellect; it is known by a man. An organic chain of mental operations links the sense perception of what is known as being to the abstraction and to the judgment through which man knows it as being. Even Cajetan's justly famous formula, *"Ens concretum quidditati sensibili,"* does not do full justice to the true nature of immediate realism, for it is sensible concreteness itself which is known as a being. The whole cycle of operations which begins in sensible intuition ends in the very same sensible intuition, and at no moment, supposing that it takes more than one, does it get out of it. We directly know perceived data as beings, so that our direct knowledge of them includes an intuitive experience of their very acts of existing.

There is no *a priori* way to deduce the possibility of such knowledge. It must be possible because it is a fact. The great discovery of contemporary existentialism, that, for man, to be is "to be in the land of the living," is at least as old as the always valid Aristotelian conception of sense perception. Idealism is so radically unreal that it does not even bear to be overcome. A product of pure thinking, it is wholly irrelevant to knowing. There nowhere is, except in the mind of thinkers, a knowing subject that knows nothing, yet wonders how it could possibly know. There nowhere is in reality such an existing subject as that of Kirkegaard, whose very existence puts him in a final state of separation from all the rest. No man is alone, because, as a spiritual substance, were he alone, he could not know and he could not *be*. If to be is, for him, to know, to be is necessarily "to become another," and for me "to become another" exactly is "to be myself." I am myself through ceaselessly becoming another, owing to a constant assimilation of essences which, in me, are my own existence. My own "I am" is always given to me in an "it is," and each "it is" is either given in or related to a sensory perception. Sensory perception is the vital exchange which constantly takes place between existing intellectual souls and actually existing things. It is, in fact, the meeting point of two distinct acts of existing.

This is why sensible perception is a first principle of human knowledge. Where thinking is mistaken for knowing, sensible perception can be no such principle, but, where knowing properly so called is at stake, knowledge begins in perception, and its end is in its beginning. To perceive is to experience existence, and to say through judgment that such an experience is true is to know existence. An intellectual knowledge of existence is therefore possible for an intellect whose operations presuppose its vital experience, as an existent, of another existent. In other words, intellectual knowledge conceives existence, but the fruit of its conception then is not the representation of some essence; it is an act which answers an act. Exactly, it is the act of an operation which answers an act of existing, and such an operation is itself an act because it directly flows from an act of existing. An epistemology in which judgment, not abstraction, reigns supreme, is necessarily required by a metaphysics in which "to be" reigns supreme in the order of actuality.

Yet, such a philosophy remains a philosophy of being. Just as essentialism is a metaphysics of being minus existence, existentialism is a philosophy of existence minus being. Hence the peculiar characters of the experience of existence upon which it rests. It can be described as a bare sensation of existence experienced by a sensibility which, for a few moments, is cut off from its intellect. It is, so to speak, a downward extasis, wherein finite acts of existing are merely felt in themselves, wholly unrelated to their essences and therefore deprived of all intelligibility. No concept there, nor even judgment, but the bare experiencing of an *is* which is not yet a *being*. No wonder, then, that, for contemporary existentialism to experience existence is to experience anguish, nausea and the utter absurdity of everything. But, where there is no thing, there can be no all. Such an experience is but too real, yet it merely proves that essence and purpose are part and parcel of actual being. Should they be removed, be it for a split second, what is left no longer makes sense: it is that whose only essence and meaning is to have neither essence nor meaning. He who allows himself thus to sink into his own sensibility cannot but experience a metaphysical giddiness, a sort of existence-sickness, whence he will later conclude that existence itself is but a sickness of being.

How could it be otherwise? There is only one way to reach pure existence, and the mystics have always known it. Not the way that leads, through the denial of essences, to the maddening experience of some existing nothingness, but the one that once lead Augustine, Bonaventura and John of the Cross, through overcoming all essences without ever losing them, to reach their common source, itself beyond essences yet containing them all. Not despair, but perfect joy, is the reward of such an experience, and it is true that philosophy alone cannot achieve it; but this is not the only case in which philosophy points out a goal which it itself is unable to reach. Contemporary existentialism is right in asking questions about existence, but one may well wonder if its fundamental mistake is not to ask existences to account for themselves, instead of looking at being for their cause. Distinct as they are from being by that only which in them is not, nothingness necessarily becomes their specific difference. We are thus left face to face with Platonic becoming, without the world of Ideas to grant it what it may have of intelligibility; or with universal motion without the self-thinking Thought of Aristotle to sway it from on high; or with a world created out of nothing, which, having lost its Creator, must needs be created by nothing. Existentialism has not discovered existence; its only metaphysical discovery is to ask how existence can still make sense, if nothingness remains the sole principle of its intelligibility.

In fact, being itself is neither existence nor essence; it is their unity, and this is why it is whole and sound. Just as to be a being is to be, so to be is necessarily to be a being. Any empirically given existence is that of a given being, and our knowledge of existence is therefore bound to be that of an existing being. This is why there are no concepts without judgments nor any judgments without concepts. Not even the simple apprehension of being can be without a judgment. Since an *ens* is·an *esse habens*, all that which is conceived as a being is also judged to be an *is*. It must be so, since "to be" is part of "being." But the reverse holds true. Actually, to be is always to be in an intelligible way. In short, reality is neither a wholly inexpressible mystery, nor is it a mere collection of materialized concepts; it is a conceivable reality hanging on an act which itself escapes representation, yet does not escape intellectual knowledge, because it is included in every intelligible enunciation. We do more than experience existence; we know it through any judgment of existence about actual being. There is an act of judging which escapes the classical definition of judgment as the linking together of two objective concepts by a copula; it is the judgment of existence, *x is*, which affirms that a subject exercises the trans-essential act of existing. The proposition, *"being is,"* can therefore be understood in two different ways. As developed into the attributive proposition, *"being is being,"* it yields the supreme law of all abstract knowledge, but also the most formal of all cognitions and consequently the emptiest of all. In this case both Parmenides and Hegel are right: being is nothing but the pure selfhood of thought, grasping itself as an object. But *"being is"* may mean something quite different, namely, that being is actual in virtue of its own "to be," in which case it becomes, though the most general, yet the fullest of all metaphysical truths. For, what it then signifies is that, in each and every particular case, the greatest mistake which a metaphysician can make about being is to overlook the very act whereby it is a being.

It may well be asked what there is to be gained foɪ real knowledge by positing an act which it should suffice to take for granted. To which the answer is that the recognition of such an act is our sole safeguard against an infinite number of speculative errors whose practical consequences are but too obvious. Contemporary thought seems to be beset by a passionate desire for purity, and the purity it aims to achieve is always that of some essence. Idealism has burned itself to death by achieving the purity of a self-consuming act of thinking. Poetry has attempted to achieve the purity of its own essence by expelling from itself all that belongs to that other essence, prose. In order to be pure of prose, it has purified words, first from their usual meaning, then from all meaning, and, having thus become senseless, it is now beginning to wonder if, after all, the essence of poetry does not include another one, that of intelligibility. Painting, too, has attempted to become pure. Since what makes it to be an art is what the artist himself adds to nature, why should not painting eliminate the whole contribution of nature and keep only what it owes to art? Could it only be achieved, the result would indeed be pure art. Yet, it is beginning to appear that, though painters can go very far indeed along that road, they cannot go the whole way. Where it achieves its non-representative purity, painting loses itself in some sort of impure geometry, just as pure poetry dissolves into an impure verbal music. All such attempts are bound ultimately to fail, because concreteness is but another name for essential impurity. All that which is concrete is metaphysically impure. In human experience there are no such things as pure self-subsisting essences, and man himself is far from being one: mind and body, forms and matter, substances and accidents are simultaneously given in actual complexes of mutual determinations. Each concrete essence is a sharing in several different essences, and it is not from looking at them in particular that we can see how they can fit together. Existence is the catalyser of essences. Because it itself is act in a higher order than that of essences, it can melt them together in the unity of a single being.

For, having overlooked the transcendence of existence, essentialism has entertained the curious illusion that, since, in order to be, a being must at least be possible, the root of being lies in its possibility. But possibility is a word of several meanings. It may mean the simple absence of inner contradiction in an essence, and, in such cases, all non-contradictory combinations of essences are equally possible, but none of them is one step nearer its actualization than another one. It may also mean that an essence is fully determined, so that it is actually capable of existing. Such possibles are in the condition which Scholastics would have called that of proximate potency to existence. But such a possibility still remains pure abstract possibility. Is it true to say, with so many philosophers, that, when all the conditions required for the possibility of a thing are fulfilled, the thing itself is bound to exist? Scarcely. When all those conditions are fulfilled, what is thereby fulfilled is the possibility of the thing. If any one of them were lacking, the thing would be impossible, but, from the fact that all those conditions are given, it does not follow that the thing is required to exist. The possibility of its essence does not include that of its existence, unless, of course, we count among its required conditions the very existence of its cause. But, if we do, the being of the cause is the reason why the possible is a possible being. *Omne ens ex ente:* all being comes from another being, that is, not from a possible, but from an existent.

To overlook this fact is completely to reverse the actual relation of essences to existences. In human experience, at least, there are no such things as fully determined essences prior to their existential actualization. Their *esse* is a necessary prerequisite to the fullness of their determination. They cannot be what they are unless they first become it. It is so with human lives, and it is so with human works. The *Matthaeus Passion* was not an essence hovering in a limbo of possible essences where Johann Sebastian Bach caught it, so to speak, on the wing. As soon as there has been a Bach, the *Matthaeus Passion* has become a possible being, but, conversely, it has had to become in order to conquer the fullness of its determinations, and it became when Bach actually wrote it. We know that the three Organ Chorales of César Franck are possible because he has written them; but the fourth one is not possible, because Franck died without having written it. Its existence is impossible, and, as to its essence, we shall never know it, because, in order to know what his fourth Organ Chorale might possibly have been, Franck himself would first have had to compose it. The primary cause making human works to become determined possibles is the very existence of the artist.

But the irrepressible essentialism of the human mind blinds us to that evidence. Instead of accounting for potency by act, we account for act by potency. We rather forget that what is at stake is neither existence nor essence, but being, which is both. We fancy that essences, which owe their complete determination to existence, are eternally independent of existence. Everything then proceeds as though the essences of possible beings had been eternally conceived, by a divine mind, apart from the very act through which they would some day become actual beings. Thus conceived, existence does not enter the concrete determination of essences; it fills them up.

It is not so, at least it is not so in a Thomistic metaphysics of being, because wherever there is being, there is *esse* (to be): the *esse* of each being is included in its divine idea. Different things are different because they imitate God in different ways, and each particular thing imitates God in its own way because, as Thomas Aquinas says, each of them has its own *esse*, which is distinct from any other: *"Diversae autem res diversimode ipsam [divinam essentiam] imitantur, et unaquaeque secundum proprium modum suum, cum unicuique sit proprium esse distinctum ab altero."*[25] This is precisely why, in the same metaphysics, although God has eternal knowledge of all that He could create, He does not know what is not created in the same way as what He creates (*non tamen eodem modo*). What determines which ideas are to be created, among an infinity of possible creatures, is the divine will. Such ideas then are determinately in God as ideas of creatures,[26] and, because they include a determination of the divine will, they are not only the pattern after which creatures are made, they are the very makers of those creatures: *"Similitudo rei quae est in intellectu divino est factiva rei,"* and for the likeness of a thing to be in God simply means that the thing participates in *esse* (to be) through God: *"Secundum hoc similitudo omnis rei in Deo existit quod res illa a Deo esse participat."*[27] In God, infinitely more than in things, existence is the root of essences, including their very possibility.

If it can affect our attitude towards reality, such a notion of being cannot fail to affect our general conception of philosophical knowledge. There are philosophies, William Ernest Hocking aptly says, which rest *on assumption*, while some others rest *on seeing*. The philosophy which naturally follows from the above-defined conception of being definitely rests on seeing. And it does not do so in virtue of any assumption. The only excuse there is for a philosopher to make an assumption is that he does not see. He who assumes *thinks*, but he who sees *knows*, and, though it be true that no limits can be set to the amount of thinking which can be involved in the process of actual knowledge, modern physics teaches us that years and years of mathematical speculation never become knowledge until, through art or chance, its results are confirmed by a sometimes almost instantaneous sense perception. Philosophy itself, including metaphysics, should obey the same law. At least, it should do so inasmuch as it aims to be knowledge. The magnificent "systems" of those idealists who

[25] *Ibid.*, qu. III, art. 2, Resp. [26] *Ibid.*, qu. III, art. 6, Resp.
[27] *Ibid.*, qu. II, art. 5, Resp.

bear the title of "great thinkers," and wholly deserve it, belong in the realm of art more than in that of philosophy. It is probably not by chance that Germany is the country of both idealistic metaphysics and of music. Hegel, Schelling, Fichte can assume a metaphysical theme and weave it into a world with no less freedom than Bach can write a fugue. Such metaphysical fabrics are far from lacking beauty, but Bach was right because, as an artist, his end was to achieve beauty, whereas Hegel was wrong, because, as a philosopher, his end should have been to achieve truth. No more than science, philosophy cannot be a system, because all systematic thinking ultimately rests on assumption, whereas. *qua* knowledge, philosophy must rest on being.

Such a notion of being and of the metaphysics it involves has been already conceived, and this as early as the thirteenth century, but it would be interesting to know how many philosophers have paid attention to it. Speaking of his own contemporaries, a certain Bernardus Lombardi, who was teaching in Paris about the year 1327, did not hesitate to say: "There are two ways of speaking: the first is that of Doctor Saint Thomas, who asserts that, in all beings short of God, essence differs from existence; the second is that of all the other Parisian masters who unanimously maintain the opposite."[28] We need not trust Bernardus Lombardi implicitly, and his statement may well have been an overstatement, but it is a fact that a notion of being such as that of Saint Thomas is a rare thing to meet in the history of metaphysics. Yet, unless it be thus conceived, what is left of being is little more than its empty shell. Why should philosophers use such an empty shell for their first principle of human knowledge? Any particular aspect of being is then bound to look preferable because, be it even abstract quantity, it corresponds at least to some "thing."

At the beginning of this inquiry we asked how it was that, if being is the first object of the human mind, so few philosophers have seen it as the first principle of philosophical knowledge. The answer is now at hand, namely, the overwhelming tendency of human understanding to sterilize being by reducing it to an abstract concept. Wherever that tendency has been allowed to prevail, being has still remained a formal rule of rational thinking, but it has ceased to be a principle of real knowledge; in short, it

---

[28] "Est duplex modus dicendi: primus est doctoris sancti Thomae, qui ponit quod in omnibus citra Deum differt esse ab essentia; secundus est omnium aliorum concorditer parisiensium, qui ponunt oppositum", in J. Koch, *Durandus de s. Porciano* (*Beitr. zur Gesch. der Phil. d. M.-A.*), Vol. XXVI, I), p. 330. See also G. Meersseman, *Geschichte des Albertismus*, (Paris, R. Haloua, 1933), Vol. I, p. 51.

has ceased to be a "beginning." Where being no longer plays the part of a beginning, another beginning has to be found. If, as seems to be the case, existence truly is a constituent element of being, the hole created by its removal can claim to be filled up, but nothing else than existence itself adequately corresponds in shape to that hole. Once existence has been removed, there always remains, in being, something for which existenceless being provides no rational explanation. The chronic disease of metaphysical being is not existence, but its tendency to lose existence. To restore existence to being is therefore the first prerequisite to the restoring of being itself to its legitimate position as the first principle of metaphysics.

To do so would by no means constitute a philosophical discovery, but it would put an end to the all-too-protracted neglect of an ancient truth. Such a metaphysics would do justice to all the metaphysical discoveries which have already been made in the past. It would grant to Parmenides that, when posited as a purely abstract essence, being is one with pure conceptual thinking. It would grant to Plato that essentiality is selfhood. It would grant to Aristotle that substance is both act and source of operations according to its specification by form. It would grant to Avicenna that existence is a determination which happens to finite essence in virtue of its cause. Last, but not least, it would grant to Thomas Aquinas that existence happens to essence in a most peculiar way, not as some sort of accidental determination, but as its supreme act, that is, as the cause of its being as well as of its operations. As to those metaphysics with which it cannot agree, it can at least understand why they arose and went their own several ways. For, indeed, the cognition of being entails an all-too-real difficulty, which is intrinsic to its very nature. When confronted with an element of reality for which no conceptual representation is available, human understanding feels bound, if not always to reduce it into nothingness, at least to bracket it, so that everything may proceed as though that element did not exist. It is unpleasant for philosophy to admit that it flows from a source which, *qua* source, will never become an object of abstract representation. Hence the ceaselessly renewed attempts of philosophers to pretend that there is no such source or that, if there is one, we need not worry about it. Yet the history of philosophy is there to show that the awareness of existence is the beginning of philosophical wisdom. It does not do so in its capacity as history, whose only business it is to relate, but by providing philosophy with a fitting matter for critical reflexion. History

214

does not bind us to the past, nor does it make us break away from the past through recognizing it as past. History takes us back to the past as to something which we can make to be present again through personal appropriation. There is no "once upon a time" to which, so long as he lives, man cannot lend his own "now." From its endless journeys into the past, history brings back, along with many errors, some precious nuggets of truth. Historians then marvel how it is that such treasures have been allowed to lie so long neglected, and this should at least safeguard them against any undue optimism concerning the future; but it should not prevent them from knowing truth when they see it, nor should it dissuade them from stating it as true.

A critical examination of the data provided by the history of philosophy leads to the conclusion that "to be" does not contradict being, since it is the cause of being, and that judgments do not contradict concepts, since all judgments are finally rooted in the existential act of what first falls under the apprehension of understanding, that is, being. Such a metaphysics does not reveal to us any new essence, but it directly concerns our attitude towards all essences. All real essences are known through abstraction, yet their abstraction does not entail their separation from existence. Such a separation never occurs until essentialism begins to deal with them as with abstractions from abstractions. Essences then become *entia tertiae intentionis*, and they are dead. The confusion or the divorce of essence and existence are two errors equally fatal to philosophy. A true metaphysics of being alone can reconcile history with objective knowledge, existence with essence and time with eternity. It provides the only ground on which philosophy can ask the question to which religion is the answer. No less fond of concepts than that of Hegel, no less related to the philosopher and to man than that of Kirkegaard, such a metaphysics is neither a system nor the self-expression of a solitary existence. It is, before anything else, wisdom, and it aims to insure the progressive adequation of human knowledge to actually existing being. A never-ending task indeed, yet not a fruitless one. For, if "to be" escapes all abstract representation, it can be included in all concepts, and this is achieved through the judgment of existence, the always available response of an existent endowed with intellectual knowledge to other acts of existing.

Appendix

Sapientis enim est non curare de nominibus.[1]

On Some Difficulties of Interpretation

Among the criticisms directed against the positions upheld in the present work, the most important bear upon our description of the intellectual apprehension of being. The particular nature of our philosophical undertaking exposed it almost inevitably to such objections. Some of them having been both foreseen and answered beforehand, we have no intention to discuss them anew. Others have been neither foreseen nor, consequently, answered. Such are, for instance, the critical remarks of Fr. Louis-Marie Régis. Their importance is obvious and we feel particularly anxious to use them as a remedy against some confusions which the complexity of our own position might cause in the minds of our readers concerning the true position of Saint Thomas Aquinas. It is difficult to philosophize from the principles of the Angelic Doctor without involving him in statements for which he is in no way responsible. It is still more difficult to discuss modern philosophical problems, be it in the light of his own principles, without using a language of which he would have probably disapproved. The remarks of Fr. Régis are a pressing invitation for us to reestablish, beyond our own formulas, the historical truth of those of Thomas Aquinas himself. We feel grateful to him, and to the publishers of *The Modern Schoolman*, for permitting us to reprint part of his own text. Any attempt to sum it up would have resulted in arbitrary deformations, and rather than ruin its unity by subjecting it to a continuous discussion, we have preferred to keep it whole. Our own remarks on the subject will be found in a distinct section of this appendix. Let us therefore begin by reading Fr. Régis himself: THE KNOWLEDGE OF EXISTENCE IN ST. THOMAS AQUINAS.[2]

[1] Thomas Aquinas, *In II Sent.*, 3, 1, 1, Resp.
[2] *The Modern Schoolman* XXVIII, 2, Jan. 1951, pp. 121-127.

216

I. CRITICAL OBSERVATIONS OF FR. L.-M. RÉGIS, O.P.

The problem of the knowledge of existence is the alpha and omega of our author's book. It is with this problem that he begins his inquiry into being as being and it is with its solution that his inquiry terminates. From the very first pages, we have a very clear indication of the road which M. Gilson is taking as a result of his categorical refusal of the concept as a means of knowing existence. Here is the text:

> It is not enough to say that *being* is conceivable apart from existence; in a certain sense it must be said that *being* is always *conceived* by us apart from existence, for the very simple reason that existence itself cannot possibly be *conceived*. The nature of this paradoxical fact has been admirably described by Kant . . . "Being," Kant says, "is evidently not a real predicate, or a concept of something that can be added to the concept of a thing" (p. 3).[3]

The entire chapter on the knowledge of existence is but an elaborate commentary on the affirmations we have just recalled. First of all, there is the distinction between the *conceptus*, which is the term of apprehension, and the *judicium*, which is the term of the second operation of the mind which composes or divides two concepts (p. 190). Then we have the study of propositions, and of their division into *one-term* and *two-term propositions*, a study which manifests the nonpredicability of the verb "to be," since it is not a concept and every predicate is a concept (pp. 190-202). Finally we have the inevitable conclusion that, since the knowledge of existence cannot be had through a concept, it must result from the judgment, which meets all the conditions of concreteness and actuality necessary for a grasp of this concrete act par excellence which is the "to exist" (pp. 202-13).

1. THE INCONCEIVABILITY OF "TO BE"

As to the "copula," it is not really a term, because it designates, not a concept, but the determinate relation which obtains between two terms. For this reason the copula cannot be a noun; it is a verb. In point of fact, it is the verb *is* (p. 190).

[3] Cf. pp. 124-26.

No one will contest that the verb is not a noun, for its function in the enunciation is radically opposed to that of the noun;[4] but it is quite a different matter to affirm that the verb is not a *concept* because it is not a noun, and I fear very much that it would be impossible to justify such an affirmation in Thomism, even by using the epistemological vocabulary used by M. Gilson. If indeed the term of every act of apprehension deserves the name of concept in the strict sense of the word (p. 190), it seems impossible to me that the name of concept be denied to the verb, since it is undoubtedly the fruit of the first operation of the mind. Here are a few texts:

> . . . the meaning of a sentence differs from the meaning of a noun or verb, because a noun or a *verb* means a *simple understanding*, but a sentence means a composite understanding.[5]

> It is to be said that, since the operation of the intellect is twofold, as was said above, he who expresses a noun or a *verb* by itself, establishes an understanding as far as the *first operation* is concerned, which is the simple conception of something.[6]

There are other interesting texts on this same point.[7]

But the verb "to be" is the verb par excellence; used alone in the present tense, which is the verb *simpliciter*,[8] it is not capable of expressing truth or of constituting the enunciation and hence does not belong to the second operation of the mind.[9]

2. THE IMPREDICABILITY OF "TO BE"

If the proposition, *"Peter is,"* means anything, it means that a certain man, Peter by name, actually is, or exists. *Is* does not predicate anything, not even existence; it posits it . . ." (p. 201).

---

[4] *In I Periherm.*, lect. 5.

[5] ". . . significatio orationis differt a significatione nominis et verbi: quia nomen vel verbum significet simplicem intellectum; oratio vero significat intellectum compositum," (*ibid.*, lect. 6, no. 2).

[6] "Sed dicendum est quod cum duplex sit intellectus operatio, ut supra habitum est, ille qui dicit nomen vel verbum secundum se, constituit intellectum quantum ad primam operationem, quae est simplex conceptio alicujus" (*ibid.*, lect. 5, no. 17).

[7] *Ibid.*, lect. 1, no. 5; lect. 3, no 11; lect. 8, no. 17; *In II Periherm.*, lect. 1, no. 1.

[8] *In I Periherm.*, lect. 5, no. 22.

[9] *Ibid.*, nos. 17, 18, 19-22.

Why this unwillingness to make a predicate of the verb "to be?" Because it is not a concept and every predicate must be a concept. But we have just seen that the verb is a concept and that the verb "to be" is the first analogate of all verbs, since it always expresses an act, an actual act, and that existence is the actuality par excellence. Hence under this aspect, there is no reason to take from the verb "to be" its function as a predicate, and the following affirmation does not seem to be justified in any way in Thomism: "In short, existence is a prerequisite for the truth of any predication, but it does not directly fall under the scope of predication" (p. 196). And the conclusion derived therefrom is not any more justified: "We thus find ourselves confronted with the fact that, since *is* does not mean either a predicate or a subject, its meaning must needs be *wholly contained in itself*" (p. 196).

The truth, in Thomism, is that the verb is the predicate par excellence: ". . . since predication seems to pertain more properly to the composition, it is the *verbs that are predicated*, rather than means predicates."[10] Now, in existential propositions, the verb "to be" is predicated per se: ". . . this verb *is* is sometimes *predicated by itself* in an enunciation, as when it is said, 'Socrates is.' By this we do not intend to mean anything other than that Socrates is in reality."[11] Furthermore, the propositions *de tertio adjacente* are not so called "because, in them, the predicate is the third word" (p. 191), but because the verb *is* is added to the principal predicate and does not have its function as per se predicate.

Sometimes [*is*] is not predicated per se, as *principal predicate*, but as conjoined to the principal predicate to connect the latter with the subject. For example, when we say "Socrates is white," the meaning is not to assert that Socrates exists in reality, but to attribute to him whiteness by means of this verb *is*. Therefore, in such propositions, *is* is predicated as added to the principal predicate. It is said to be the third, not because it is a third predicate, but because it is the third expression in a proposition, and *together with the noun which is predicated makes one predicate*.[12]

[10] ". . . cum praedicatio videatur magis proprie ad compositionem pertinere, ipsa verba sunt quae praedicantur, magis quam significent praedicata" (*ibid.*, lect. 5, no. 9).

[11] ". . . hoc verbum *est* quandoque in Enunciatione praedicatur secundum se; ut cum dicitur, *Socrates est*: per quod nihil aliud intendimus significare quam quod Socrates sit in rerum natura" (*In II Periherm.*, lect., 2, no. 2).

[12] "Quandoque vero [*est*] non praedicatur *per se*, quasi principale praedicatum,

The metaphysical reason on which this function of the verb "to be" in all enunciations is based comes directly from its object, which is not existence in general, but the actual and present "to exist":

> For [is] means that which is understood after the manner of absolute actuality. For is, when it is expressed without qualification, means to be in act, and therefore it has its meaning after the manner of a verb. But the actuality, which is the principal meaning of the verb is, is indifferently the actuality of every form, either substantial or accidental act. Hen^{ce} it is that when we wish to signify that any form or act actually inheres in any subject, we signify it by this verb is, either simply or according to some qualification—simply, in the present tense; according to some qualification, in the other tenses.[13]

Consequently the knowledge of existence is had through and in a concept in Thomism, not a noun concept but a verb concept. It would be strange if by definition all concepts were abstract and only had the function of causing the quiddities of things to exist in the soul. It is not of the essence of a concept to be abstract: there are even concepts which cannot be abstract because their intelligibility requires an absence of abstraction.[14] Neither the concept of being as a noun nor that of being as a verb can be the result of an abstraction: for "being" as a noun implies essentially habens esse or quod est, and "being" as a verb

---

sed quasi conjunctum principali praedicato ad connectendum ipsum subiecto; sicut cum dicitur, *Socrates est albus*, non est intentio loquentis ut asserat Socratem esse in rerum natura, sed ut attribuat ei albedinem mediante hoc verbo *est*; et ideo in talibus, *est*, praedicatur ut adiacens principali praedicato. Et dicitur esse tertium, non quia sit tertium praedicatum, sed quia est tertia dictio posita in enunciatione, quae simul cum nomine praedicato facit unum praedicatum . . ." (*Ibid.*, lect. 2, no. 2).

[13] ". . . [est] significat enim primo illud quod cadit in intellectu per modum actualitatis absolutae: nam *est*, simpliciter dictum, significat *in actu esse;* et ideo significat per modum verbi. Quia vero actualitas, quam principaliter significat hoc verbum *est*, est communiter actualitas omnis formae, vel actus substantialis vel accidentalis, inde est quod cum volumus significare quamcumque formam vel actum actualiter inesse alicui subiecto, significamus illud per hoc verbum *est*, vel *simpliciter* vel *secundum quid:* simpliciter quidem secundum praesens tempus; secundum quid autem secundum alia tempora" (*In I Periherm.*, lect. 5, no. 22).

[14] *In de Trin.*, 5. 3.

implies necessarily the subject of existence whose act it is.[15] This notion of *concept* would be absurd in Kant since the concept is made up above all "of a priori conditions of understanding;" and existence is not an a priori condition but a fact, an act which is observed and known but is not thought. Consequently, there are concepts in Thomism which neither are nor can be quidditative, because the reality which they signify is not quiddity but being. All analogical concepts enter into this category, and being is the first among them.

3. THE AFFIRMATION OF EXISTENCE

If we admit that "to exist" can and must be known in and by a concept of apprehension, we also admit that there is a second knowledge of "to exist" which comes after the first, controls, and completes it. This is affirmation, an act of judgment, whose soul is neither the subject nor quiddity, nor even the verb or the act of existing but the *synthesis* of the two, the unification of the substance and of its act par excellence, "to exist." In this synthesis, being is not conceived as a potency to exist, as a correlative of potency-act, but as a substance, as a *quod* which has its act in actuality. Everything that M. Gilson tells us about the nature of the act of judgment and the points of contact between the two acts (that of the objective being which is the reality and the subjective act which is the judicative activity) seems to me admirably expressed and endowed with great metaphysical and epistemological value (pp. 202-15). One can only envy the keenness of this intellect which has so capably grasped what constitutes the proper value of judicative knowledge in the Angelic Doctor.

And though there be a few divergences between M. Gilson and the present writer on the meaning of certain Thomistic doctrines, it is nonetheless true that if I were to add a name to the Thomistic genealogical tree I would say in all sincerity: *Thomas genuit Gilson.*

II. COMMENTARY ON FR. RÉGIS' REMARKS

The remarks of Fr. Régis are fully justified. No Thomist, aiming to express the point of view of Thomas Aquinas as he himself would express it, should write that existence (*esse*) is not known by a concept. Historically speaking, our own formulas are inaccurate, and had we foreseen the objections of Fr. Régis, we

[15] *In I Periherm.*, lect. 5, no. 20.

would have used another language, or made clear that we were not using the language of Saint Thomas. We should avoid, as much as possible, unnecessary misunderstandings. The question is: can these misunderstandings be completely avoided?

The incontrovertible texts quoted by Fr. Régis make it abundantly clear that, in the language of Saint Thomas, every cognition is a "conception." We ourselves said so (p. 190). Moreover, Fr. Régis seems to consider *conceptio* as synonymous with *conceptus*, and we feel inclined to accept this equivalence as fundamentally correct. Consequently, it is true to say that, in the language of Saint Thomas, every cognition is a concept, including verbs. If *esse* is an object of cognition, which it undoubtedly is, it is known by way of concept. As we said in the same passage, even a judgment is a "conception" (p. 190, n. 1), hence a *conceptum*. In this broader sense of the term, we have not only not denied, but affirmed, that the act of being can be, and is, conceived.

On the other hand, the word "concept" is susceptible of a more restricted sense, which, however we may regret it, has become its most commonly received one, and which it has acquired precisely in consequence of the success of the "essentialist" interpretation of the metaphysical notion of being. Thomas Aquinas is in no sense responsible for the fact, but it cannot be said that no representatives of the Thomistic school or tradition are responsible for this development. Whatever his personal philosophical tenets, which we do not know, the indignant denunciation of our own position, signed E. A. M., in *The Journal of Philosophy*,[16] clearly show that the *philosophia perennis* as a whole, and not only Thomism, is considered as put in jeopardy as soon as the suggestion is made that something else than essence is included in our cognition of being. In point of fact, all the "Thomists" who, for some reason or other, have refused to ascribe to being a composition of essence and *esse*, are bound to reduce concepts to as many simple apprehensions of essences and our judgments to as many correlations of essences apprehended by way of concepts. Merely to suggest that reality includes something "other than" essence is sure to provoke a violent reaction. Is not metaphysics a "science"? And is not science a cognition of essences by way of concepts? No essence, no concept; no concept, no science. We do not have to invent the objection for dialectical purposes. In *The Journal of Philosophy*,[17] discussing the very same positions examined by Fr. Régis, our critic simply concludes that we leave no room "for anything that could be called a metaphysics in the

[16] Oct. 1951, p. 616.　　　　[17] *Op. cit.*, p. 615.

traditional sense of a *science* of being as being." In short, "Professor Gilson seems to leave no alternative except an empiricism and positivism which most people would consider to be anti-metaphysical." Such is the penalty one has to pay if, in his desire to recapture in its fullness the Thomistic notion of being, he insists on composing it of essence and of an *aliquid* "other than essence." Call that *aliquid* what you please; since it is not essence, it is not conceivable and the whole structure of metaphysics breaks down once and for all.

In such a situation a Thomist is entitled to maintain the language of Saint Thomas himself, which is the only correct one; and there is no question that Fr. Régis is right in doing so, but he has not a ghost of a chance of making himself understood. Rather, speaking to other philosophers than Thomists who accept the composition of *esse* and *essentia*, the terminology of Saint Thomas is likely to confirm a regrettable misunderstanding. All Suaresians will grant Fr. Régis, against our own language, that *esse* is known by a concept, but to them this will mean that he agrees with them on the very point where we both disagree with them, namely that actual being is not composed of essence and *esse*. And no wonder, for indeed the very reason why they refuse to accept the presence in being of an *actus essendi* is that, since such an act would have to be other than essence, there could be no "concept" of it.

The situation is not a comfortable one, but there it is. Desirous as we were to make ourself intelligible to the tenants of being conceived as *realis essentia*, we have introduced a distinction of our own between *conceptio* and *conceptus*, reserving for the latter the narrower sense of "simple apprehension of an essence" which it evokes in the minds of most of our own contemporaries. In consequence, every time we said that *esse* is "inconceivable," we intended to convey that, not being an essence, it cannot be grasped by a *conceptus*. Naturally, this does not prevent it from being an object of "conception." Otherwise, how could it be known? But it cannot be known by the simple conceptual apprehension of an essence, which it is not.

Would Saint Thomas himself condone such a terminology? We don't know. He sometimes went rather far in order to carry the conversation; for instance when he conceded that, *improprie loquendo*, the act of *esse* can be called an "accident." At any rate, we are not recommending our own terminology, and everybody should feel free to reject it: *sapientis est non curare de nominibus*.

The same remarks apply to the problem of the predicability of *esse*. For the very same philosophical reasons, the meaning of the words "predicate" and "predication" has undergone important transformations since the thirteenth century. In Thomas Aquinas himself, as in Aristotle, to predicate is to say. All that which is said of a subject is predicated of it. If I say that Socrates is white, I predicate whiteness of Socrates. If I say that Socrates is, or exists, I predicate existence of Socrates. It is both evident in itself and clear from the texts quoted by Fr. Régis that, in the thought and language of Saint Thomas Aquinas, existence can be predicated. But this does not imply that, in the modern sense of the word, *esse* is a "predicate." Naturally, there is no reason why a Thomist should worry about the modern meaning of the word "predicate" unless he wishes to make clear to his own contemporaries the thought of Thomas Aquinas. For if we tell them that existence is a predicate, they will certainly understand that, according to Thomas Aquinas, actual existence, or *esse*, can be predicated of its essence as one more essential determination.

Here, however, a philosophical problem arises in our very interpretation of the texts of Saint Thomas. We do not claim to hold the key to its solution. In his commentaries on Aristotle does Saint Thomas always express his deepest personal thought on a given question? Unless we admit that logic is a strictly formal science wholly unrelated to metaphysics, it is hard to imagine that the true Thomistic interpretation of a logic applicable to *habens esse* can be identically the same as that of a logic applicable to a metaphysics of *ousia*. This general remark cannot be used in a discussion where the nature of *to be* is at stake. We could not do so without begging the question. The fact remains, however, that Thomas himself has distinguished three fundamental meanings of *esse*: first, "ipsa quidditas vel natura rei," as signified by its definition; second, the very act of essence itself (*ipse actus essentiae*), which is his decisive contribution to the metaphysics of being; third, the copula signifying the composition or division in judgments.[18] The first and the second *esse* are real; the third does not point out something existing in real nature, but only in the intellect uniting or dividing our concepts of the natures of things.[19] Whether or not we call it a "concept," the meaning of *est* is not the same in all three cases. When we use it in logic, even following the language of Thomas Aquinas, *est* is not a *tertium praedicatum:* in "Socrates est albus," "est-albus" makes

[18] *In I Sent.*, 33, 1, 1, ad 1m.   [19] *Quodl.*, IX, 2, 3, Resp.

up a single predicate. In this enunciation, Thomas says, the copula *est* "simul cum nomine praedicato facit unum praedicatum."[20] Naturally, whatever language we choose to use, we all concede that in fact "est-albus" is a predicate known by a concept.

What about the case when *est* signifies actual existence? In saying "Socrates est," we mean to say simply that "Socrates sit aliquid in rerum natura." In Thomas' own terminology, even this particular kind of *est* is a predicate: Socrates is then posited as the subject of which it is predicated that he *is*. Hence our own problem, whose answer is not to be found in the excellent texts so aptly quoted by Fr. Régis. In "Socrates est-albus," we have a two-term proposition, "Socrates" and "est-albus," where *est* appears as a copula *de tertio adjacente*. In the proposition "Socrates est," we still have a proposition made up of two parts, but one in which the predicate is a verb: "praedicatur per se quasi principale praedicatum." Obviously, the term "Socrates" refers to an essence; but does its predicate refer to an essence as in the case of "albus"? There is no problem as to its conceivability: I have the concept of "existing Socrates," which is the intelligible import of this judgment. Our own question is: if *est* is a predicate, what kind of a predicate is it?

Let us agree that in Thomas Aquinas the verb *est* is a predicate; what is the nature of the cognition which we have of what it predicates? This is no longer a logical problem; it is a problem in noetics and in metaphysics, because it deals with the nature of being and of our knowledge of it. When we predicate *est*, we are not predicating the "quidditas vel natura rei." Nor, for that matter, do we predicate something that belongs to the essence of Socrates (such as "homo"), or that inheres in it (such as "albus"). Logically speaking, it could be said that *esse* inheres in the subject Socrates, but metaphysically speaking, it does not, because where there is no *esse* there is no Socrates. Granting that *est* is a logical denomination of Socrates as existing, the metaphysical status of the denominated still remains an open question. Among those who refuse the composition of essence and *esse*, quite a few have been misled precisely by the fact that their metaphysical inquiries were being conducted in terms of logic. For indeed, as soon as we do so, *est* becomes a predicate like all other predicates, and we imagine ourselves in possession of a distinct concept of *esse* in itself, apart from the concept which we do have of "Socrates-conceived-as-existing." This is the preoccupation which has led us to argue about logical formulas in order to convey to non-

[20] *In II Periherm.*, 2.

Thomists the feeling that, even in logic, there are visible traces of the difficulties raised by the metaphysical composition of being.

The distinction of these two orders was familiar to Thomas Aquinas. He knew not only that being is not considered in the same way by the logician and by the metaphysician, but that among the things which interest the metaphysician, not the logician, the most important is existence: "Logicus enim considerat modum praedicandi et non existentiam rei."[21] Thomas was acutely aware of the fact that "secundum logicam considerationem loquitur Philosophus in Praedicamentis."[22] The logician considers things in as much as they are in the intellect, "sed philosophus primus considerat de rebus secundum quod sunt entia." This is why some types of predication are both logically possible and metaphysically impossible. For instance, a logician can predicate substance *de subjecto*, but a metaphysician cannot, because where there is no substance there is no subject. "Man is a substance" is a perfectly possible logical predication, because "substance" can be predicated of "man"; but no metaphysician, at least no Thomist, will imagine that, conceived as a being, "man" can be posited as a subject distinct from the substantiality attributed to it by logical predication. In other words, substance can be logically predicated *of* man because it can be metaphysically said to be *in* man. In the mind of the metaphysician, Thomas says, "non differt esse in subjecto et de subjecto."[23] As far as we can see many of those who refuse the composition of essence and *esse* are overlooking this fundamental distinction. How could *esse* be distinct from *essentia*, they say, since unless it exists essence is nothing? How can essence be composed with that apart from which it is not? And, true enough, the thing is logically impossible; but it is metaphysically possible because to the metaphysician "Socrates est" does not mean that Socrates *has* the predicate *to be*, but that Socrates *is* a being. The metaphysician says that there is in the being Socrates, as the act of its formal essence, "aliquid fixum et quietum in ente,"[24] namely *esse*, in virtue of which Socrates is a "being." For indeed, outside of being there is nothing.

To sum up our explanation of Chapter VI, let us say that we fully subscribe to the criticism directed by Fr. Régis against our terminology on the level of logic. Naturally, we still more wholeheartedly concur with him in stressing the point that, speaking of actual existence as of *"de* subjecto," the verb *est* is a predicate.

[21] *In VII Metaph.*, 17, n. 1658.
[23] *Ibid.*
[22] *Op. cit.*, VII, 13, 1576.
[24] *Cont. Gent.*, I, 20.

On the other side, which is the metaphysical one, we still incline to maintain that the remarkable scarcity of logical considerations about existential propositions in classical logic is a useful warning to us not to confuse these two orders. Unless we consider it necessary to identify *praedicare* and *dicere*, there is some justification for distinguishing between the metaphysical conception of *esse* and its logical concept.

III. CRITICAL OBSERVATIONS OF FR. J. ISAAC, O.P.

The remarks made by Fr. Isaac in the *Bulletin Thomiste*[25] are in no way less pertinent nor less constructive than those of Fr. Régis, only they approach the same problem in a different way.

In the light of his previous contribution to a solution of the difficulty,[26] Fr. Isaac reminds his readers that we should distinguish in the doctrine of Saint Thomas between the level of dialectics and that of metaphysics. Roughly speaking, the level of the dialectician is that of the physicist or of the biologist, and it has often remained the level of Aristotle's speculation even in metaphysics. Hence the discussions about his "idealism" or, more exactly, about the remnants of Platonism still visible in his own philosophy. Incidentally, it is notable that in his 1950 lecture on *Method in Metaphysics*[27] Fr. J. Henle, S.J. had also stressed, with both force and penetration, the difference there is between the extension of knowledge "by way of addition of distinct intelligibilities or notes"[28] and the properly metaphysical moment in knowledge, which implies a "deepening of insight" into the meaning of being. The reality of the problem seems to be confirmed by the spontaneous convergence of these two independent lines of thought.

The next question is: how far does this remark help us in clearing up the nature of our cognition of being? Fr. Isaac agrees with the objections of Fr. Régis concerning the predicability of verbs. Our explanations to Fr. Régis will no doubt help him in understanding why, instead of speaking the language of Saint Thomas' commentary on Aristotle's logic, we have chosen to discuss some of his modern scholastic interpreters. Let us add that, in our mind, the existence of such divergences among Neo-Scholastics con-

---

[25] VIII, 1, (1951), pp. 39-59.
[26] "La notion de dialectique chez saint Thomas," in *Revue des Sciences Philosophiques et Théologiques* XXXIV, 1950, pp. 481-506.
[27] Marquette University Press, Milwaukee, 1951.
[28] *Op. cit.*, p. 41.

cerning the thought of Saint Thomas is in itself an important philosophical problem. It is a fact, but an intelligible answer should be given to the problem of its very possibility. In order to eliminate error, the first condition is to understand it *qua* error, that is to say, to define it in each case as the particular deviation from truth which it is.

The answer of Fr. Isaac to our problem is that a noun and the corresponding verb do not express two ideas, but solely two different ways of grasping one and the same thing.[29] Applying this remark to the verb *est*, or *is*, we would say that its import does not differ in kind from that of the corresponding noun. Both are therefore "concepts," since one and the same intellectual representation presides over our two different ways of grasping *ens* and *esse*.[30] A perfectly intelligible statement indeed, but one which in its turn raises considerable difficulties.

We all agree, I suppose, that there is a concept of being, or, in other terms, that being is grasped in a concept. It should be no less clear that in the doctrine of Saint Thomas *ens* and *esse* are two notions inseparably related because they both refer to the same object. It is because "it has *esse*" that a thing is an *ens*. Last, not least, it should be likewise agreed by all those who accept the definition of *ens* as a "having *esse*," that the simple apprehension of any given being implies the apprehension of its *esse*, to be later on explicitated by way of judgment. But this is where our personal hesitations begin. Does the verb *is* express just the some object as the noun *ens*, or is it the other way around?

The least we can say about it is that the answer is not evident. Thus to equate the content of *is* to that of *ens* is quite satisfactory from the point of view of Suaresian being, which is a real essence actually posited in reality outside of its causes. In this case, *is* simply means that a certain completely determined essence is an existent. In the metaphysics of Saint Thomas himself, the objects of our simple apprehensions are indivisible units made up of an *essentia* and an *esse*. The question then is to know if *is* does not point out, within Thomistic being, its act of *esse*. In our own interpretation, the verb *is* signifies, not being grasped in a certain way, but the *actus primus* of which Thomas Aquinas says that it turns an essence into an actual "being." It is the verbal expression of an act which, after explicitating it in the judgment *"x is,"* we can conceptualize under the form of a wider simple apprehension: *x* known as an existing being, and not as a mere abstract possibility. If the concept of *ens* is the simple apprehension

[29] *Op. cit.*, p. 56.   [30] *Op. cit.*, p. 57.

of *habens esse,* it includes *esse.* But this applies to possible being as well as to actual being. On the contrary, in the judgment *"x is," is* points to the actual existence of *x.* If it is true to say with Thomas Aquinas that in the enunciation "Socrates est," the verb *est* signifies the fact that "Socrates sit in rerum natura," what it answers in reality is what in Socrates makes him to be a being, that is, its *esse.* This is so important that, in the doctrine of Thomas Aquinas (not in that of Aristotle), the ultimate foundation for the truth of an enunciation concerning any actual being is not its essence, but its *esse:* "veritas fundatur in esse rei magis quam in quidditate."[31] If there is a case where the proper foundation for the truth of a judgment is to be found in the *esse* of its object, it should be that of the judgment which says that its object is or exists. In Aristotle, and in all the interpretations of Saint Thomas which identify his metaphysics with that of Aristotle, the truth of an enunciation ultimately rests upon the fact that a certain thing actually is; in the doctrine of Thomas himself, it ultimately rests upon the act which, in the thing, makes its existence to be an actual fact. Thomas Aquinas then has an excellent personal reason to maintain that, of the two operations of the human intellect, judgment and simple apprehension, judgment is the more perfect, for indeed, "ipsum esse est perfectissimum omnium, comparatur enim ad omnia ut actus; nihil enim habet actualitatem, nisi inquantum est."[32]

There is a divine beauty in the sequence of these metaphysical intuitions when their order appears in its fullness. Unless we keep them always in sight, we are liable spontaneously to relapse into the facilities of abstract conceptual thinking, instead of, following the sound advice of Fr. J. Henle, deriving our metaphysics from experience, "through a constantly purifying reflexion."[33] Imagination then soon takes the upper hand. Because being is composed of act and potency, we begin to speak as though each categorical being were made up of two other beings, the one *essentia,* the other *esse.* But there is no *essentia* outside of some being, nor is there any *esse* outside of some being. Fr. Isaac then is absolutely right in saying that all our conceptions, either verbs or nouns, are about beings or being. This is a point on which Aristotle and Thomas fully agree: taken alone, *is* means nothing. Moreover, Fr. Isaac is again right in saying that in a being all is being, its essence no less than its *esse.* Yet, when all is said and done, the metaphysical composition of categorical being remains in it as

[31] *In I Sent.,* 19, 5, 1, Resp.   [32] *Sum. Theol.,* I, 4, 1, ad 3m.
[33] J. Henle, *op. cit.,* p. 55.

the mark of its finitude, and the duality of our intellect's operations remains in it as a means to maintain the unity resulting for finite being from its composition. Just like being, intellectual knowledge is one, but God alone is simple. Naturally, it is tempting for us to simplify the structure of finite being at the same time as human knowledge. The only question is: can we know its unity without acknowledging its complexity?

The gist of the difficulty, at least in our own mind, lies in an obscure metaphysical feeling, groping for its correct verbal formulation. Whether or not our conceptions of verbs should be called "concepts" is, outside of history, of secondary importance. What does matter is to know if nouns and verbs express cognitions of the same nature and if they point out the same constitutive element in the metaphysical structure of being. A sign that such is not the case can be found in the fact that, in human knowledge, essences are many, distinct from each other and susceptible of definitions. This is so true, in Saint Thomas himself, that essence is for him what is signified by the definition: "quod quid est esse est id quod definitio significat."[34] Incidentally, this is why science is about essences, and consequently, together with science, dialectics. Now, since truth ultimately rests upon *esse*, there is no science without some cognition of *esse*, and yet there is no discursive cognition of *esse*, either in science or in dialectics. All that we can say about existence is: *est, est, non, non*. Discourse may be needed in order to establish *esse*, but there can be no discourse about it. Such is the nature of our intellect: "Quidditas rei est proprium objectum intellectus."[35] Since it has no essence, *esse* has no quiddity, and therefore it does not yield itself to discursive knowledge; existence, Thomas says, is "extra genus notitiae," that is to say, outside of the order, not of cognition, but of discursive and of scientific knowledge. So long as we agree on this fundamental distinction, it does not matter very much whether we call our cognition of *esse* a "conception" or a "concept." Our agreement is a real one if we understand our concept of *esse* as that of the element of being which, because it is not essence, is not susceptible of quidditative definition.

There now remains for us to ascertain the exact relation of verbal nouns, such as *ens*, to their verbs, such as *esse*. Let us quote a suggestive text: "Ens autem non dicit quidditatem, sed solum actum essendi."[36] What would some Neo-Scholastics say if we had written this *solum* without warning that it is found

[34] *In VII Metaph.*, 5, n. 1378. [35] *Sum. Theol.*, I, 17, 3, ad 1m.
[36] *In I Sent.*, 8, 4, 2.

230

in Saint Thomas? The reason for this is clear. "Nomen autem rei a quidditate imponitur, sicut nomen entis ab esse."[37] How then could there be a science of *esse*, since each of every particular being has its own? "Non enim idem est esse hominis et equi, nec hujus hominis et illius hominis."[38] Too particular for scientific knowledge, it is also too universal, for all things are likewise "beings": "Res ad invicem non distinguuntur secundum quod esse habent, quia in hoc omnia conveniunt."[39] And again: "Hoc esse ab illo esse distinguitur in quantum est talis vel talis naturae."[40] All these propositions are true, each of them in its own context and in its own place. They all point out the same metaphysical distinction between *esse* and *essentia*, which entails the logical distinction between simple apprehensions and judgments, as well as the grammatical distinction between nouns and verb.

From this point of view, the expressions used by Fr. Isaac do not seem to adhere more closely to the authentic terminology of Thomas Aquinas than our own. Yet neither one of us has any other intention than to express the thought of our common master. According to Fr. Isaac, a noun and the corresponding verb express, not two "ideas," but the same one grasped in two different ways. "When I think *running*, and when I think *to run*, or, still better, *runs*, I have the same abstract concept in mind, namely, what constitutes what we call *running* or that one *runs*. In the first case, however, what I am grasping under this same character is a subject; in the second case, it is the act of a subject, which is only possible in a judgment, for it is impossible to think the act of a subject without being able distinctly to grasp both this subject and its act."[41]

Obviously, one cannot understand the meaning of *runs* without understanding that of *running*, but there is no *x* common to both which can be grasped, now as a subject, now as an act. The only reality there is in this case is the act of running, signified *in abstracto* by the noun and *in concreto* by the verb. The same illusion, which we were trying to dissipate, appears in full in this interpretation of Thomas Aquinas. *Running* can be used as the subject of a logical proposition, but it *is* not a subject. It is our abstract cognition of a concrete act. Thomas has often quoted the text of Aristotle, *vivere viventibus est esse*,[42] and he always quoted it with approval; but when someone tried to infer from it that the life of a living being was its essence, Thomas absolutely

[37] *Cont. Gent.*, I, 25.
[39] *Cont. Gent.*, I, 26.
[41] Fr. J. Isaac, *art. cit.*, p. 56.

[38] *Sum. Theol.*, I, 3, 5, Resp.
[40] *Q. D. De Potentia*, VII, 2, ad 4m.
[42] *In II De Anima*, 7, n. 319.

refused to accept the inference. *Vita* does not point out the essence, but the act of that which lives. *Running* does not signify an essence; that which runs has an essence, but running itself is an act. On the contrary, the noun *essentia* correctly designates that which has *esse:* "Vita non hoc modo se habet ad vivere, sicut essentia ad esse; sed sicut cursus ad currere: quorum unum significat actum in abstracto, aliud in concreto. Unde non sequitur, si vivere sit esse, quod vita sit essentia."[43] But the true noun answering to the verb "to be" is not essence, it is being. *Ens* signifies *in abstracto* the act concretely signified by *is.*

Because essence is the proper object of human understanding, we feel inclined to imagine that all that which we conceive as related to some essence is itself an essence. Not so in Thomas Aquinas, according to whom, although each and every finite being has an essence, something other than essence enters the metaphysical structure of reality. First, the *actus primus* of finite being, which is its *esse;* next, all its secondary acts, or operations, which, according to its essence, follow from the prime act in virtue of which it is a "being." Thomas Aquinas had said this time and again, under all possible forms of philosophical language. We read him; we learn that *ens dicit solum actum essendi,* not the essence or quiddity, and straightway we proceed to reduce being to its essence or quiddity. It was in order to protect ourself against this always recurring illusion that we got used to distinguishing, among conceptions, the "concepts" which are the grasping of true essences. We do not see why others should follow our example. Besides being non-Thomistic, the distinction is perfectly useless to those who, like Thomas Aquinas and unlike ourself, do not constantly relapse into the fallacy of misplaced essentiality.

[43] *Sum. Theol.*, I, 54, 1, ad 2m.

232

INDEX

233